Writers in Retrospect

Writers in Retrospect

{ *The Rise of*
American Literary
History, 1875–1910

CLAUDIA STOKES

The University
of
North Carolina Press
Chapel Hill

Designed by Kimberly Bryant
Set in Cycles by Keystone Typesetting, Inc.
Manufactured in the United States of America

The paper in this book meets the guidelines for permanence
and durability of the Committee on Production Guidelines for
Book Longevity of the Council on Library Resources.

Chapter 3 has been reprinted with permission in revised
form from "Copyrighting American History: International
Copyright and the Periodization of the Nineteenth Century,"
American Literature 77 (June 2005): 289–315.

Library of Congress Cataloging-in-Publication Data
Stokes, Claudia, 1970–
Writers in retrospect : the rise of American literary history,
1875–1910 / Claudia Stokes.
p. cm.
Includes bibliographical references and index.
ISBN-13: 978-0-8078-3040-6 (alk. paper)
ISBN-10: 0-8078-3040-2 (alk. paper)
ISBN-13: 978-0-8078-5720-5 (pbk. : alk. paper)
ISBN-10: 0-8078-5720-3 (pbk. : alk. paper)
1. American literature—History and criticism—Theory, etc.
2. Criticism—United States—History—19th century. I. Title.
PS25.S76   2006
810'.9—dc22   2006010780

cloth   10 09 08 07 06   5 4 3 2 1
paper   10 09 08 07 06   5 4 3 2 1

In memory of my father,
SHERMAN MAXWELL STOKES

Contents

Acknowledgments ix

Introduction 1

PART I   The Lay of the Land: Nation and the
          Responsibilities of Literary History

    1   A Culture of Retrospection: The Rise of Literary
        History in the Late Nineteenth Century 17

    2   Preservation and Assimilation: Brander Matthews
        and the Silences of Literary History 33

PART II   Class, Authority, and Literary History

    3   Copyrighting American History:
        International Copyright and the Periodization
        of the Nineteenth Century 77

    4   A Higher Function: Literary History
        and the Advent of Professionalism 103

    5   Rancor's Remains: Barrett Wendell
        and the New England Renaissance 139

        Epilogue: Relevance and Its Discontents 187

        Notes 195

        Index 225

Acknowledgments

This book examines the personalities, relationships, and institutional cultures that shaped American literary historical research at the turn of the last century, and it is with pleasure and sincere gratitude that I acknowledge the profound influence of many of these same forces on my own work in American literary history. This project has been nurtured, encouraged, guided, and polished by so many people, and my debts are considerable. Though this book bears scant resemblance to my dissertation on American literary realism, my initial thinking for this project began in response to the probing, wonderfully helpful questions of Richard Bushman, Jonathan Levin, and Priscilla Wald at my dissertation defense, and I thank them for providing the germ that grew into this book. I particularly wish to acknowledge Priscilla Wald, whose influence—intellectual and otherwise—cannot be adequately summarized here. My mentor, teacher, and valued friend, she has served as a role model of scholarly rigor, ethical integrity, and impeccable character for an entire generation of Americanists. I have much to thank her for, as does the entire profession.

I researched and wrote this book in my first few years at Trinity University, which has been as supportive and nurturing an institution as I could have hoped. This book has benefited enormously from the support that Trinity has offered me at every turn, from generously providing financial resources for travel and research to the enriching and sustaining intellectual community I have found there. Upon arrival at Trinity I was awarded the Tom and Mary Turner Faculty Fellowship, which provided financial support for three consecutive summers. I cannot overstate the importance of that fellowship to the research and writing of this book, and I am grateful to Trinity University's Office of Academic Affairs for awarding it to me. I also owe considerable thanks to the English department chair who arranged that fellowship on my behalf, Peter Balbert, and to his inestimable successor, Victoria Aarons. In their boundless encouragement, support, and reassurance, Peter and Vicki created an intellectual environment that made the writing of this book possible. I am also grateful to Fred Loxsom for inviting me to present part of chapter 5 at a faculty research dinner, and to the many colleagues in attendance for their warm enthusiasm, helpful comments, and valuable questions. I also thank Jed Deppman, formerly Trinity's sponsored research officer, for indispensable help preparing grant proposals.

This research was made possible by several fellowships. I am grateful to the Gilder Lehrman Institute of American History for a grant that enabled me to spend a summer at Columbia University's Rare Book and Manuscript Library. At that archive, I thank Jean Ashton for her assistance. So, too, do I express gratitude for the William Dean Howells memorial fellowship in American literature (1860–1920) at Harvard's Houghton Library and the kind, helpful staff there who aided me in numerous ways: Elizabeth A. Falsey, Susan Halpert, Leslie Morris, and Roger Stoddard. At the Harvard University Archives, I wish to thank Michelle Gachette and Andrea Goldstein for their generous and always good-humored assistance.

I wish to express my sincere thanks to my editor, Sian Hunter, for her faith, support, and guidance in bringing this project to fruition. I also thank Paula Wald for supervising the production of this book. I owe more thanks than I could ever express to two enormously generous anonymous readers, who told me just what I needed to hear and who contributed to this book in ways that they (and Sian) alone fully grasp. Thanks are due, too, to Frances Kerr, managing editor of *American Literature*, for her exceedingly helpful edits to chapter 3.

I am fortunate to have so many friends and colleagues, at Trinity and elsewhere, who deserve my thanks for their invaluable recommendations, important advice, and availability for conversation. Renée Bergland, Judith L. Fisher, Lisa Fluet, Larry Kutchen, Richard K. Reed, Willis Salomon, and Michael Soto all served as trusted readers and all made important recommendations. I am grateful to Rachel

Cohen, Nina Ekstein, Susan Goodman, Carl Leafstedt, and Douglas Pfeiffer for fielding what must have seemed like very peculiar queries. Thomas Jenkins offered transportation to an archive I never would have reached otherwise. John D. Kerkering and Glenn Hendler provided much-needed assistance in navigating academic publishing, and their help has made all the difference for me. Amid his own impossibly busy schedule, Char Miller read every chapter of this book, sometimes more than once, and helped me refine my argument in vital, strategic ways. And it's difficult for me to weigh the full extent of my debt to Michael A. Elliott, whom I met on the first day of graduate school at Columbia University. Since that time, he has been a cherished interlocutor, collaborator, and friend. He has read every word in this book at least once and provided me with boundless encouragement and sage advice. I am grateful for his generosity and for his friendship.

My family has contributed to the research and writing of this project in more ways than they perhaps realize. My brother, Brian Stokes, has always been my most fierce champion, and I thank all of my parents for their encouragement and support. I have much to thank my husband, David Liss, for, but I will restrict my thanks here to an acknowledgment of his perpetual willingness to discuss my research and his miraculous ability to fabricate time and space when I needed them. I began work on this book shortly after the birth of our daughter, Eleanor, and I have no doubt that the joy she has brought to my life made the research and writing of this book all the more pleasurable.

Finally, it is with a very heavy heart that I acknowledge my father, Sherman Maxwell Stokes, who died unexpectedly while I was making the final revisions to this book. His searching intellect and deep commitment to political justice have profoundly shaped my life and this project. It is to him and to his memory that I dedicate this book.

Writers in Retrospect

Introduction

As a discipline, American literary history has had mixed fortunes in the twentieth century, its stock pitched between steep rises in popularity and equally precipitous plummets in professional interest. When the twentieth century began, American literary history had already enjoyed several decades of prosperity due to the blossoming of interest in the American past during the last quarter of the nineteenth century.[1] Between about 1875 and 1910, publishers solicited literary histories, literature professors regularly wrote slapdash literary histories to satisfy mounting requirements for promotion and tenure, and writers such as Thomas Wentworth Higginson and Julian Hawthorne tried to pass off literary gossip as literary history. By the close of the nineteenth century, readers had at their disposal countless options to satisfy this interest—author biographies, anthologies, textbooks, ambitious surveys, and more modest primers. Though most of the contributors to this period of vast productivity in literary history were themselves literary authors writing about their friends, acquaintances, and predecessors, these decades proved enormously influential, so that, by the time work began in the second decade of the twentieth century on the first expansive academic American literary history, the *Cambridge History of American Literature* (1917–21), much of the groundwork of the discipline of American literary history had already been laid, with the production of knowledge that has been in wide circulation ever since.

The first half of the twentieth century saw continued productivity in American literary history, visible in the steady publication of many important contributions to the field, among them Vernon L. Parrington's *Main Currents in American Thought* (1930–38), Van Wyck Brooks's *Flowering of New England* (1936) and *New England: Indian Summer* (1940), and Robert E. Spiller's *Literary History of the United States*

(1948). In the preface to his widely influential literary history, Spiller famously declared that "each generation must define the past in its own terms" and therefore should "produce at least one literary history of the United States."[2] However, shifting disciplinary interests and demands derailed Spiller's hopes for the continual revision and production of American literary history, and for forty years his 1948 work remained the standard national literary history, consulted and relied upon by several generations of Americanists, until the publication of the *Columbia History of American Literature* (1988), the introduction of which speaks explicitly to Spiller's unfulfilled hopes for the continual production of literary history.[3] The literary interests of those intervening decades are well known, as the dictates of the New Criticism and then of some schools of poststructuralism made literary history seem not only retrograde and stodgy but also directly obstructive to textual interpretation. But after nearly forty years of inactivity and indifference, the late 1980s witnessed a marked revival of interest in literary history. Since that time, literature graduate students in all fields have been enjoined to follow Fredric Jameson's famous dictum, "Always historicize!" and reading texts within historical context— whether literary, political, or material—is now an accepted, expected interpretive practice.

These recent years of undeniable prosperity in literary history have reaped considerable rewards, among them the rediscovery of neglected writers, texts, and genres, and the production of knowledge that has altered both our perception of the literary past and the ways in which we assay literary value. Because of the important archival and interpretive work that has recovered, for instance, the place of women and people of color in our knowledge of the literary past, it would be very easy to imagine that the current discipline of American literary history bears scant resemblance to its forebears, both at the time of Spiller's central 1948 work and even earlier, at the time of the discipline's origination in the late nineteenth century. However, such an exceptionalist perception of contemporary work in literary history is altogether erroneous, for, if anything, the recent revival of interest in American literary history has moved the profession closer to its antecedents at the beginning of the last century than we would perhaps expect or even desire.

The striking similarities between the research of current practitioners of American literary history and that of a century before can tell us quite a lot about both the conditions that breed intellectual trends and the ways in which those conditions seep into and shape the knowledge they produce. In the first chapter, I discuss at greater length some of the stimuli that prompted the first outpouring of interest in literary history at the turn of the last century, but even the most cursory glance at the work produced in that era reveals that it more than a little resembles the current twenty-first-century revival. For example, American literary historians in both the late nineteenth and late twentieth centuries persistently confronted the problems of writing a national literary history in a climate of increasing internationalism, both literary and otherwise. Whereas late nineteenth-century literary histories were visibly motivated by mass immigration and anxieties about foreign cultural influences (the subject of chapter 2), their counterparts a century later engaged the American literary past through the lens of twenty-first-century globalization and its discontents.[4]

Literary history seems to emerge and reemerge in the company of a host of other expressions of anxious nationalism, such as heated debates about family structures and maternity—which appoint the family a particularly vulnerable synecdoche of the nation at large—and renewed interest in racial classification as a way of taking stock of a national population believed to be in jeopardy from menaces abroad. In her recent study of academic labor and intellectual property, Corynne McSherry discusses the entanglement of the university with the nation, with the university serving as the appointed protector of national culture. As McSherry argues, the decline of one—or the perceived decline of one—invariably coincides with the seeming decline of the other.[5] The persistent reemergence of this academic subfield during periods of anxious nationalism certainly accords with this observation, for the threat of compromised nationalism leads specialists in the literature of this nation to return to national literary history as an apparent microresponse to this larger crisis. During periods of increased anxiety about porous national borders and controversy about the expansion of those borders abroad, American literary histories chart the limits of national literary culture by producing scholarship that firmly designates and centralizes a literary and cultural metropole constituted by its relation to ever-widening margins. Though the work of contemporary literary historians often complicates these binaries implicit in national literature, the very medium of national literary history serves as reassuring intellectual ballast in periods of debate about what it means to be an American.[6]

The continuity between the national literary histories authored during these two intellectual moments does not stop there, however. For instance, works of literary history authored in both periods evince a concerted preoccupation with literary labor. Whereas late nineteenth-century literary historians documented with fastidious detail the work habits and finances of American writers, their descendants a century later also have attended to the conditions of textual production emphasized by such materialist interpretive methods as New Historicism. This shared interest in the material conditions of literary labor may derive from the immediate conditions of *academic* labor that propelled literary history in both the late nineteenth and late twentieth centuries. Literary history markedly rises in value during periods of increased skepticism about intellectual labor for its own sake, and allows literary academics to position themselves in opposition to predecessors whose work had been derided and deemed at odds with the requirements of an ever more demanding academic marketplace. Literary history, that is, emerges when the status of literary faculty members as vital contributors to the academic marketplace is thrown into question and reliably allows them to demonstrate their social and material usefulness.

As I discuss in a later chapter, late nineteenth-century literary historians relied upon historical research to compete in an increasingly professionalized academy. Their late twentieth-century descendants, too, turned to history amid similar questions about the market value and material uses of their discipline. The rise of literary history in the late 1980s correlates with the contraction of resources—financial and otherwise—in the literary academy. Universities and colleges habitually failed to replace retiring faculty, relied increasingly upon adjunct teachers so as to avoid expensive tenure-track hires, dramatically raised requirements for tenure and promotion, and engendered a torpid and exceedingly competitive academic job market—all the while being publicly denounced by legislators and conservative critics for the seemingly cushy jobs and inflated salaries of humanities academics.[7] This financial belt-tightening overlapped with a virulent public backlash against critical theory, which was roundly denounced for being at once too aloof from and too stridently meddlesome in its criticisms of the laity. These two controversies dovetailed in widespread criticisms of curricula and course offerings, whether in the creation of courses in popular culture or in the perceived replacement of "Great Books" courses with classes in popular culture or in the literature of minorities and women. The publicized protests that greeted these courses complained not only that critical theory had effectively eroded the barriers separating high culture from low culture, but also that parents were consequently no longer getting their money's worth. This confluence of complaints shows how concerns about academic market value resulted in skepticism about knowledge for its own sake: increasingly cost-conscious parents demanded that their children acquire literary knowledge whose association with the cultural elite would result, they hoped, in their later professional membership in that elite. In the explicitly market-conscious climate of the late twentieth century, intellectual labor was increasingly deemed valuable only insofar as it paved the way for lucrative careers.

It was in this highly fraught academic climate that historicism emerged to take the place of theory as the dominant preoccupation of the literary academy, as evidenced by the increasing prominence of such historicist journals as *American Literary History*, the rededication of *Modern Language Quarterly* to literary history, and a *New York Times Magazine* article announcing the preeminence of New Historicist interpretive methods.[8] Just as it had a century before, history in the late twentieth century offered literary academics a vehicle by which they could protect themselves and compete in an increasingly demanding marketplace. It allowed faculty to substantiate these highly publicized and politicized curricular changes and to seek refuge from the widespread attacks leveled against critical theory by producing scholarship bolstered less by philosophy and argument than by material support. Whereas critics could attack theory for being at once too abstract and transparently motivated, the dependence of literary history on archival and material research rendered it seemingly invulnerable to attack.

The debates about the relationship between literary study and careerism concerned not only students and parents but also faculty themselves, who were increasingly required by shrinking financial support to showcase their own market value. In sharp contrast with the often deliberately languorous meditations widely associated with theory, literary history flaunted itself as recognizably arduous work—marked by voluminous footnotes and impressive lists of consulted archives—and therefore constituted itself as meriting professional advancement within the university's contracting reserves of resources: to demonstrate their own material value, literary academics turned to materiality, as it were, by way of literary history. And so it is no accident that literary histories that painstakingly document the conditions of literary labor of the past indirectly showcase the considerable labors of their authors. Similarly, these disputes about the value of academic labor extended during both periods into debates about copyright and the literal value of intellectual work. In chapter 3 I discuss at length the extensive involvement of the international copyright movement of the 1880s in the disciplinary rise of American literary history, and an important study is yet to be written examining the concurrence of the present revival of literary history and the renewal of discussion about the effect of copyright laws on intellectual labor, both of which affirm the literal value of literary labor.[9]

As a practitioner of literary history, I by no means claim to be somehow above or beyond or in some other geographical relation to the upheavals that reanimated literary history in recent decades. Trained during these fractious, professionally difficult years, I happily clasped what Cary Nelson has called "history's handshake," and my interests, methods, and field of vision no doubt bear the unmistakable fingerprint of a literary academy in dire fiscal crisis.[10] I vividly recall being urged throughout my training to make research decisions based on market demand, but this well-meaning advice caused me primarily to recognize the ways in which knowledge is motivated, sometimes transparently and sometimes not, by the institutional culture and climate that frame it. Historicist, materialist methods have illuminated how the conditions of a text's production are inevitably inscribed on the text itself, and the preoccupations of current literary history evidence that works of scholarship are equally permeable.

My recognition of this consonance has led me to the late nineteenth century, to another fraught academic climate but one whose foundational research findings in American literary history have proved resilient and enduring. Though current literary historians have made important interventions in the way we understand the American literary past, we continue to rely heavily upon late nineteenth-century research, methods, and beliefs. The names Charles F. Richardson and Moses Coit Tyler may have long been forgotten, but the flowering of American literary history in the late nineteenth century in which they worked has proved enormously influential in dictating the shape and direction of the discipline of American literary study. The turn of the last century produced both foundational texts, such as Edmund Stedman's *Library of American Literature* (1888–90) and Barrett Wendell's *Literary History of America* (1900), and foundational knowledge, such as the discernment of a New England liberal tradition and the identification of Harriet Beecher Stowe as a progenitor of late-century literary realism. This late-century wellspring of literary history also produced some of the most basic tools of the discipline: the canon of American writers and texts deemed suitable for study and admiration, the periodization of American literary history, the embrace of nonliterary writers such as Jonathan Edwards and Benjamin Franklin as important literary forebears, and the institutionalization of evaluative criteria that privileged literary craftsmanship over popularity. Though embattled efforts in the 1980s to widen the scope of the American literary canon have caused some changes to that product of the literary late century, these inventions of the late nineteenth century have been transmitted largely intact from one generation of Americanists to the next, and have essentially organized the very discipline of American literary study. However, to continue to rely upon the intellectual fruits of the late nineteenth century is to overlook the ways in which knowledge is both motivated and prescriptive. And because knowledge is developed expressly to resolve particular problems or concerns, it has distinct functions and vectors; to build uncritically upon the scholarship of the late nineteenth century is to submit one's work to the directed energies and mission encoded there. To do so is in effect to allow one's own work to follow the programming of scholarship authored under different conditions and in response to different stimuli.

Because the recent revival of interest in literary history has caused the profession to consolidate its commitment to the intellectual legacy of the late nineteenth century, a historicist analysis of the foundations of our discipline has never been more needed, and this book proceeds from the assumption that we can better handle the tools of our profession if we know more precisely the conditions of their origination, and therefore the nuanced vibrations that may go unheard consciously but that nevertheless resonate in their use. To that end, *Writers in Retrospect* returns to the first eruption of interest in American literary history between 1875 and 1910 to provide a long-overdue historical analysis of some of the most basic terms, assumptions, and tools of this again thriving discipline. In examining the forgotten contexts that produced knowledge that for over a century has been so incontrovertible as to be practically invisible, *Writers in Retrospect* examines the visions of American literature implicit in those tenets that we, in our professional dependence on them, unconsciously cling to.

It is a truism that research into the past always entails the historian's bringing the present to bear on the events of the past. As June Howard elegantly put it, "When we study the past we recursively double and redouble our involvement in it; for we too can be understood only in history, yet we exercise agency within it."[11] At its foundation, historicism is always utopic, for our visions of the past are inevitably informed by our ideas of how things ought to be. Recent scholarship in literary history is by no means exempt from this unavoidable circumstance, as evidenced by the spate of literary histories that impugn writers of the American past—Phillis Wheatley, Ralph Waldo Emerson, William Dean Howells, to name just a few—for adhering to moral, political, and economic belief systems that fall short of a mark that is unmistakably constituted by late twentieth- and early twenty-first-century academic standards. As this recent strain of literary scholarship evidences, the line between the historical and the transhistorical is very fine indeed. To be sure, the horizon at which the historian's own historical moment comes into view in his or her engagement of the past is the focus of this study. In revisiting the vogue for literary history at the turn of the last century, this book investigates the ways in which the founders of this discipline in the late nineteenth century both candidly and reflexively brought their own moment to bear on the American literary past they studied and codified. Our vision of the American literary past, I aim to show, is inevitably filtered through the lens of the literary nineteenth century that produced it.

I have organized the book's chapters as a series of concentric circles with the common center of literary history. Though the book moves roughly chronologically, it follows a narrowing thematic focus, beginning with discussions of such broad collectives as nation and moving to discussions of more restricted subcommunities, such as those engendered by regional or academic affiliation. Similarly, the two parts of this book begin with discussions of communal literary efforts and move toward chapters on the workings of individuals within and sometimes at odds with those groups. Commencing with these larger tectonic conditions and homing in, as it were, on some particularly influential, enduring microresponses to these circumstances, this book engages episodes and characters of particular importance in the disciplinary formation of American literary history. Though each chapter relies upon chronology to tell a story, my reliance upon chronology and narrative for the sake of clarity should not give the unfair impression that the disciplinary formation of American literary history took place in a methodical, orderly, and chronological fashion, for it most certainly did not. Moreover, chapter organization itself, though a commonplace and even necessary textual arrangement, conveys the mistaken impression of separateness and distinctness between the various discussions staged here; rather, the topics of these separate chapters were often concurrent and indistinctly demarcated, but the necessity of chapter organization may suggest otherwise. It will, and should, become clear that these chapters spill over into each other: the marked reappearance of the same cast of characters, texts, themes, and settings throughout the book belies the implicit logic of separateness imposed by chapter organization.

The chapters here put in synoptic focus the various conditions in late-century literary culture that infused literary history with importance and directly contributed to the emerging generic conventions, core methods, and responsibilities of literary history. To show the continuing influence of the late-century circumstances that gave rise to the literary history boom, each chapter offers a history of a late-century relic that has survived into our own time, such as the lingering preeminence of New England antebellum letters within the national canon, the continuing omission of Native narrative from American literary history, and the enduring struggle of intellectual laborers for public respect. Such an endeavor entails balancing a discussion of the internal workings of the university in this period with a discussion of the larger literary culture in which all the architects of this discipline lived and worked. In so doing, this book documents both the permeability of the literary academy at that time and the untidy confluence of forces—both academic and extra-academic— that underlay the development of this particular literary discipline. The history of American literary history often extends beyond the limits of the academic departments in which it currently finds its home and outside the walls of the university itself.

One particular theme that threads throughout the book, from chapter to chapter, is the use of literary history in struggles for power —political, institutional, and literary. Because literary histories were originally authored by literary men—novelists, playwrights, poets, editors, critics—writing about their friends, enemies, predecessors, and successors, these texts were perceptibly motivated by a desire to secure their writers' own places in literary history. They therefore pay visible homage to their allies and are equally transparent in their partisan dislikes. One particularly sensitive subject around which clustered considerable disagreement, activism, and internecine hostility is the class status of literary work. The dramatic changes in the business of writing in the late nineteenth century are well known, as is the opening of literary work to writers of varied backgrounds such as Hamlin Garland, William Dean Howells, and Mark Twain, all of whom came from relatively humble origins and received minimal formal education. The mid-to-late nineteenth century saw little friction between writers of elite backgrounds and those of less prestigious origins, as the many warm friendships across these class lines attest. However, because the practice of literary history often entails documenting the conditions of literary work—writing habits, earnings, business arrangements—the vogue for literary history in the late century proved to be an irritant in class relations between writers, for it provided an opportunity for writers of various class backgrounds and philosophies to shore up their own opinions on the proper position of literary writing in the continuum of class. Consequently, literary history at the turn of the century often proved fractious, widening the gulf between writers who clung to the vestigial associations of authorship with gentility and privilege and those pushing for the inclusion of the writer among the ranks of other middle-class (and occasionally even lower-class) workers. As I will show, disagreement about the class status of literary work not only propelled the vogue for literary history at the turn of the last century but also appears as a persistent undercurrent in the knowledge produced then and that we continue to rely upon and circulate.

THE RISE OF LITERARY HISTORY in the late nineteenth century did not emerge unprompted, and so *Writers in Retrospect* begins with an introductory chapter examining the confluence of forces that made literary history particularly appealing and relevant in the late century, both for writers and for readers. As this first chapter shows, the academic discipline of literary history was fueled by various extra-academic influences, among them the deaths of many elderly American writers during the 1880s and the mass immigration that overwhelmed the period. The second chapter elaborates on the influence of these nationalist anxieties on late-century literary histories. Taking as its starting point the conspicuous silence of literary histories about Native narrative traditions, this chapter examines the pedagogical, nationalizing responsibilities of literary histories, as they circulated uncomplicated narratives of cultural achievement at odds with the period's fraught debates about how best to incorporate aliens into the national fabric. This second chapter uses as a case study the literary historical writings of the Columbia University professor Brander Matthews, who is best remembered today as a New York bon vivant of the late century, but Matthews found his greatest professional success with his best-selling *Introduction to the Study of American Literature* (1896). In that work, as well as elsewhere, Matthews broke with generic convention to address the responsibilities of literary histories to Native peoples. Though he failed in his efforts to constitute literary history as a site for the preservation of the irretrievably lost, Matthews illuminated the generic conventions and political allegiances of late-century literary history authored in such a climate.

The third chapter figures as a transition from these discussions of the context of nationalism to an extended consideration, carried out over several chapters, of the foundation of late-century literary history in the changing nature of intellectual work. The third chapter examines how late-century writers' desires for adequate compensation and public respect produced one of the more durable, resilient products of this late-century flurry of literary history: the periodization of the nineteenth century. At the center of this inquiry is the international copyright movement, which in the 1880s galvanized writers and literary workers intent on securing financial rights and editorial control over their work across national borders. To generate public sympathy and combat widespread associations of authorship with aristocratic privilege, copyright activists preyed upon already tense Anglo-American literary relations and generated literary histories that banished the literary aristocracy to a distant, Anglophilic past. In so doing, late-century literary activists constituted themselves as patriotic populists and self-made men, producing an enduring narrative of literary history that has gone unchallenged since its inception in the 1880s.

I follow this discussion of periodization with a chapter on professionalism and its impact on the literary academy. As universities began to change their requirements for hiring, promotion, and tenure, generalist English professors who had been hired on the basis of their social contacts and literary sensibilities suddenly found themselves expected to compete with the researches of their highly trained philologist colleagues. It was in this climate that literary history emerged as a vehicle for these men to publish scholarship and comply with mounting institutional expectations. While professionalism may have instituted scholarly quality control, it also left less laudable marks on the literary histories produced under its aegis, such as the frequency with which literary historians manipulated the data at their disposal to tell narratives that established the social importance of literary experts and critics. In this way, literary histories regularly incorporated already circulating narratives about the dangers of unsupervised reading to transform the antebellum literary critic Margaret Fuller into a poster child for the civic necessity of literary professionalism, a tactic that destroyed her reputation until feminist critics began rehabilitative work in the 1970s and 1980s.

Whereas Brander Matthews found significant success both as a professor at Columbia University and as a popular writer, his counterpart at Harvard, Barrett Wendell, was a famous underachiever whose efforts at both fiction and literary history failed to generate the attention he hoped for. If he is known at all today, it is for the vicious review his *Literary History of America* (1900) received at the hands of the novelist and critic William Dean Howells. The final chapter traces the prehistory of that review to investigate the origins of Wendell's most lasting legacy in American literary history: the anointing of antebellum New England as the apex of American literary achievement.

As a discipline we forget how truly unlikely this belief was, as the late century saw the critical depreciation of such antebellum luminaries as Holmes, Longfellow, and Lowell, and this chapter investigates the improbable survival of this core argument of Wendell's literary history, despite Howells's public denunciation of the regional and class biases he saw underlying it. Indeed, the endurance of Wendell's controversial argument reveals the survival in American literary history of these same alliances of region, class, and academic affiliation that Howells decried.

In keeping with all historical inquiries, this book is no less transparently idealistic, for my perception of the profession's past, and present, derives from my hopes for a disciplinary future more willing to historicize itself, more willing to examine how our work calculatingly and explicitly defines our own subject positions as professionals, as teachers, as researchers, scholars, historians, and critics. Until we do so, we fall prey with "apparent obliviousness to the rhetorical content of what [we] present as historical facts," in the words of Lora Romero.[12] To that end, *Writers in Retrospect* probes the origins of the field of American literary history so that we may determine whether the literary, cultural, and political vision implicit in the intellectual foundations of our discipline is one we necessarily want to promote.

PART I

{ *The Lay of the Land:*
Nation & the Responsibilities
of Literary History

CHAPTER 1

A Culture of Retrospection

The Rise of Literary History in the Late Nineteenth Century

In 1891, Julian Hawthorne, the son of Nathaniel Hawthorne and a popular late-century novelist in his own right, observed that "American literature has of late been receiving considerable attention," and he cited the works of the critics Charles F. Richardson, Edmund C. Stedman, Moses Coit Tyler, and Charles Dudley Warner as examples of the trend he had detected.[1] Hawthorne's observation was apt, for the preceding decade had seen an upsurge of critical interest in American literature, but his announcement is hardly news to current specialists in American literature, as in recent years both David R. Shumway and Kermit Vanderbilt have published important studies of the rise of American literature as an academic discipline in the late nineteenth century.[2] In spite of its seeming self-evidence, however, Julian Hawthorne's remark reminds us of the specific conditions under which American literature began to receive such concentrated critical attention. All his examples of important contributors to American literary study—Richardson, Stedman, Tyler, among others—had achieved renown in the 1870s and 1880s for their published research in a specific branch of American literary scholarship, namely, American literary history. It was in the form of literary history that American literature was first taught at American universities by such men as Richardson and Tyler and was first written about in scholarly studies and monographs, a fact about itself that the profession has long forgotten. To chart the history of American literary history, as it were, is to chart the earliest history of American literary study itself, for it was under the aegis of literary history that the study of American literature emerged in the late nineteenth century.

As early as the 1870s, American literary history became a full-fledged fad, with the publication of countless texts in any number of genres—magazine articles, literary biographies, anthologies, textbooks, lectures, and book-length studies—that attempted to chronicle the growth and achievements of American letters. Enthusiasm for literary history extended beyond the limits of the American university, with such varied figures as Julian Hawthorne, Thomas Wentworth Higginson, William Dean Howells, Donald Mitchell (who published under the pseudonym Ik Marvel), the publisher George Haven Putnam, and the poet Edmund Stedman all trying their hands at this fashionable new genre. This spate of productivity lasted roughly until the second decade of the twentieth century, when World War I, the emergence of literary modernism, and the publication of the seemingly definitive *Cambridge History of American Literature* (1917–21) together turned literary scholars' attention elsewhere. Public and academic appetites for these histories seem to have been considerable, as evidenced by the high sales of Brander Matthews's *Introduction to the Study of American Literature* (1896), which sold over a quarter of a million copies, and Barrett Wendell's *Literary History of America* (1900), which flew off the shelves in early 1901 and remained in print until the 1940s. In addition to the many academic publishers that issued literary history textbooks, more mainstream publishers readily made room for literary histories on their lists, and all the major publishing houses of the period—Harper's, Houghton Mifflin, Macmillan, Putnam, Scribner's—issued high-profile literary histories to considerable fanfare. Even children's magazines participated in this fad, as with the *St. Nicholas* magazine, which in the 1890s ran a series of author biographies tailored to young readers.

In addition to broad historical surveys of American literature, the era saw the publication of specialized studies of particular aspects of American literary history, as with Moses Coit Tyler's numerous treatments of early American literature, William Peterfield Trent's works on the American South, and Edmund Stedman's various histories of American poetry. The period also saw the publication of reference books such as *Appleton's Encyclopedia of American Biography* (1887); book-length monographs, typically titled "time lines," that compared events in American literary history with those of national politics and social history; and comparative surveys that overlaid American literary history on a larger account of European or British literature. Other literary histories aimed for sheer breadth, such as the massive eleven-volume *Library of American Literature* (1888–90), edited by Edmund Stedman and the *New-York Tribune* book editor Ellen M. Hutchinson, an anthology whose catholicity is apparent in its highly unusual inclusion of such typically overlooked genres as Negro spirituals and sentimentalist narrative. At the turn of the century, literary history became such a fixture in American letters that, by the first years of the twentieth century, literary histories began including self-referential histories of the genre itself, as with Theodore Stanton's *Manual of American Literature* (1909), which included a brief history of American literary history that mentioned the accomplishments of Brander Matthews, Charles F. Richardson, Moses Coit Tyler, and Barrett Wendell. Similarly, Edmund Stedman included a chapter from Charles F. Richardson's literary history in the eighth volume of the *Library of American Literature*, an inclusion that suggests the perception of literary history itself as a literary historical event.

The literary histories published during that thirty-year span employed a wide array of methodologies, organizational strategies, and ambitions, both stated and implied, but they were nonetheless united by a desire to narrate the American literary past and by a presumed belief that such historical narratives were of interest to American readers. Though today the names Charles F. Richardson and Moses Coit Tyler hardly resonate even for specialists in American literature, these men and their cohort of avid literary historians produced knowledge about American literature that has been instated as received wisdom and still endures today. They organized American literature into periods; discerned within each of those periods dominant literary figures, texts, and influences; and traced trends and patterns believed to thread through American literature over time. And in publishing a steady stream of texts and textbooks tailored to young readers, these literary historians enabled American primary and secondary schools to include American literature in their curricula for the first time. Though we may not formally acknowledge these men as disciplinary founders, they collectively and individually produced the most basic tools and assumptions of the discipline of American literary history.

The attraction to the American literary past that saturated literary markets during those years defies any simple explanation, for a constellation of factors and motives together bred a culture of literary retrospection at the turn of the last century. In his fine history of American literary study during the twentieth century, David R. Shumway isolates immigration and the consequent struggle to define the limits of American culture as primary motive forces for the rise of American literary study, a dynamic I will discuss more fully in the following chapter. American literature, he argues, was enlisted both defensively and offensively in response to the crisis of immigration, with American-authored texts constituted as primers of American culture whose reading was believed to enable the immigrant's acclimatization to American culture.[3] Shumway's analysis may account for the prominence of New York-based writers and institutions—for example, the Columbia University professors George Rice Carpenter, Brander Matthews, and William Peterfield Trent—in the turn-of-the-century eruption of American literary history, for their position in the epicenter of national immigration may have made these concerns immediately pressing and rendered their work in American literary study politically germane and timely.

This argument, however salient and important, does not sufficiently account for the larger appetite for historical chronicles in the period, and we cannot discount a variety of other circumstances in turn-of-the-century culture that equally contributed to such avid literary retrospection. One vital feature of American life worth remembering in this context is the culture of commemoration that characterized the late century. The conclusion of the Reconstruction era, which had been fraught with rabid anxieties—both racial and economic—about the nation's future, conveniently coincided with a sequence of national centenary events that provided abundant opportunities for national retrospection. Beginning with the 1876 celebration of the national centennial, the following decades of the century were studded with commemorative galas and holidays celebrating the hundredth anniversary of numerous national events, among them the ratification of the Constitution and Washington's two inaugurations. In an era replete with many print media outlets all competing for market share, this sequence of centenary celebrations required the repeated production of texts that both revisited these originary moments in American history and attempted to synthesize quickly and efficiently the ensuing hundred years in American life. American history in general witnessed a considerable surge in interest and productivity amid this climate, and the historical retrospective in particular became a frequent feature of magazines and periodicals in the last quarter of the nineteenth century.[4]

Because these centenaries necessitated the celebratory exhibition of national accomplishments during the preceding century, American literature became a regular fixture for the exercise of national retrospection in this era. At least since Sydney Smith's famous question, posed in the *Edinburgh Review* in 1820, "Who reads an American book?," no aspect of American life has been more used as an index of cultural vitality than its literature; consequently, the pressing need to affirm American cultural achievement in the late century necessitated the accumulation of evidence attesting to American *literary* achievement. In this context, literary history often served as a proxy for a more comprehensive survey of national culture, which may account for the persistent presence of historians, natural scientists, orators, statesmen, and theologians in literary history. It is therefore no coincidence that, after over twenty years of dormancy since the enthusiasm for poetry anthologies in the 1840s and the 1855 publication of Evert and George Duyckinck's prodigious *Cyclopaedia of American Literature*, literary histories began to emerge in the late 1870s in conjunction with these centenary celebrations.

Literary histories often frankly announced their formal ties to the centenary celebrations of the late century, as with Henry Beers's *Century of American Literature 1776–1876* (1878). Perhaps the most successful and lauded literary history published in the immediate aftermath of the centennial was Moses Coit Tyler's *History of American Literature*

(1878), the success of which was due in large part to its focus on the years preceding the Revolution, which had been the subject of much attention in the wake of the centenary. Tyler's early American literary history was so admired that, in the words of Alan Heimert, it was "already in 1890 a classic," relied upon and cited by subsequent literary historians.[5] The popularity of history following the 1876 centennial proved a boon for literature professors more generally and for teachers of American literature in particular. In chapter 4, I discuss the significant changes in the literary academy during the late century, but it bears remarking that history provided the ballast necessary for the legitimation of American literary study, a subfield that had tenuous status at best.[6] History added rigor and scholarly authority to the study of American letters, both in American universities and in wider transatlantic literary opinion.[7] Just as Moses Coit Tyler had had to become a professor of history in order to study and teach American literature, so history offered late-century literary men a scholarly vehicle by which they could engage American literature without suspicion of laxity.[8]

To be sure, the use of literary history as evidence of national cultural achievement had a European context, for the genre had already flourished abroad with the publication of Spanish, German, and English literary histories, among others. This precedent spurred the production of American literary history intent on showcasing the comparable stature and fitness of the new nation. The papers of the Columbia University professor and literary historian Brander Matthews indicate an acute consciousness of these European antecedents in the drafting of his 1896 *Introduction to the Study of American Literature*, as evidenced by the many excerpts from various European national literary histories included in his archived files on American literature. Many of the most prominent American literary histories were visibly indebted to European forebears, as with Selden L. Whitcomb's *Chronological Outlines of American Literature* (1894), which explicitly announced its derivation from Frederick Ryland's *Chronological Outlines of English Literature* (1890). Similarly, the American Men of Letters series, which published high-profile if slim literary biographies, seems to have taken its cues from a British precursor, the English Men of Letters series. The European literary history that provided the most explicit model for late-century American literary historians was the Collection of British Authors series, more widely known as the Tauchnitz edition, founded in 1841 in Leipzig by the German publisher Baron Bernhard Tauchnitz with the aim of "promot[ing] the literary interest of . . . Anglo-Saxon cousins, by rendering English literature as universally known as possible beyond the limits of the British empire."[9] Quite a lot can be said about this statement by the son of the founder of the Tauchnitz edition—its imbrication of the spread of British imperial power with the circulation of British literature is particularly noteworthy—but the intersecting language here of consanguinity and national separateness presages the similar rhetoric that would be deployed later in the century by American literary historians such as Charles F. Richardson, who used American literature both to demarcate the racial limits of American culture and to proffer that literature as a vehicle of assimilation; histories of national literatures in the nineteenth century were designed at once to differentiate and to amalgamate.[10]

The emergence of literary history in the late century may have also been due in some measure to the consequences of the turn of a century, which, as we have seen in our own time, engenders a climate of retrospection and cultural accounting. Just as the turn of the twenty-first century saw the proliferation of "best of" lists that appraised and ranked the cultural achievements of the past century (or millennium, as the case may be), the turn of the twentieth century saw a similar cultural impulse, as with the wealth of anthologies and omnibuses issued in this era, all of which claimed to have edited literature down to its finest artifacts. For example, Charles Dudley Warner, editor of the American Men of Letters series, also edited the massive thirty-volume *Library of the World's Best Literature Ancient and Modern* (1898), and Charles Eliot Norton oversaw the Heart of Oak Books, a series of anthologies that claimed to use quality literature to cultivate the reader's literary taste.[11] Similarly, the novelist and critic William Dean Howells attempted to develop a "Library of Select Literature," which, though it went unpublished, aimed to whittle literature down to its greatest specimens. In doing the work of selecting American writers and texts they deemed of particular significance, the many American literary histories published in this period were of a piece with the larger cultural compulsion to inventory and rank generated by the turn of a century. The context of cultural accounting necessarily puts such texts as Albert H. Smyth's *American Literature* (1889) and William C. Lawton's *Introduction to the Study of American Literature* (1902) in the company of such works as *The Harvard Classics* (1910), perhaps the most famous example of the curatorial cataloging of literature in the period. Popularly known as "Dr. Eliot's Five-Foot Shelf of Books" and edited by Harvard president Charles W. Eliot upon his retirement, it was composed of fifty volumes of world literature he had personally selected. An important study is yet to be written interpreting the late-century vogue for self-education within the context of the cultural compulsions generated by the turn of the century, as the urge to catalog cultural achievements produced texts, literary histories among them, explicitly designed for informal and formal programs of adult education.[12]

The culture of commemoration also had a more direct incentive for turning to literature. The last quarter of the century witnessed not only a wealth of centennial celebrations but also a series of events that confirmed for the first time a transfer of power from one literary generation to another. The last two decades of the nineteenth century saw the deaths of many American writers associated with an earlier time in American letters: Louisa May Alcott, Ralph Waldo Emerson, Oliver Wendell Holmes, Henry Wadsworth Longfellow, James Russell Lowell, and John Greenleaf Whittier all died in the last quarter of the century. Writers who ascended to prominence after the Civil War— among them Hamlin Garland, William Dean Howells, Henry James, and Mark Twain—were vividly aware of the superannuation and fragility of their forebears, and so these deaths were often preceded by well-publicized gala dinners at which younger writers feted the lives and achievements of their literary predecessors, as with the infamous 1877 dinner in honor of Emerson, Holmes, and Longfellow during which Twain delivered a notoriously unsuccessful speech lampooning the guests of honor before an appalled audience. The public appetite for centenary celebrations would eventually coincide with this awareness of literary mortality, and the centenaries of American writers such as Washington Irving and Nathaniel Hawthorne became opportunities for the celebration of national literary achievement; for example, the 1903 centenary of Emerson's birth was marked by a particularly eventful two-week-long gala that included Thomas Wentworth Higginson and Julia Ward Howe as participants.[13]

These events produced countless valedictory celebrations of the literary past, whether through obituaries of the dead or through commemorative public addresses that, in memorializing the lives of writers whose national significance had only recently been confirmed by literary historical writings published in honor of the centennial, produced an environment sympathetic to literary retrospection. It is therefore unsurprising that the genre of the eulogy figures so prominently in the texts it indirectly inspired. Many of the entries in these literary histories often served as de facto obituaries for recently deceased writers, as with the markedly sorrowful tone that often imbued discussions of Emerson, who died in 1882. The frequent appearance of published tributes among the archived papers of numerous literary historians suggests that these postmortem valedictions may very well have served as resources culled for data in research. Eulogies for the literary dead frequently made their way into literary histories, as with Emerson's eulogy for Henry David Thoreau and William Cullen Bryant's eulogies for both James Fenimore Cooper and Washington Irving. These speeches were excavated for pithy epigrams—as with Emerson's oft-quoted description of the underachieving Thoreau as "the captain of a huckleberry-party"—and treated as literary events in and of themselves, which suggests a high regard in this era for the literary memorial, a genre of which literary history was part.[14]

This widely publicized generational demise contributed directly to a particular enthusiasm for a subgenre of literary history—the author biography. One particularly visible product was the American Men of Letters series of the Riverside imprint at Houghton Mifflin, edited by

Charles Dudley Warner.[15] Commissioned upon the success of Warner's 1881 biography of Washington Irving, the American Men of Letters series published a flurry of high-profile literary biographies that showcased and even profited from this generational shift. As with the biography of Oliver Wendell Holmes by western-novelist Owen Wister and a biography of Emerson authored by Holmes himself, the more popular volumes published in the American Men of Letters series were typically authored by younger writers who had personally known their subject, and in so doing they formally announced a literary generational succession. The American Men of Letters series and the conditions that inspired it exerted considerable influence on literary history by the emphasis on "the cult of exemplarity," the isolation of the individual author's life as a synecdoche of a wider movement or trend.[16] Although this methodology was first advocated in the nineteenth century by the French critic Hippolyte Taine and was already firmly in place in Continental and British literary history, the American Men of Letters series helped institutionalize an individualistic thrust in American literary history that depicted the American literary past as an orderly, diachronic succession of Great Men.

Although the series ultimately failed to live up to the publisher's expectations, it offers important insight into literary history in the late century. The series' authors were drawn in roughly equal measure from English professors intent on broadcasting their expertise and literary writers drawing upon their own memories and experiences. This heterogeneity resulted in an unevenness of tone and content, as the series mediated between the scholarly and the gossipy, between the production of knowledge and the recitation of personal anecdotes. This mixture was characteristic of late-century literary history as a whole, and it indicates the difficulty faced by the genre in balancing the increasingly separate domains of the academic and the popular, between the specialized and the mass market. This uneasy negotiation contributed to Warner's editorial decision to counterbalance volumes of wider appeal with volumes, for the sake of historical thoroughness, about less popular writers such as Nathaniel Parker Willis.[17] In this way, the American Men of Letters series typified the challenges and decisions faced by literary historians marketing intellectual content for a mass audience.[18] The series' financial disappointment also tells us something about readers of literary history, who resisted purchasing the entire series, preferring to buy individual volumes instead. Similar problems afflicted the sales of Edmund Stedman's eleven-volume *Library of American Literature*, whose considerable expense rendered it financially inaccessible to the lower-class and middle-class markets targeted by salesmen. The ambitious planning of both series signals the wide hopes of publishers seeking to profit from popular interest in literary history, though it would seem that readers were less interested in cultivating expertise in the field than in acquiring a more generalized knowledge—that is, readers were less inclined to commit to multivolume series that provided depth and range but instead reached for the convenience and economy of condensed, single-volume works. In this way, publishers overestimated American readers' interest in literary history, which occupied a subordinate role in readers' wider campaigns of self-improvement and self-education.

The preoccupation with the past, both literary and national, may at first glance seem out of keeping with the stated interests of some of the more commanding, forceful literary critics of the late century, such as William Dean Howells. According to the inexact intellectual practice that is periodization, the late century is typically associated with the loose consortium of writers and editors grouped together by their espousal of an aesthetic of realism, which entailed the rejection of many established literary conventions they deemed outdated, and the partiality for literary texts they believed more accurately documented the texture and rhythm of American life. But to assign the literary late century solely to realism is both to overstate its popularity and influence and to downplay the resistance to realism leveled by many of the era's most influential and respected literary critics— among them Edmund Clarence Stedman, Barrett Wendell, Richard Grant White, and George Edward Woodberry—who were grouped together by their aesthetic idealism, their distaste for the vulgarity they detected in realism, and the decline of values they associated with the literary past. The late century was riven by wide disagreement about the ethical and aesthetic merits of realism, but this discord was couched in a wider disagreement about the proper attitude toward the literary past. To use the enduring language trenchantly offered by Van Wyck Brooks in 1918, this conflict had at stake the methods of creating "a usable past." The antirealists—labeled by later critics as the "Genteel Tradition"—often resemble prim Victorians in their nostalgia for a literary past they idealized and strove to preserve through their writings, whereas the realists worked at every turn to rescue literature from what they felt to be a literary past that had outlived its natural limits, and consequently prevented the literary present from assuming its rightful place as successor.[19] Whereas the Genteel Tradition deemed the literary past usable because of its ability to work as a moral and aesthetic compass orienting the literary present, realists had very different opinions about the utility of the past, and literary histories seemed poised to aid both the realists and their opponents in their respective positions toward the literary past.

It is not necessary to rehearse here the complications and impracticalities of a literary aesthetic essentially at cross purposes with the very media of fiction and literary invention, but realism was at its core present-oriented and, as such, assumed a contentious stance toward the literary past.[20] William Dean Howells famously used his columns in both *Harper's Weekly* and *Harper's Monthly* to urge American writers and readers to reorient their literary tastes toward texts that offered faithful depictions of the substance of life and that therefore took a more skeptical attitude toward such durable literary conventions as the marriage plot, which seemed to him to exaggerate the drama of such events in the lives of Americans. Realists deplored what they believed to be the imitativeness of American fiction, which, they argued, took its cues less from the immediate conditions of late-century American life and culture than from the conventions popularized decades before in British and Continental fiction; rather than reflecting the conditions of its own immediate production, fiction, the realists maintained, had become anachronistic in its subservience to its own generic history.

In an 1887 *Harper's Monthly* column, Howells offered a technique of literary evaluation that he hoped would help differentiate the technically derivative from the technically good. "For our own part we confess that we do not care to judge any work of the imagination without first of all applying this test to it. We must ask ourselves before we ask anything else, Is it true?—true to the motives, the impulses, the principles that shape the life of actual men and women?"[21] In his column published the following month, Howells announced: "Let fiction cease to lie about life; let it portray men and women as they are, actuated by the motives and the passions in the measure we all know; let it leave off painting dolls and working them by springs and wires . . . let it not put on fine literary airs; let it speak the dialect, the language, that most Americans know—the language of unaffected people everywhere."[22]

Recommending the reduction of the fictionality of fiction leads Howells here and elsewhere to call for a nearly ethnographic commitment to exactitude, and realists as diverse as Hamlin Garland, Howells, Henry James, and Mark Twain advocated, to varying degrees, tempering literary imagination with fieldwork spent in intent observation, the results of which would be channeled in literary texts distinguished by their anthropological accuracy.[23] In works of criticism as varied as Henry James's "The Art of Fiction" (1884) and Twain's "Fenimore Cooper's Literary Offenses" (1895), writers working in this idiom disdained texts that depended for their research chiefly on the style and plots of other novels.

In its advocacy of present-oriented fiction, realism constituted yet another late-century engagement in American literary retrospection, for its principal grievance lay in what it believed to be the excessive enthusiasm of Americans for the literary past. In essence, realists saw the late-century culture of retrospection as a dire impediment to American literary achievement and regarded with consternation the American aestheticizing of the past at the expense of a healthy appreciation for the present. This is not to suggest that literary realists opposed the proliferation of literary history in this period. On the contrary, realists emerged as some of the most ardent supporters of literary history. And though it provided a vehicle by which Americans could direct their attention away from the immediate present so valorized by realists, literary history was nonetheless fully compatible with their goals and flourished in part because of the sponsorship of realists. The impact of Howells's sponsorship alone cannot be overstated.[24] He reviewed all the major contributions to literary history and many of the minor ones, too, and, in so doing, publicized these books to a national literary market attuned to his recommendations and taste. As I will discuss in chapter 4, Howells's reviews initiated an important, highly influential discussion about the social responsibilities of the literary historian, and in this way he educated readers in the emerging generic conventions of literary history. Howells even dabbled in the genre himself with the occasional historically oriented review and with his own two-volume *Heroines of Fiction* (1901), in which he charted the treatment of women in the Anglo-American novel. Howells himself encouraged the playwright and Columbia professor Brander Matthews to write his *Introduction to the Study of American Literature* (1896), asking, "Why don't *you* write a history of fiction for scholars and colleges? Nobody else could do it so delightfully and so well."[25]

In an 1896 review of two different literary histories—Matthews's volume and Albert H. Smyth's biography of Bayard Taylor in the American Men of Letters series—Howells helped account in part for the realist appreciation of literary history. Acknowledging the popularity of American literary history during "the last twenty or thirty years," he expressed his belief that such work signaled "that we have freed ourselves, in a measure unknown before, from our awe of alien criticism, and that what we had lately written was from an impulse of our own life, without the fear or affection of any public beyond our borders."[26] That is, literary history betokened in part the fulfillment of one of the realists' aims: the production of criticism free from European influence and committed to American life and letters. But what seems to have been at the center of realist sponsorship was the help that literary histories promised to offer in mapping a literary past that had become unwieldy and indistinctly delimited; literary histories seemed poised to chart the literary past for both readers and writers unaware of the obsolescence and origin of their literary tastes. Through discussions that situated various literary styles within the contexts of their origination, literary histories promised to disentangle the literary past from the literary present, and so would make it possible for readers both to recognize its stylistic footprints and to grow more sensitive to realist aims.

But this is not to suggest that antirealists had been inimical to literary histories because of a perception of these histories as somehow subservient to realist interests. Rather, opponents of realism made enormously important contributions to literary history, as with Edmund Stedman's eleven-volume anthology of American literature and his numerous histories of American poetry.[27] Similarly, the Columbia professor George Edward Woodberry authored biographies of Emerson, Hawthorne, and Poe, as well as the 1903 literary history *America in Literature*. For these antirealists, however, literary history seemed designed not to secure the final ejection of the literary past but to preserve it in amber, as it were, and to burnish its sheen to a high polish. For example, in the introduction to *The Nature and Elements of Poetry* (1892)—a collection of lectures given in 1891 under the aegis of the Percy Turnbull lectureship of poetry at Johns Hopkins University—Edmund Stedman situated his lectures on the history of poetry in the context of late-century tastes, which he found wanting. "Perhaps it is only natural," he wrote, "that such intention [of these lectures] should be overcome by a striking illustration of the fact that, under stress of public neglect or distaste, the lovers of any cause or art find their regard for it more unshaken than ever. . . . It seemed to me a notable and suggestive thing that at such a time, though many think of poetry as the voice of the past, a few should still consider it a voice of the future also, and that there should be found what I may call practical idealists."[28] Literary history offered Stedman a vehicle by which he could respond to and correct popular literary tastes, an aim he shared with the realists, but Stedman expresses here a hope that, in cultivating an appreciation for the past, literary histories will secure its enduring influence.

Unsurprisingly, the literary histories authored by realists and antirealists differed profoundly in their attitude toward the literary present, which was depicted either as auspicious or as apocalyptic, depending on the author's attitude toward realism and the literary present. Despite the fact that these men were members of the same cohort of turn-of-the-century literary men—who worked in the same literary genres, joined the same literary and social clubs, contributed to and read the same periodicals, and often worked side by side in activist causes such as the international copyright movement—it is important to remember the divisiveness engendered by these widely different, if principled, attitudes toward the literary past. Some of the most ugly and infamous skirmishes of the literary late century took place between men on opposing sides of this rift, as with the 1886 hostilities between Howells and Stedman that ensued when Howells published a review that took Stedman to task for his literary idealism; the antagonism between Brander Matthews and his Columbia colleague George Woodberry, which could be resolved only with the institutional reorganization of literary studies into several departments; and Howells's ongoing wrangles with Barrett Wendell about literary taste. If these episodes of literary antagonism can tell us anything about the literary culture of the late century, it is that these differing attitudes toward the literary past were deeply felt, often because they provided a cover by which literary men attempted to articulate and establish a literary climate tailored to their exact specifications. In narrating the literary past, literary historians were implicitly voicing their vision of a literary present and a literary future—and of their own place in them. The chapters that follow will examine particular episodes in the narration of the American literary past to show at once the long-forgotten context that produced some of the most important tenets in the discipline of American literary history and the visions of American literature that we, in our disciplinary attachment to these tenets, unconsciously cling to.

CHAPTER 2

Preservation & Assimilation

Brander Matthews and the
Silences of Literary History

Numerous scholars in recent years have ex-
amined the popular national enthusiasm for Native peoples and their
artifacts during the turn of the last century, a fervor in sharp contrast
with a long-standing national policy of extermination, deracination,
and, as the century wore on, assimilation and forcible cultural renun-
ciation.[1] Evidence of such popular interest abounds: from countless
juvenile adventure novels and theatrical adaptations of Longfellow's
Hiawatha to Frederic Remington's paintings and numerous literary
texts with a Native setting (among them Hamlin Garland's 1902 novel
The Captain of the Grey-Horse Troop and Zitkala-Sa's short fiction published in the *Atlantic Monthly* and in her 1901 collection, *Old Indian
Legends*), this interest is visible in a variety of media, cultural settings,
and social strata. Enthusiasm extended into the researches of turn-of-
the-century academics, as with the work of anthropologists such as
Franz Boas and Paul Radin examining Native cultures and the published transcriptions of Native tales by such figures as Natalie Burlin
Curtis, George Dorsey, and Boas himself. Considering this climate,
it can be presumed that the inclusion of Native narrative artifacts
in late-century literary histories would have been greeted favorably
in both popular and academic settings. However, despite this widespread enthusiasm and the ready access to Native narrative, American
literary histories published between 1875 and 1910 are conspicuously
silent about Native peoples and their narrative traditions. Such an
omission is all the more striking because of the interest that literary
historians often showed for other kinds of indigenous oral artifacts,
such as the many Bre'r Rabbit stories transcribed to great popularity
by Joel Chandler Harris and the proliferation of local color and realist
writings that put an aesthetic premium on oral narration; the *Library*

of American Literature (1888–90), the nation's first comprehensive literature anthology, even devoted an entire section to Negro spirituals.[2]

The omission of Native narrative and people can be attributed to some of the larger political and social ambitions of turn-of-the-century literary history. David Shumway has shown how American literary studies derived from late-century anxieties about the urgent need for uniformity of belief and practice among a citizenry of increasingly diverse provenance.[3] Histories of American literature, too, gained luster from this political context by manufacturing a literary tradition that would defend the cultural fort from foreigners (and the literary traditions they brought with them) and by producing an educational curriculum in American values, aesthetics, and history. In documenting a continuous chain of literary transmission and innovation, literary histories offered a reassuring narrative of national achievement uncomplicated by strife or the threat of alien incursion. American literary histories, that is, emerged as one of many strategies in the late century designed to prevent the United States from joining Native peoples in the company of vanished civilizations, for it was hoped that the reading of American literature would cultivate national values among foreign students and breed national cohesiveness through the circulation of a uniform body of knowledge.

Alan Trachtenberg has recently examined the importance of Native peoples to these turn-of-the-century responses to immigration.[4] In a policy that visibly channeled anxieties engendered by immigration about the dangers of isolated cultural pockets within the nation, the Dawes Severalty Act of 1887 advocated the elimination of Native peoples less by explicit violence than by assimilation. To that end, private property ownership and labor were designated vital routes by which Native peoples could be Americanized, and tribal landholdings were divided into individual agricultural plots to be worked by Native tenants. Education emerged as one of the key vehicles for the execution of assimilationist policy, with the establishment of schools and curricula expressly designed to weaken attachments to indigenous cultural traditions and to inculcate in Native students more mainstream national beliefs, practices, and history.[5] Often used as pedagogical instruments, literary histories complied by excising Native narrative and peoples from the record of national literary achievement altogether. The cloak of silence about Native peoples that enveloped literary histories in the late century is nothing less than a literary extension of the national program to eliminate the distinctiveness of Native peoples within the larger national collective, for such was the effect of literary histories that failed even to notice Native peoples.[6]

There is one exception, however, and that is the work of Brander Matthews, a Columbia University professor whose extensive contribution to American literary history included *An Introduction to the Study of American Literature* (1896), a secondary school textbook that cumulatively sold over a quarter of a million copies. Matthews did not incorporate Native narrative per se into his literary histories, but his work nonetheless remains pivotal to a political historiography of the genre because of its attempts to steer literary history away from propagandistic silence and toward greater frankness about Native peoples in American history and literature. American literary history, he proposed, ought not to contribute to the historical erasure of Native peoples but instead ought to commemorate and preserve their history. Matthews's work therefore stands alone in turn-of-the-century literary history, championing literary texts that depicted Native peoples and discreetly alluding to national events and policies banished from more hagiographic works. That said, Matthews was neither radical nor aggressive in making these claims. A canny promoter and marketer, he never resorted to extremist tactics that might jeopardize his sales or standing; he instead relied upon subtle allusions and equivocation that skirted controversy but still made clear his political sympathies and generic preferences. It is very difficult to talk about silence, but Matthews's techniques and varied work allow us to see more clearly the conventions and obligations that enabled the suppressions of other literary histories of the period. His work in diverse genres and media compulsively returned again and again to Native peoples, and he persistently paired these engagements with considerations of education and its instruments in the elimination of Natives. In so doing, Matthews made visible and explicit the pedagogic, nationalist responsibilities that led turn-of-the-century literary history to proffer uncomplicated narratives of national achievement in decided contrast with widespread panic about the nation's future.

A playwright, drama critic, and important advocate of the academic study of American literature, Brander Matthews reflected throughout his career on the heavy nationalist responsibilities shouldered by educational institutions, particularly by teachers of literature. Though best remembered today as a socialite and chronicler of the glittering social lives of elite New Yorkers, Matthews was one of the earliest and best-known public intellectuals in American academic history.[7] His status was such that in 1910 he became the nominal representative of the entire profession in his election to the presidency of the Modern Language Association.[8] Matthews used his considerable muscle to lobby for American literary studies, both at Columbia and in the profession at large, and in this way made invaluable contributions to the nascent fields of American literary study and American literary history. In publishing essays on American writers in such periodicals as the *North American Review*, the *Atlantic Monthly*, and *Harper's*, Matthews attempted to cultivate public interest in such material, but he also did important work in the establishment of a specialized academic field of study. He developed the first course in both American literature and American literary history at Columbia University and helped Columbia develop a reputation as the leading institution in this field. His work as a writer and teacher paved the way for the first comprehensive work of American literary history, the *Cambridge History of American Literature* (1917–21), a collection sponsored by Columbia and edited by the Columbia professors John Erskine, William Peterfield Trent, and Carl Van Doren, and that featured essays by Columbia English faculty, including Matthews himself. His study of American culture extended into his voluminous work as a literary writer, which often drew inspiration from American history. As with his play *Peter Stuyvesant, Governor of New Amsterdam*

(1899), Matthews often revisited and imaginatively re-created early moments and figures in American history.

This interest in American culture and use of literature as an agent of historical elaboration spilled over into a lifelong interest in Native peoples. An avid collector of masks, Matthews amassed an impressive and diverse collection of Native American masks. While doing the initial research for his 1896 literary history, Matthews collaborated with the composer Charles Villier Stanford on the one-act ballet *Pocahontas* (1894), a highly conventional version of the fictionalized narrative of Pocahontas's fabled romance with Captain John Smith.[9] Matthews's enthusiasm for Native relics and representations certainly accords with late-century tastes and trends, but by the early 1880s Matthews made Native imagery his own personal insignia or trademark, an identification that may account for his unusual later opinion. In 1882, just as national literary history was beginning to prosper, he commissioned a bookplate that offered a more sentimental depiction of the Native American past than he would produce a decade later. Drafted by Edwin Austin Abbey, an artist best known for his illustrations of dramatic scenes and paintings drawn from Shakespearean drama, this image is in some respects typical of the late century in its flat, iconic, and allegorized depiction of Native peoples as well as its ostensible celebration of assimilationism.[10] It nonetheless qualifies as Matthews's first venture into American literary history and as the literal template for all his later discussions of Native people, which he would repeatedly revise and reference. While serving as a visual metaphor for the powers of education in general, this image merits consideration, for, in its depiction of an imaginary moment of cultural contact, it explicates the allure of literary histories in the late century, whose recountings of past national achievements in assimilation assuaged late-century anxieties about the national future.

Dated March 1882, the image is circular, with a thin frame around the image containing a quotation attributed to Molière, "Que pensez-vous de cette comédie?," taken from *La Critique de l'école des femmes* (1663), and which means "What do you think of this comedy [or

Edwin Austin Abbey, "J. Brander Matthews hys Bokeplate," March 1882.
(James Brander Matthews Papers, Rare Book and Manuscript Library,
Columbia University; reproduced by permission)

play]?"[11] Inside the frame is an image of a Native man, bald except for a thin scalp lock at the top of his pate and wearing only a loincloth and feather. He kneels on a flat, grassy plain and holds an outsized mask into which he peers. Directly above his head and flanking him on both sides are Matthews's initials, which provide an internal frame in concert with the banded quotation. The original pen and ink drawing that became the template for the bookplate reads "J. Brander Matthews hys Bokeplate," words that, though they would be omitted from the plate itself, tether this image to its commissioner. Matthews retained and used the bookplate throughout his life. Upon his death, he bequeathed Abbey's original drawing and the printing plate made from it to Columbia University, a gift that indicates his perception of the image as of lasting value and importance.

Matthews's bookplate clearly stages an allegorical encounter, a meeting of cultural antipodes. The mask appears to be a found object, the residue of past inhabitants or travelers. It remains uncertain where the mask originated, but it is clear that it is not a Native one familiar to the kneeling man, for the grotesque profile of an upturned, strained grin clearly denotes the Greek mask of comedy, a denotation reinforced by the Molière allusion to comedic theater. The image of the Native man is replete with a visual vocabulary of primitiveness: his nakedness, the unself-conscious artlessness of his body language, his literal closeness to the earth, and the minimalism of the feather that is his sole adornment. The mask, too, contains a wealth of signification. Because of its origin in fifth-century B.C.E. Athens, long regarded as the navel of Western culture, the mask conjures at once antiquity and modernity. It emblematizes an evergreen narrative of ancient Greece as the cradle and author of civilization, but, as the indispensable accompaniment of Athenian theater, the mask also summons the literary and artistic creations of that ancient culture and its modern descendants: theater, cinema, literature, and the performing arts more generally. The product and ritual object of many civilizations, the mask often has less lofty associations, but the Athenian comedy mask evokes the hypercivilized through its association here with class privilege, those elite few with access both to high culture and to humanities curricula without immediate vocational applications. The allusion to Molière and inclusion of a French quotation corroborate the esoteric sympathies suggested by the Athenian mask. The effect of this juxtaposition of an icon of premodernity and an icon of an elitist fantasy of humanistic civilization depends upon the Native man's apparent receptivity to and interest in the mask, evident in his attentive study. Implicit in this image is an assumption that the mask is capable of shrinking the wide cultural chasm between the two and that the Native man's exposure may engender cultivated tastes and sympathies; the mask, that is, seems poised to socialize the Native man, and in this way the bookplate depicts the commencement of a humanities education.

And so it is not accidental that Matthews made this image his bookplate, for it stages in visual terms a narrative about the social and political applications of his own lifework as an educator and literary man (as well as a specialist in drama). Tacit in this image is the assumption that the encounter between the Native man and the mask is a first encounter; the man would not be so rapt and attentive to an already familiar object. This image stages an originary moment in American history, the moment of first contact between Native Americans and British settlers. Like his sentimentalized ballet *Pocahontas*, which replaced the history of violence between Jamestown settlers and Powhatan with a more benign and passive romance, this rendering of first contact replaces Western settlers with the more benevolent, passive figure of the mask. What emerges in Matthews's bookplate is a revision of a fraught, strife-ridden American political history as a peaceful, uncomplicated American literary history, in which the arts—drama, literature—play a central role in this ur-moment of the conquest of North America. And in depicting the occupation of North America as the work of artistic sympathy, the image reconstructs history by recasting violence as cultivation and conquest as education. In this way, Matthews's bookplate shows how American literary history may serve as a reassuring, partial substitute for a more thorough, and therefore unpleasant, account of American political history.

With the establishment of the Brander Matthews Dramatic Museum at Columbia University in 1911, this image came to be associated with an institute of higher learning. The result of both Matthews's considerable clout at Columbia and his authority as a creator of disciplinary knowledge, the Dramatic Museum adopted this image as its own insignia and plate, suggesting that this visual rendering of education had been both legible and appealing to custodians of higher learning, who implicitly endorsed this rendering of education as well as its narrative of American literary history. The connotations of Columbia University's name, derived from that of Christopher Columbus, neatly comport with the image's allusions to North American conquest, and Matthews's bookplate came to represent institutional policy at the university that fostered some of the most important researches in Native narrative tradition but whose name nonetheless broadcast its embrace of assimilationist policy. In its portrayal of the civilizing powers of education, the plate revisits a moment in the American past that would have been of immediate significance to an institution surrounded by large numbers of immigrants and urban poor. The image celebrates the past successes of assimilative programs to forecast their continuing successes in an increasingly diverse nation: mediating between the exigencies of the past and the present, the mask ominously suggests that the fate of Native peoples will also be the fate of immigrants.

Coiled beneath this seemingly sentimentalized image, however, are several easily overlooked but nonetheless noteworthy departures from late-century literary historical convention: its unusual inclusion of Native peoples in a chronicle of American literary history, its acknowledgment of literature's involvement in their assimilation, and the suggestion that American literary history commence with a discussion of the prior cultures of North America. Matthews's use of stock tropes allowed these potentially contentious proposals to go unnoticed, a savvy mediation between the politically and generically conventional and the politically broad-minded that would become typical of his engagements with Native peoples in his later works of literary history, in which he routinely used compliances with convention as shields for less conventional opinions.

Indeed, his 1896 literary history not only elaborated more fully on the discreet suggestions implicit in the bookplate but also similarly relied upon conservative camouflage for less popular positions. A textbook designed for the secondary-school market, the book began as a series of seven essays on individual American writers published in 1895 in the well-respected children's magazine *St. Nicholas*. In large part because of Matthews's celebrity as a public intellectual and socialite, as well as his own extensive experience doing promotion in the New York theater, his literary history received extensive promotion from its publisher, the American Book Company. It received reviews in countless local publications and national magazines such as *The Nation* and *Harper's Weekly*, which took the unusual step of reviewing a school textbook, though it was abundantly clear that this latter review was undertaken as a favor to Matthews from his friend the editor William Dean Howells. The wealth of publicity paid off for Matthews, and the book went through numerous printings. In the first four years after its initial publication, it sold 96,000 copies, and as late as 1922 Matthews received royalties on sales of over 4,000 copies.[12] Its long life on the backlist enabled Matthews in 1917, twenty years after first publishing it, to revise and reissue the book with new chapters on Lincoln and Webster and a revised chronology. Though designed as a schoolbook for young students, *An Introduction to the Study of American Literature* even attracted the attention of the Chautauqua movement, which tried to publish an edition for adult general education and self-improvement.

In numerous ways, Matthews's literary history complied with generic expectation and convention, as with his use of literary biography to teach American values to foreign students: he transformed Benjamin Franklin into an icon of frugality and industry, William Cullen Bryant into an exemplum of moderation, and Longfellow into a paragon of fortitude during times of personal strain.[13] Matthews spoke directly to this pedagogic expectation in his introduction, with remarks about the burden borne by literature in a national climate destabilized by immigration and expansionism abroad. Matthews explicitly touted the utility of common-language literature in forging a collectivity out of a cultural hodgepodge. He wrote:

> We believe that there is a difference between the American and the Englishman—although it is not easy to declare precisely what that difference may be. We believe that there is such a thing as Americanism. . . . This Americanism has left its mark on the writings of the authors of the United States. It is perhaps for this reason, and perhaps, because we all like to find ourselves in the books we read, that American writers are of more interest to us. . . . American

literature reproduces for us our own life; it records our feelings, our thoughts, and our deeds; it enables us to see ourselves and our neighbors as we really are. . . . [I]t explains us to ourselves. (13–14)

Matthews here explicitly invites the reader to perceive his book as a primer of American character and to search out the various traits that compose it. According to Matthews, reading American literature enables self-knowledge via knowledge of the national collective: American literature presumably manufactures national unity by enabling the self-recognition of its constituent citizens, thereby folding idiosyncratic distinctiveness into a recognizable national character.

Matthews capitalized on late-century anxieties about nationalism and assimilation by asking his old friend Theodore Roosevelt to review his textbook, and Roosevelt's lengthy, spirited review in *Bookman* generated such media attention for Matthew's literary history that it became as well known and as well circulated as the book itself.[14] Roosevelt was an apt choice that signaled to readers the political relevance of Matthews's literary history; a famously enthusiastic and wide-ranging reader of American literature, Roosevelt took seriously the political uses of literary texts and sponsored the works of writers whose politics he championed, such as Israel Zangwill's assimilationist 1908 play *The Melting Pot*.[15] The seriousness with which Roosevelt regarded the relevance of the humanities to national policy is evident in his "cowboy cabinet," a consortium assembled during his presidency of unofficial advisers on Indian policy, composed of such turn-of-the-century American writers and artists as Hamlin Garland, Frederic Remington, and Owen Wister. Roosevelt's persistent depiction of literature as a unifying force able to override differences in culture and history made him an especially astute choice as reviewer. In the first volume of his multivolume study *The Winning of the West* (1889–96), titled *The Spread of English-Speaking Peoples* (1889), Roosevelt appointed shared language, and not shared heritage, as the more powerful agent of national cohesiveness. In a construction similar to one Matthews used in his literary history, Roosevelt used literature as a metonym of colonial expansion. Intertwining literary history with political history, he wrote, "During the past three centuries, the spread of the English-speaking peoples over the world's waste spaces has been not only the most striking feature in the world's history, but also the event of all others most far-reaching in its effects and its importance," visible in the global familiarity with "the names of the plays that Shakespeare wrote [,which] are household words in the mouths of mighty nations."[16] To track the world's familiarity with English-language literature is to map the Anglo-American expansionist juggernaut.

Roosevelt's review proved enormously helpful in generating attention for Matthews's book, for other reviews routinely reprinted long excerpts and used Roosevelt's words as surrogates for their own. In 1917, when Matthews revised and reissued the textbook, the American Book Company circulated a brief pamphlet on the book's uses, titled *Suggestions for Teachers of American Literature*, that prominently featured a widely reprinted passage from Roosevelt's review. This excerpt is worth quoting in full, for it evidences both the responsibilities attributed to literary histories in the late century and the grounds for Matthews's success.

> The book is a piece of work as good of its kind as any American scholar has ever had in his hands. It is just the kind of book that should be given to a beginner, because it will give him a clear idea of what to read, and of the relative importance of the authors he is to read; yet it is much more than merely a book for beginners. Any student of the subject who wishes to do good work hereafter must not only read Mr. Matthews's book, but must largely adopt Mr. Matthews's way of looking at things; for these simply written, unpretentious chapters are worth many times as much as the ponderous tomes which contain what usually passes for criticism; and the principles upon which Mr. Matthews insists with such quiet force and good taste are those which must be adopted, not only by every student of American writings, but by every American writer, if he is going to do what is really worth doing. There is little room for division of opinion as to the excellence of Mr. Matthews's

arrangement as a whole, and as to the soundness of his judgments. He presumes always the difficult balance between sympathy and justice. . . . In short, Mr. Matthews has produced an admirable book, both in manner and matter, and has made a distinct addition to the very literature of which he writes.[17]

Quite a lot can be said about this logically and rhetorically tangled passage, but the most dominant chord is its dependence upon assimilationist language. The political strain of his praise is apparent in Roosevelt's preoccupation with enforced unanimity and uniformity: all students and writers must read this book, and everyone must agree with the book's organization and selections—gross exaggerations that illustrate how national literary history provided an opportunity for the insistence on national unity and engendered a vision of harmony of practice and opinion. Roosevelt's linkage of national literary history with homogeneity and the elimination of difference evidences his astute command of the undercurrents in late-century literary history. In this light, his overstatement that "there is little room for division of opinion" about the book's organization is telling, for he resorts to the assimilationist rhetoric he had used in such works as "True Americanism" (1894) and "American Ideals" (1895). In the former text, for example, Roosevelt voiced his strong belief in the necessity of educating immigrants in the culture and values of their adopted nation, for, he argued, if immigrants "remain alien elements, unassimilated, and with interests separate from ours, they are mere obstructions to the current of our national life."[18] Roosevelt's fervent belief in the necessity of national homogeneity also extended to his position on Native Americans, and his advocacy of assimilative education derived from a wider belief in the responsibility of "civilized" nations to uplift lesser peoples through conquest and colonial settlement.[19] Difference in those quarters was not to be tolerated, and Roosevelt resorted to the characteristically strong language of that debate to assert that difference is not to be tolerated in the opinion of Matthews's literary history, a text with announced ambitions of breeding national unity.

As the recent critics Priscilla Wald and John Kerkering have shown, literary form in the American nineteenth century was inextricably entangled with politics.[20] In this case, the literary convention of chapter organization, of mandatory separation and distinction within a text, elicited transparently political language earmarked in this period for the discussion of other forms of separation and distinction believed to be at odds with nationalist unity. Roosevelt does not oppose chapter organization per se but reaches for the tempering concord of interpretive consensus: some kinds of division seem to be inevitable and customary, but they require the counterweight of other unifying forces, such as agreement of opinion. And implicit in Roosevelt's freighted language and forceful syntax is the suggestion that criticism of Matthews's literary history is divisive, and therefore unpatriotic.

Roosevelt's review, however, failed to acknowledge the marked ambivalence in Matthews's literary history about such assimilationist programs, especially as they collided with Native peoples. Matthews refused to adopt an unambiguously celebratory tone and broke with literary historical convention by reminding readers of what had predated the settlement of North America, again using the humanities as a metonym of British colonization. The literary history was limited to discussions of deceased writers (as Matthews said in his preface, "No living author is named in the text"), a restriction that infused his educational text with a sense of loss.[21] This decision constituted literary history as a vehicle for the commemoration and preservation of the irretrievably lost. Matthews launched into this elegiac project right away, with the very first words of his literary history. It was typical for literary historians to begin their volumes with the origins of American literature in seventeenth-century British politics, but Matthews commenced his literary history with a more sweeping vision of what had preceded British settlers; he began with the very beginning, as it were, of Western civilization itself, with a discussion of antiquity that quickly reveals itself to be a cloaked substitute for a discussion of the more immediate predecessors of American culture. He refrained from the elevated pitch and American exceptionalist celebrations typical of other works of its kind and, in a mournful tone, alluded to the many great vanished civilizations of the past, such as those of the ancient Israelites, Greeks, and Romans. Though they are now gone, their "literature . . . helps us to understand the lives of the peoples of the past" (9). To drive this point home, Matthews allotted a sentence to each of these cultures, stating that "Greek literature tells us how the Greeks lived" and that "through Latin literature we get to know the ways of the old Romans" (9). Literature, that is, both safe-guards against the total disappearance of cultures and provides a vehi-cle for cultural memory. It is only after this reflection that Matthews turns to the more recent past, but he again situates the flourishing literary culture of England within the context of these lost civiliza-tions of antiquity: he notes, "English literature is the record of the thoughts and the feelings and the acts of the great English-speaking race. This record extends a long way back into the past. . . . Greek literature is dead, and Hebrew literature is dead; but English literature is alive now" (10).

As with the Athenian comedy mask in his bookplate, Matthews here references a cherished myth of Western culture as the successor to and inheritor of Greco-Roman civilization and its literary tradi-tions. However, this measured, historical way of approaching his sub-ject matter, as he winds his way through the vanished civilizations of the West to arrive, finally, at the American present, produces another effect. Matthews frames American literary history within a context of grief and memory of the fallen civilizations that have paved the way for our own national literature and, in so doing, reshapes American literary histories of the late century from the celebrations of national achievement to a kind of national elegy. This somber climate of retro-spection inevitably summons the more recent past and the civiliza-tions indigenous to North America whose destructions more directly and literally allowed for the creation of the United States of America. The logical structure of Matthews's introduction therefore invites the commemoration of the Native histories, narratives, and peoples otherwise expunged from texts of its kind.

In going about this business as he does, Matthews exposes some of the motives that may underlie our national attachment to antiquity, a myth of cultural origin that may derive in equal parts from national vanity and the displacement of national memories of our own vanished civilizations: borrowing from Mark Antony, we praise the Greeks and Romans so as to avoid remembering whom we buried, as it were.[22] Matthews's introductory formulation of the role of literature and literary history in national memory does similar work. He wrote, "Since the invention of the art of writing, the story of the past is no longer kept alive by word of mouth only. . . . It has been set down in black and white, by means of letters, so that we to-day can read the record of the feelings, the thoughts, and the acts of the people of two thousand years ago. . . . When this record is so skillfully made as to give pleasure to the reader, it is called literature" (9). Literature, that is, "enabled men to keep an account of the things they wished to remember" (9). Within the immediate context of his efforts to demonstrate the value of studying American literature and its history, Matthews suggests that omissions from the literary record are no less meaningful, for they indicate precisely the things a culture wishes to forget, a suggestion that bespeaks the latent motives of late-century literary historians themselves in omitting Native peoples and narrative.

The very first words of the literary history indirectly fill in these blanks, in their assertion that "[s]ince the invention of the art of writing, the story of the past is no longer kept alive by word of mouth only, the father telling the son, and the son, in turn, telling the grandson" (9). Embedded in these remarks about the preservative value of writing is a story of modernization and conquest, with oral narrative and written language serving as stand-ins for the kinds of cultures that respectively use them. Matthews's story about the replacement of one with the other uses the conceit of narrative technologies to tell a cloaked political story: a history of literacy—literary history at its most elemental—functions here as a substitute for political history. As with his bookplate, contact between these two cultures appears to be a benign form of progress and advancement, and Matthews again uses literary accoutrements—theatrical masks, stories, written texts—as benevolent proxies for a story of violence and expansion that he seems compelled and yet unable to tell. In narratological terms, the placement of these allusions in the introduction to his literary history is telling, for it bespeaks his own recognition that the beginning of American literary history must engage the Native peoples who predated colonial settlement and therefore elaborates on an implicit argument made over a decade earlier in his bookplate. Renée Bergland has examined the ways in which spectral images of Native Americans in the nineteenth century functioned as a kind of "national uncanny" incarnating repressed national memories.[23] In these allusions to the unspoken prehistory of North America and the peoples who inhabited it, Matthews's own language and arguments seem positively haunted.

Matthews's literary history was born out of controversy over some prior writings in which he had carefully approached a discussion of the responsibilities of literary history to Native peoples. In a series of published exchanges, Matthews directly challenged the limits of the literary realist aesthetic criteria widely used by literary historians for the evaluation of texts' relative importance and merits. The synthesis of literary realist aesthetics with literary history is readily apparent in Matthews's own fervent belief in the historical significance of literary verisimilitude, which documents the "feelings, the thoughts, and the acts of the people" (9). This realist-informed belief led Matthews, in his literary history and elsewhere, to assert the uses of literature for the preservation of the irretrievably lost and, against the grain of his contemporaries, to appoint literature as a bulwark against the rapid disappearance of indigenous cultures. Just as realists appraised literary quality in part by the accuracy of a text's depictions, so Matthews accorded special attention to literary texts that spoke directly and honestly about Native peoples, and, in a series of writings in the 1880s and 1890s, recommended that such texts receive special consideration from literary historians because of their special contribution to national memory. However, as he came to see it, literary realism went only so far as a literary historical heuristic device before other evaluative criteria kicked in, criteria that had more of a foothold in national policy than in a genuine command of American literary achievement.

The controversy that greeted these published assertions began when Matthews unexpectedly broke with realist party lines by publishing several essays in praise of the historical novelist and realist scapegoat James Fenimore Cooper. In the culture of centennial commemoration discussed in chapter 1, Matthews in 1889 published an article in the *Century* in honor of the centenary of Cooper's birth. While conceding the "overabundant detail," occasional lifelessness, and "incongruities and lesser errors" in Cooper's prose, Matthews attempted to rehabilitate Cooper's reputation in a literary climate that found his writing stiff and stylized to a fault.[24] He played to nationalist sympathies by hailing Cooper as "the first of our American novelists and the first American author to carry our flag outside the limits of our language" (796), a statement of dubious accuracy, as Washington Irving had been the first American writer to achieve international renown. For his Leatherstocking Tales steeped in American history, geography, and idiom, Matthews anointed Cooper "the first who proved the fitness of American life and American history for the uses of fiction" (796), and consequently designated him the progenitor of the autochthonous literary nationalism that coursed through American literary realism. Furthermore, Matthews credited Cooper's literary rendering of upstate New York with inventing the American literary regionalism that permeated late-century literature, for Cooper "was the prospector of that little army of industrious miners now engaged in working every vein of local color and character, and in sifting out the golden dust from the sands of local history" (796). "Though they carried more modern tools," late-century regionalists such as George Washington Cable were "but following in Cooper's steps" (796).

These arguments had some merit and were somewhat insulated by the precedent established by the widespread designation of another much-maligned writer, Harriet Beecher Stowe, as a similar pioneer of realism and late-century local color writing. However, what did stand apart in Matthews's encomium was his praise of Cooper's depictions of Native Americans, which had already been roundly and widely criticized by such disparate figures as Bret Harte and James Russell Lowell. Matthews deviated from this opinion and spoke strongly in

defense of these characters. He wrote, "Cooper's Indian has been dis-
puted and he has been laughed at, but he still lives. Cooper's Indian is
very like Mr. Parkman's Indian—and who knows the red man better
than the author of 'The Oregon Trail'? . . . They are Indians, all of
them; heroic figures, no doubt, and yet taken from life, with no more
idealization than may serve the maker of romance. . . . They were the
result of knowledge and of much patient investigation under conditions forever passed away" (797). Matthews sounds a realist note
here in his comparison of Cooper with the historian Francis Parkman,
who documented his personal experiences with Native peoples in his
travel narrative *The Oregon Trail* (1849) and wrote extensively about
Native tribes in early American history, as with his study *The Conspiracy of Pontiac* (1851). In arguing that Cooper's characters derive from
the same sources and authorial experiences as Parkman's histories,
Matthews turns to the realist playbook to posit that Cooper's novels
are important cultural artifacts of authentic historical and anthropological value. His melancholy reminder that Cooper's Native characters were composed and researched "under conditions forever passed
away" only sharpens this assertion, for Matthews implies that the
cultures of Native peoples documented in Cooper's novels are now
part of the same cohort of vanished civilizations as Greece and Rome.

And it is no accident that Matthews builds his argument around
Cooper's 1826 novel, *The Last of the Mohicans*, whose title and plot corroborate this mournful sense of disappearance. Though these characters were "taken from life" under conditions that are "forever passed
away," it is through these documents that they "still live." It is at this
point that Matthews appeals to the discourse of the vanishing Indian
that authorized the omission of Native peoples from literary history.
Native peoples are not gone, he affirms, if only because of their literary preservation, and, as such, they merit acknowledgment and special treatment at the hands of literary historians in the last line of
defense in the survival of Native peoples. To effect this aim, literary
historians and critics must encourage the survival of Cooper's novels,
for the disappearance of Cooper's readers will result in the total elimi-

nation from national memory of the events and peoples documented in his novels. That is, the survival of Native peoples depends upon the continuing survival of Cooper's readers.

According to Matthews's argument, the realist emphasis on verisimilitude ought to have made Cooper the hero of late-century critics, and Matthews hints that something else may be behind the widespread distaste for Cooper in the late century. In protesting the treatment of Cooper by late-century critics and historians, Matthews implies that the terms of these treatments have imported national policy toward Native peoples into the literary arena. For example, he observes that "We see Cooper's Indians nowadays through mists of prejudice due to those who have imitated them from the outside. 'The Last of the Mohicans' has suffered the degradation of a trail of dime novels, written by those apparently more familiar with the Five Points [a New York slum often featured in popular fiction] than with the Five Nations" (797). In his attempt to extricate Cooper's own reputation from that of his lesser imitators, Matthews's reference to the "degradation of a trail of dime novels" "suffered" by *The Last of the Mohicans* alludes obliquely to the Trail of Tears, the forced removal of the Cherokee Nation from Georgia to Oklahoma. According to Matthews, the reception history of Cooper's novel parallels the history of Native peoples themselves, a confusion between the literary sign and the referent that bespeaks the novel's uncanny authenticity. Matthews hints here that the late-century persecution of Cooper evidences the absorption of politics into literary history, as literary critics and historians carry out national policy by attacking the only traces of Native peoples available to them. Realist orthodoxy dictates that documentary preservation of historical memory necessitates respect and adulation for Cooper's novels, but the refusal of late-century critics to do so exposes for Matthews the social entanglements of literary aesthetics used by literary historians as a pretext for the diminution of Cooper's reputation and future readership. And in preventing Cooper from being read, late-century critics menacingly threaten to expunge from the literary historical record the little documentary evidence of what has already "passed away."

These opinions were met with a very public response from Mark Twain, who organized his celebrated 1895 essay "Fenimore Cooper's Literary Offenses" as a series of direct rebuttals to Matthews's praise.[25] Of the many works published in the late nineteenth century that appraise and organize the American literary past, Twain's essay is among the very few that continue to be read and taught in literature courses. Its enduring popularity can be attributed in part to its usefulness to teachers of nineteenth-century American literature, who have long used Twain's essay to differentiate the literary aesthetics of the midcentury from those of the late century, as Twain famously brought late-century literary realism to bear on Cooper's 1841 novel, *The Deerslayer*. However, Twain's essay was composed not only within the context of late-century literary realism but also within the flurry of literary history in the late century, when it was desirable—even expected —for literary men to contribute to the growing body of knowledge about the American literary past. In intertwining late-century literary realism with the appetite for literary history, "Fenimore Cooper's Literary Offenses" constitutes Twain's own contribution, however limited, to the flowering of the latter genre. But in making this contribution, Twain singled out for special ridicule Brander Matthews's published comments about Cooper. Matthews and Twain had been friendly acquaintances, and Twain on several occasions sought out Matthews's scholarly expertise, writing him, for example, to inquire about the aesthetics of Sir Walter Scott.[26] According to Lawrence Oliver, Twain respectfully admired Matthews's erudition, but this admiration did not prevent him from publicly skewering Matthews for his published praise of a writer Twain despised.[27]

The essay begins with three epigraphs in praise of Cooper, one of them authored by Matthews. Twain responded directly to these quotations by remarking that "It seems to me that it was far from right for the . . . Professor of English Literature in Columbia [among the authors of the other two epigraphs] to deliver opinions on Cooper's literature without having read some of it."[28] In listing with unremitting zeal many examples of Cooper's errors of style and judgment, Twain returns again and again to Matthews's epigraph praising Cooper's command of "the delicate art of the forest," and turns these words on their side to expose both Cooper's flaws and Matthews's own in overlooking them. Halfway through the essay, Twain breaks from this more discreet form of ridicule to address Matthews directly, remarking that "We must be a little wary when Brander Matthews tells us that Cooper's books 'reveal an extraordinary fullness of invention' " (334). After admitting that "as a rule" he is "quite willing to accept Brander Matthews's literary judgments and applaud his lucid and graceful phrasing of them," Twain asserts that this "particular statement [about Cooper] needs to be taken with a few tons of salt" (334).

Chief among Twain's criticisms was his particular disdain for Cooper's characters. Twain rearticulated the realist emphasis on verisimilitude with his declaration that literary characters "shall be alive" (331), and in this way ventriloquized Matthews's own assertions that Cooper's Native characters "live" and are "taken from life." For example, in stating that this evaluative criterion has "been overlooked in the *Deerslayer* tale" (331), Twain directly counters Matthews's claims about the realism and vitality of Cooper's Indians. Just as he would turn Matthews's words about the "delicate art of the forest" against him, so Twain presses this point throughout the essay, returning to it repeatedly, as with his assertion that literary criteria "require that the personages in a tale, both dead and alive, shall exhibit a sufficient excuse for being there. But this detail also has been overlooked in the *Deerslayer* tale" (331). Similarly, Twain took particular issue with the inauthenticity of the dialect spoken by Cooper's characters, remarking that "When the personages of a tale deal in conversation, the talk shall sound like human talk" (331). By directly dismantling Matthews's published opinions about Cooper, Twain lightheartedly threw into public question Matthews's own loyalty to realist doctrine. But in methodically illustrating that Cooper "seldom saw anything correctly" and "suffers noticeably from the absence of the observer's protecting gift" (335), Twain pronounces that nothing truthful or of genuine historical value has been preserved or documented in Cooper's novels, other than Cooper's own faults. This is especially the case with Cooper's Native characters, for "The difference between a Cooper

Indian and the Indian that stands in front of a cigar-shop is not spacious" (337).

Twain's essay did not fail to make an impression on Matthews. Though it began as a series of author biographies in 1895, Matthews's literary history can also be regarded as an unlikely spin-off of Twain's essay, for he used it to address directly the specifics of Twain's criticisms and to affirm his own literary loyalties. Though Matthews avoided explicitly saying as much, the presence of Twain and his essay is unmistakable, for the 1896 literary history responds directly to Twain's implicit, though hardly serious, question about Matthews's fidelity to realism. Matthews's slim literary history was organized into eighteen chapters, each devoted to a particular writer or period in American letters, and the book begins right away, in its introduction, by establishing its realist credentials. In attempting to explain to his presumptive audience of secondary-school students the value of studying literature, Matthews downplayed the aesthetic and imaginative to stress heavily the historical and material content of literature, just as Twain had done the year before. In language that strongly echoed the declarative statements of realist credo in wide circulation in this period, Matthews asserts that literature "is the reflection and the reproduction of the life of the people" (9), words he would tellingly repeat no fewer than four times in as many pages, as if to affirm the sincerity and significance of this claim.[29] Throughout the book, Matthews offers a version of American literary history that plays to many of the concerns and preoccupations of realists. For example, it highlights the material foundations and historical referents of literary texts, such as the political sources of John Greenleaf Whittier's abolitionist poetry or the authenticity of Oliver Wendell Holmes's dialect in *The Autocrat of the Breakfast-Table* (1858). Matthews's focus on literary biography was similarly attuned to realist interests, for it cultivated among student readers an implicit association between the literary and the empirical, between the writers' own lived experiences and the texts they wrote. Much like Twain, Matthews posited literary greatness as a by-product of authorial experience and to that end omitted any mention of the imaginative, aesthetic, or generic components of the literary, anything that might frame literary production within an abstract or philosophical context. "To arouse the student's interest in the authors as actual men," Matthews interleaved the volume with authors' portraits, samples of their handwriting, pictures of their homes, and, as was typical of literary histories at the time, a chronology of American literature (6).

While all of these concessions to realist doctrine are more implied than stated, Matthews reserved his most direct rebuttal for the chapter devoted to Cooper, as one would expect. Whereas his discussion before had been brief and confidently declarative, Matthews now resorted to lengthy argumentative elaboration made from a defensive crouch. Just as he had in 1889, Matthews attempted to repair Cooper's reputation by crediting him with making the novel an American genre and inventing American regionalist writing. While it may be that "other novelists have a more finished art nowadays," Cooper "did a great service to American literature by showing how fit for fiction were the scenes, the characters, and the history of his native land," thereby sowing the seeds of literary nationalism that would grow into realism (68). Putting a positive spin on Twain's ample evidence of Cooper's inclination to falsify and confabulate, Matthews argues that Cooper should not be held to the same evaluative standards as late-century realists, for, as a "writer of romance" (67), Cooper worked in a different literary idiom with a different set of aesthetic expectations. Though in 1889 he had portrayed Cooper as "thin-skinned and hot-headed," inclined to "become involved in a great many foolish quarrels," and having "a plentiful lack of tact" (798), Matthews in 1896 attempted to justify the many faults of Cooper's prose by depicting him as "an optimist, an idealizer" who "seeks to see only the best" (67), a character trait at odds with his claim of Cooper as a protorealist and documentarian. But this predisposition, he argues, is not without historical or material value, and his defense of Cooper's realism returns to the primary locus of his original praise, Cooper's Native characters, who, he reiterates, are "true to life" (67). This time, however, Matthews hedges with his claim that these characters are "absolutely true to life—so far as they go. Cooper told the truth about them—but he did not tell the whole truth" (67). Cooper's idealizations were not falsifications, he argues, but were instead half-truths: that Cooper does not divulge the whole truth does not invalidate the truth and importance of what he does depict. Returning to his repeated assertion in the book's introduction that literature "is the reflection and reproduction of the life of the people," Matthews pronounces that it is through Cooper's novels that the "men of the forest and the plain . . . are alive" (68). Again revising somewhat the discourse of the vanishing Indian, he argues that the survival and circulation of literary records allow for the perpetuation of those unable to reproduce themselves.

Just as in 1889, when Matthews had attempted to authenticate Cooper's Native characters by hanging them on the presumed legitimacy of Francis Parkman's historical researches, so Matthews's 1896 literary history devoted an entire chapter to Parkman, an inclusion that allowed him to circle back to his earlier remarks in defense of Cooper's Native characters. The only nonliterary writer other than Franklin to receive such extensive attention from Matthews, Parkman had already risen above the ranks of other nineteenth-century political historians—such as George Bancroft, John L. Motley, and William H. Prescott—who were usually acknowledged in literary histories as pioneers in American historical writing but were not, as was Parkman, typically embraced as literary peers. Parkman's special status in literary histories can be attributed in part to his membership in the same Boston-based literary peer group as the poets Oliver Wendell Holmes and James Russell Lowell and to his 1849 travel memoir, *The Oregon Trail*, which had more in common generically with such literary memoirs as Thoreau's *Maine Woods* (1864) or Twain's *Life on the Mississippi* (1883) than with Motley's *Rise of the Dutch Republic* (1856).

Though he was financially independent and debilitated by illness throughout his life, Parkman's renowned struggles to write while in dire physical discomfort lent credence to late-century rhetoric, discussed in chapter 3, of writing as arduous labor, just as his publications satisfied the realist demand for authorial experience and extensive research. In his own treatment of Parkman, Matthews played to these late-century sympathies, describing, for example, Parkman's work as "the unhasting labor of nearly half a century," and his travels on the Oregon Trail in 1844 as a research trip designed "to help fit himself for the task" of writing the histories of North America that would occupy most of his life (210, 212). Matthews's emphasis on authorial experience leads him to the supreme assertion of realist hyperbole with his claim that "from the day when this project [of writing the history of the French and Indian War] first took shape in the mind of the young man at college, everything he did afterwards was made to contribute to its fulfillment" (211); that is, the entirety of Parkman's life was designed to channel directly into his writing.

Having primed Parkman as the epitome of realist principle and industry, Matthews turns to Parkman's efforts to "know the Indians and to understand their enigmatic character" (212). He then elaborates on the extent of Parkman's research on the topic: he "lived with the Indians, sharing their rough fare and studying their ways and their customs, and getting an insight into their character not to be had in any other manner. [He] underwent also the hardships of the Indians, the toils, the privations, the exposure; and Parkman was so enfeebled by these that he never regained his strength" (212). Matthews suggests that the collapse of Parkman's health resulted both from the severity of these trials and from the vast accumulation of data about Native peoples, as if his health had failed as the result of circuit overload. Derived from undisputed authorial experience, the *Oregon Trail* "has preserved for us the outward appearance of a state of things long since vanished forever. From it the reader can gain an understanding of the red men and of their white neighbors, and a knowledge of the motives which rule their conduct, unobtainable from any other single book" (213). Again, the literary record intervenes to preserve "things long since vanished," and, in a striking allusion to his bookplate, Matthews positions the literary as central to "an understanding of the red men and of their white neighbors," again imbricating literary history with political history. Matthews refreshes and reinvigorates the language he had used earlier in his discussion of Cooper by attaching it to

Parkman's more reputable memoir, a maneuver that feeds directly into the thrust of his argument: his assertion that Parkman's *Oregon Trail* "enables us to see for ourselves that the Indian Cooper presented in his novels is very like the real Indian, but that the real Indian had another side to him than the side Cooper chose to depict" (213). Parkman enabled Matthews to defend the legitimacy of his beleaguered remarks about Cooper and to reassert that, if truthfulness is the sine qua non of literary quality, then we must recognize Cooper's novels as necessary companions to Parkman's *Oregon Trail* and to be of national and literary value in preserving aspects of American history.

Abandoning more passive figurations of conquest such as the comedy mask, Matthews breaks from the circumlocution he had used elsewhere to speak directly about the violence requisite to the settlement of North America. Parkman's *Oregon Trail*, he writes, "helps us to explain to ourselves the unending series of wars between the white race and the red, ever since the men of our stock first set foot on the soil which the Indian claimed for his own" (213). In conceding that this violence is "unending," he departs from the silence of other literary histories on the matter, whose refusal to acknowledge Native peoples implies the presumed successes of national policies of elimination. Matthews, however, here traverses generic conventions of literary history by acknowledging the continuing presence of Native peoples within the national collective and the violence of policies portrayed elsewhere as passive and beneficial. Matthews then closes the chapter with an excerpt from Oliver Wendell Holmes's elegy on Parkman.[30] Matthews reprinted only four stanzas of a poem composed of fourteen and, in so doing, carved out a different poem with an altogether different emphasis. He chose to begin his excerpt in the very middle of the poem, with the seventh stanza:

> He told the red man's story; far and wide
>   He searched the unwritten records of his race;
> He sat a listener at the Sachem's side,
>   He tracked the hunter through his wildwood chase.

High o'er his head the soaring eagle screamed;
　The wolf's long howl rang nightly; through the vale
Tramped the lone bear; the panther's eyeballs gleamed;
　The bison's gallop thundered on the gale.

Soon o'er the horizon rose the cloud of strife—
　Two proud, strong nations battling for the prize—
Which swarming host should mold a nation's life,
　Which royal banner flout the western skies.

Long raged the conflict; on the crimson sod
　Native and alien joined their hosts in vain;
The lilies withered where the Lion trod,
　Till Peace lay panting on the ravaged plain. (218–19)

The excerpt is noteworthy for numerous reasons, but especially for
Holmes's designation of American citizens as the aliens in their own
settlements, inverting the alien-native dichotomy that preoccupied
the late century. Matthews pointedly omitted Holmes's celebrations
of military violence against Native peoples, such as the stanza claiming that a "nobler task was theirs who strove to win/The blood-
stained heathen to the Christian fold;/To free from Satan's clutch the
slaves of sin."[31] As it stands, the edited excerpt instead accentuates the
costs of this violence, as with the description of "lilies withered where
the Lion trod," a clear figuration of the destruction of Native peoples. In commencing the excerpt with a description of Parkman's
researches, Matthews's edited version frames the historian as the pre-
server or protector of what national policy had earmarked for elimination. Framed by these ongoing struggles, his focus on the "red
man's story" and the "unwritten annals" documented by Parkman
underlines the special service performed by the literary historian,
who not only preserves narrative traditions in jeopardy but also, in so
doing, preserves for future generations "the feelings, the thoughts,
and the acts" of Native peoples, a function he attributes to literature
throughout his literary history. Matthews closed the last in-depth

chapter of his literary history by using the words of the recently deceased Holmes to articulate what had been implicit throughout his book, and carved out of Holmes's elegy a poem about the importance of literary history in preserving Native narrative in the face of national policy.

HAVING ENCOUNTERED RESISTANCE in the genre of literary history, Matthews turned to other genres to speak directly about the place of Native peoples in American cultural life and the involvement of the humanities in the execution of national policy. I turn now to two texts by Brander Matthews, both of which speculate about the aftereffects of such pedagogy. Both of these texts figure as companion pieces to Matthews's literary history, for they more fully explore what he had only hesitatingly gestured at in 1896: the role of education in carrying out policies of assimilation. One of these texts, the 1892 boys' book *Tom Paulding*, found significant success among young readers, just as his literary history would do several years later. The second text, the unpublished comedy "High Spirits," failed to find a receptive publisher or audience. In their dramatization of educational programs attuned to national policy, both texts revisit and revise scenes of American literary history Matthews had depicted in 1896 and elsewhere.

Matthews's *Tom Paulding* follows the exploits of the title character, a bright and enterprising boy, as he searches for the treasure lost by an ancestor during the Revolutionary War. Motivated chiefly by his desire to pay off the mortgage that his widowed mother is increasingly unable to pay, Tom hopes to use the surplus to finance his own education at the engineering school of the neighboring university, which happens to be the place of Matthews's own employment, Columbia University. Though *Tom Paulding* was published before Matthews's literary history, the two texts had similar origins. *Tom Paulding* began, as did *Introduction to the Study of American Literature*, as a serial for *St. Nicholas*. The book received slight but largely favorable reviews, and, though it was not a best-seller, it sold its first printing of 2,500 copies and recouped Matthews's advance, allowing him to receive royalties as late as 1915. Like *Introduction to the Study of American Literature*, *Tom Paulding* remained in print for decades after its original publication because of its lasting appeal to young readers, and received a surge in sales in 1913 when it was selected by the Boy Scouts of America for its list of recommended reading.

Just as Matthews's bookplate communicated his perception of the social responsibilities expected of the literary scholar, so *Tom Paulding* has some elements of the cloaked professional autobiography. Both scions of newly poor families, both Matthews and Tom elect Columbia as their preferred route out of poverty, and both turn to research to secure their position there, whether as a faculty member or as a student, for Tom's enrollment is made possible by his extensive archival research into the probable location of the buried treasure.[32] *Tom Paulding* is not only an adventure in research but also a narrative elaboration of the process and motives that underwrite historical research, as Tom meticulously combs archival papers to reconstruct the past and generate a coherent chronology of events. Matthews would admit to this identification: in an inscription dated February 1919 in an edition of the novel in the holdings of Columbia University's library, he wrote, "Ever have I gone in quest of buried treasure!" This personal identification helps explain why Matthews would insert in this boys' book the same imagery, rhetoric, and logic that he had used elsewhere to affirm the civic importance of educators and literary historians to national policies of expansionism and assimilation.

And just as Matthews's literary history began with a discussion of the primordial origins of Western history and North America, so *Tom Paulding* commences with an allusion to the very beginning of the nation's history, a reference that situates this boys' book within a context of larger national significance. Matthews delays the introduction of the novel's characters or premise until the second chapter, but begins instead with a detailed topographical survey of Tom's neighborhood, which lies "above Central Park, behind Morningside Park, and beside the Hudson River, where the Riverside Drive stretches itself for two miles."[33]

In every city there are unexplored fastnesses as little known to the world at large as is the heart of the Dark Continent. Now and again it happens that a sudden turn in the tide of business or of fashion brings into view these hitherto unexplored regions. Then there begins at once a struggle between the old and the new, between the conditions which obtained when that part of the city was ignored, and those which prevail now that it has been brought to the knowledge of men. The struggle is sharp, for a while; but the end is inevitable. The old cannot withstand the new; and in a brief space of time the unknown region wakes up, and there is a fresh life in all its streets; there is a tearing down, and there is a building up; and in a few months the place ceases to be old, although it has not become new. (1)

The neighborhood Matthews describes is Morningside Heights, and he alludes to the upheaval that took place in upper Manhattan in the 1890s, when Columbia president Seth Low purchased a vast tract of land and arranged for the building and relocation of Columbia University's campus there. Matthews begins with a tale of urban development, in which the revitalization of an old neighborhood generates resistance from its long-term inhabitants, who bristle at their new neighbors and the changes that accompany them. Just as he had in his 1896 literary history, Matthews begins the novel at the very beginning of American history, for this story about the inevitable difficulties of settling land belonging to other people is a revision of the American primal scene visualized in Matthews's bookplate and elegized in his 1896 literary history. His comparison of Morningside Heights to "the heart of the Dark Continent," the language of expansion used by the nineteenth-century British explorer Henry Morton Stanley, signals Matthews's awareness of the political narrative underlying his description of the conflicts between residents and developers. This opening scene expands on what had been compacted in the bookplate and presumed in his 1896 textbook. Whereas the mask had implicitly served as a synecdoche of the humanities and education in general, this scene explicitly announces the involvement of educational institutions in the deracination of Native peoples, for it is the university itself, the very place of Matthews's own education and employment, that oversees the removal of local inhabitants.

The university remains suspect in the novel, and *Tom Paulding* elaborates more fully on the process by which universities become refineries of national citizenship. Just as Matthews's literary history began with a memento mori reminding readers of the many vanished civilizations that predated American cultural achievement, so *Tom Paulding* presents history less as a tidy time line of discrete events than as a series of indistinctly demarcated and repetitive cycles. *Tom Paulding* is replete with allusions to numerous disputes in American history about property rights and sovereignty, all of which seem to reenact the conflict in this opening scene of gentrification: internecine struggles among Native Americans, early American expansion and colonial settlement, the Revolutionary War, the political climate of the late nineteenth century, and, finally, the immediate context of university development.[34] At the center of these concentric circles of history is the university, which emerges as a fixed point within the repeated cycles of history. In retelling this American historical narrative in the context of university development, Matthews suggests that the former is literally built on the foundation of the latter: In identifying themselves as places where the rough and crude may be civilized and polished, universities acquire their prestige and power by recycling the rhetoric and imagery of expansionism depicted in the novel's opening chapter and Matthews's bookplate. In other words, universities announce themselves as places where the work of civilization begun in that opening scene (both of the novel and of the nation itself) may be continued and carried out over these repetitive cycles of history. It is therefore unsurprising that Columbia embraced Matthews's bookplate as an institutional emblem.

Tom Paulding intimates that one particular academic activity— the study of the American past—is particularly complicit in this process. As practiced in Tom's extensive archival researches, the study of American history abets his maturation and feeds directly into his beliefs, goals, and skills. Study of the past literally provides the motive and opportunity for Tom to develop the skills necessary for the continuing reenactment of the American primal scene. The novel begins amid the upheaval caused by university construction, though at the novel's close Tom is in the process of learning new technologies for land appropriation from his Uncle Dick, a hydraulic engineer. It is Tom's hope throughout the novel that the unearthed gold will finance an engineering education at Columbia's School of Mines, a career track that Cecelia Tichi has shown to be a professional extension of turn-of-the-century expansionism.[35] In this way, the study of the American past enables his transformation into an agent of the very civilizing process that he himself endures. Contrary to the adage that the study of the past is the best way to keep history from repeating itself, Matthews suggests that the study of the past ensures the survival and endurance of its policies.

As evidenced by his bookplate and the vast popularity of his 1896 literary history, Matthews was one of the central purveyors of such rhetoric in the late century; however, like his literary history, *Tom Paulding* shows marked ambivalence about such activities. Matthews relies on an enduring association, one also evident in his bookplate, between American boyhood and Native Americans, and constructs Tom as a symbolic stand-in for Native peoples.[36] As if to confirm the relevance of this boys' book to the history of American policy toward Native peoples, Matthews follows the novel's opening chapter about land appropriation with a boisterous scene in which Tom and his friends imitate a battle between the Sioux and Pawnee. An enthusiast for all things Native and a resident of the neighborhood disrupted by the incursion of the university, Tom is also shortly to begin the civilizing education depicted in the bookplate and in wide discussion at the turn of the century. In Tom's efforts to retrieve the plunder stolen from his family during the American Revolution, the novel follows his efforts to undo the injustices of the past that have left his formerly illustrious family poor and helpless before impersonal, faceless institutional authorities. In this way, *Tom Paulding* offers a narrative from the perspective of the displaced and powerless, and symbolically revises the conflicts between Natives and invaders referenced in the novel's opening scene. Published just two years after the massacre of Native women and children at Wounded Knee, *Tom Paulding* focuses on the special vulnerability of a widow and her son. Through the payment of reparations and the discovery of buried gold that allows Mrs. Paulding to pay off the mortgage and send Tom to Columbia, *Tom Paulding* revises American history to tell a story of social justice in which Natives profit from the upheaval caused by foreign incursion, a narrative keenly at odds with the political climate that frames the novel.

Matthews's 1893 short story "Two Letters" is a neat supplement to *Tom Paulding*. True to Matthews's typical style, it at first glance appears to justify American policies toward Native peoples by recycling stereotypes of Natives as treacherous and unreliable. The story is composed of two letters to the editor of a fictitious New York paper, the *Gotham Gazette*, recounting the adventures of an American engineer on a mining expedition in British Guiana. The engineer, Walter Stead, inadvertently offends the White Indians, a violent local tribe that lays claim to the gold unearthed by the American miners. In an elaborate series of mishaps, Stead falls prey to the White Indians and makes his way to safety first by boat and then by foot. Once again, Matthews recounts here a primordial narrative about colonial first contact. Though the story is set in South America, the obstacle to American mining is not the Guyanese people, who hardly appear at all, but is instead the mythical, seldom-seen tribe of White Indians. Though the word "Indian" was used, and still is, to denote native peoples of colonized countries, Matthews renders this South American tribe using the familiar idiom of the Native American: their technology, political structure, religious practices, and dress derive from the iconography of the American Indian. The illustrations, too, liken the White Indians to the American Indians in their reliance on the recognizable feathered headdresses, tomahawks, and high cheekbones common among images of Native Americans. And in dubbing the hostile tribe "White Indians," Matthews employed a term used in turn-of-the-century American culture to denote American enthusiasts for Native cultures, such as Tom Paulding, who donned Indian dress and imitated Native rites and battles. However, with the second letter, Matthews unwrites this story about treacherous Natives and beleaguered, heroic engineers. The second letter declares the first letter, about Stead's adventures, to be a fake designed to disguise Stead's own nefarious business dealings. In its suggestion that Native peoples would benefit from the American expansionism they so treacherously impede, the first letter ventriloquizes prevailing late-century beliefs. However, the second letter exposes how such narratives, which revise and depend upon American history, both fail to have any direct correspondence to the Native peoples they claim to document and are in thrall to American business interests. In this way, Matthew suggests that the medium of literature can more faithfully tell stories excised from or whitewashed by national literary history.

Matthews's undated theatrical comedy "High Spirits" provides an illuminating epilogue to these defiant narratives of Indian education by dramatizing the afterlife of Native peoples socialized by assimilative pedagogy.[37] Moreover, it shows the afterlife of these educational programs, which, as shown by Alan Trachtenberg, were eventually transferred to other objects of assimilation, such as the immigrant. Matthews wrote "High Spirits" with his longtime dramatic collaborator, George H. Jessop, with whom he turned out many unpublished and unproduced plays and two produced comedies, *On Probation* and *A Gold Mine* (both 1887).[38] "High Spirits" has its own archival ties to the rest of Matthews's considerable corpus, for Jessop also collaborated with the British composer Charles Villier Stanford, who had been slated to write the musical score for *Pocahontas*. Best known for grand, late Victorian symphonies, Stanford wrote several comic operas with Jessop, among them *Shamus O'Brien* (1896) and "Christopher Patch" (ca. 1897), which was never published or performed. A renowned dramatic enthusiast and critic, Matthews wrote literally dozens of plays, most of which went unproduced and which tend toward conventional drawing room comedies about courtships among the wealthy and aristocratic, in which lovers separate over silly misunderstandings and which conclude with revelations and felicitous

"The cable parted, and his foes fell into the river below." From
The Story of a Story and Other Stories *(1893).*

reunions. Neither produced nor published, "High Spirits" was also composed in this vein and follows the attempts of two engaged lovers, Rachel Redding and Jack Hazleton, to solicit her father's blessing for the match. A superstitious devotee of the occult, her father, Solon Redding, depends upon séances and spirit consultations before making any decisions, and the play begins with the anticipated arrival of several guests at the Redding house: the renowned spiritualist Theodosius Lowe; Rachel's betrothed, Jack; and Jack's college friend Modockawando, a Chippewa chief. After Mr. Redding mistakenly takes Modockawando for the spiritualist Lowe, Jack and Rachel stage a burlesque séance conducted by the Indian chief in which he convinces Mr. Redding to give his blessing to his daughter's engagement.

Matthews situates this romantic comedy in the context of a pier-building development project overseen by the New Seaside Beach Pier Company, in which Mr. Redding is a stockholder and for which both Jack and Modockawando work as engineers. As with *Tom Paulding* and "Two Letters," engineering provides the narrative backdrop here, and Matthews again constitutes engineering as a vehicle of civilization that brings decency and order along with scientific advancement and land development. Because agents of civilization such as educators and engineers require materials on which to practice their arts, "High Spirits" is also interested in the management and development of the primitive and uncultivated, whether in nature or in human behavior, and contains various characters whose unreasonable, antisocial behavior invites reform. Similarly, engineering brings these two men to the Redding residence, and their involvement and problem-solving skills restore order to the play's romantic entanglements and narrative confusion.

Though a comedy about an obstructed courtship, "High Spirits" is very much about the necessity of schooling the ignorant and uncouth, and those characters are, as in Matthews's other works, constituted by their relation to Native peoples. Whereas *Tom Paulding* and Matthews's bookplate depend on metaphor to draw this comparison, "High Spirits" conveniently includes among its cast of characters a Chippewa, the Harvard-trained engineer Modockawando, whose respectable appearance causes considerable confusion among various characters who expect a Native person to wear traditional dress and to remain a resistant object of assimilationist effort. With his evening dress and Harvard degree, Modockawando has been transformed after passing through the civilizing alembic of higher education depicted in the bookplate. As described by Jack, Modockawando is "a red Indian—but he's a white man, for all that."[39] Matthews revisited his spat with Twain in another similar remark by Jack: Modockawando "is a Harvard graduate and a Red Indian. If you want to know how a Harvard graduate looks, examine me. If you want to know how a Red Indian looks, read 'The Last of the Mohicans.' Between the two, you'll get a very fair idea of" Modockawando (7). Again affirming the verisimilitude of Cooper's renderings, Matthews splices together Cooper's suggestive title and Modockawondo's Harvard polish, to affirm both the authenticity of Cooper's novels and the disappearance of the Native peoples documented in them.

But that is not to suggest that the work of civilization begun in the American past is complete, for the play contains several characters whose suitability for civilizing pedagogy is made visible by their attitudes toward Modockawando, for the Native American figures here as an emblem of the successes of past civilizing ventures and the work yet to be done in the American present and future. With poise and polish cultivated at Harvard, Modockawando throws into relief the loutishness of other characters, and "High Spirits" attends primarily to those several characters whose ignorance qualifies them for an equally civilizing education, from Solon Redding, the family's wealthy patriarch, to Biddy, the family's ignorant Irish maid whose belief in the savagely cannibal and war-painted Indian renders her the object of much derision and humor in the play. The play's central conflicts depend upon the ignorance of Solon Redding, who, though a prominent member of society and a successful businessman, retains a belief in the occult that the play constitutes as premodern and primitive. Indeed, the notable consonance between "Red" and Redding signals that the two men have swapped the roles of civilizer and rough, a rapport confirmed by Redding's attempts to conjure Black Hawk and

Modockawando's mocking impersonation of Black Hawk to elicit Redding's blessing for Rachel's engagement.[40]

Matthews might have constructed this narrative around any number of other scenarios—for instance, a European character—to expose the characters' ignorance just as effectively. His inclusion of a Native American in this romantic comedy is entirely extraneous, for the plot relies primarily on puns, slapstick, and Irish stereotypes for its humor and narrative maneuvers. Though he seems to criticize the use of and belief in the stock trope of the Native American, Matthews's continuing use of a Native American in this play reveals his continuing reliance upon the Native as an icon of education and his inability to demonstrate the benefits of an education without one. Matthews's notes for the play substantiate this correlation, as the play had originally been designed as an academic spoof set on a college campus and peopled by both undergraduates and professors. The narrative kernel common to this early draft and the final version is its organization around an obstructed courtship in which a superstitious older man stands in the way of the marriage of his young female charge, a conflict also resolved through a comedic imitation of supernatural intervention. However, Matthews's notes describe a play that differs markedly from "High Spirits." He wrote, "We have already outlined the plot of such a play. A superstitious old man desires to marry his young ward who is in love with a handsome young fellow. The young man appeals to his uncle, a professor of . . . electricity and optics in the college in the town, to his cousins who are the champion gymnasts of the college and a friend of theirs who is a professional magician. With their assistance the old man is cured of his love for his ward. In the course of the piece, the old man attends a spiritualist séance [in which he is duped]."[41] Elsewhere Matthews documented his intention of giving the play an explicit academic setting, locating the first act in the professor's office and the second act in the school gymnasium.[42]

Matthews and Jessop revised the play's premise quite significantly before they began the actual writing. In their intermediate version of the play, which predates the final version of "High Spirits" distributed to literary agents in 1905, Matthews and Jessop altogether omitted the academic setting, replacing both the location and the college professor with the setting and characters that would appear in "High Spirits." The play in this incarnation is titled "Mr. Lo," an allusion to Modockawando's college nickname, "Lo, the poor Indian," which the guardian, now Mr. Redding, confuses with Mr. Lowe, the renowned spiritualist.[43] In this revision, the campus is replaced with an engineering expedition, and the academic personalities who intervene on behalf of the engaged couple—professors and students—are replaced with the Indian Modockawando, who now oversees the deception of the superstitious guardian. Despite the excision of the academy, the play retains a dramatic interest in education and enlightenment, a concern compatible with the new backdrop of engineering. While this exchange may not illustrate an interchangeability per se between engineering and higher education, it does show Matthews's perception of a similarity in cultural function between them.

As in *Tom Paulding*, Matthews constitutes such programs of instruction as evangelical, so that the endurance of assimilation causes the student to become an envoy of the civilizing process: Modockawando's Harvard education renders him a civil engineer, causing him to participate in the very expeditions that Matthews had elsewhere depicted as both threatening and rehabilitative to Native culture. The orality of the theater afforded Matthews with an opportunity to use puns and homonyms to express the entanglement of Native peoples with the engineer. When Modockawando arrives at the Redding residence, he meets the Irish maid, Biddy, who notifies him of the other expected guests.

> BIDDY: They're expectin' an Indian here.
> MODOC: They *do* expect me, then.
> BIDDY: No, no. An Ingin, I said; not an eggineer [*sic*].
> MODOC: Then I'm not an Ingin? I'm an Ingineer, am I?
> BIDDY: That's what you said yourself. (9)

Though played for a laugh, this scene nevertheless blurs together the Indian and the engineer, a striking conflation of two antagonists on opposing ends of the colonialist spectrum. The addition of a single syllable is all that separates these two words, just as the addition of an education is all that it takes to turn the Native person into the engineer.

In "High Spirits," the scantily clad Native in Matthews's bookplate is a thing of the past, and higher education has successfully overseen the relocation of the Native from a prehistoric, precivilized past to the technologically sophisticated modern era. "High Spirits" replaces the originary moment of first contact between the Native and the settler that proved a mainstay of Matthews's work with a narrative about the assimilation of immigrants. Biddy, the Redding maid and an Irish immigrant, offers the play its biggest laughs with her naïveté about Indians, her malapropisms, and her blustery manners. While "High Spirits" does not stage Biddy's first contact per se with American culture, its dramatization of the disorientation and mistakes of an immigrant revises the American originary narrative that reappears in Matthews's work. Biddy, however, is unable to relinquish the originary narrative and recognize herself as its new object. Having heard cautionary tales about the Native American, she remains convinced that Modockawando will scalp and devour her, despite abundant evidence attesting to his refinement. This misunderstanding provides much of the play's comedy, but it also provides Matthews and Jessop with a pretext for Biddy's own civilizing education. Her belief in the savage Native is meant, in part, to signal her own suitability for the civilizing education that has rendered this original narrative obsolete. In being disabused of this misconception, Biddy herself undergoes civilizing education in miniature and, in finally recognizing Modockawando as a polished professional, she witnesses up close the benefits and results of an American civilizing education. In a scene that strikingly resembles the image on Matthews's bookplate, Biddy has to look into the face of another to recognize herself as the rough in need of cultivation. And just as in Matthews's bookplate and literary history, the play reminds the audience of the past accomplishments of such programs to provide assurance of their future successes among a different constituency.

The beliefs and practices that underlay Matthews's literary history and that he elaborated on in his fiction continue to pose very real challenges to current literary historians trying to make a place for Native narration and history in American literary history. Late-century literary histories either banished Native peoples altogether or reduced the Native presence in American literature to that of an icon and the passive recipient of instruction rather than an active contributor. Against our best efforts to do otherwise, the profession still recapitulates those late-century founding parameters of our discipline. In a recent article analyzing the placement of a Chinook story of the trickster Coyote in recent editions of the *Norton Anthology of American Literature*, Michael A. Elliott exposes the lingering residue of these late-century beliefs in current, though well-meaning, literary histories trying to rectify earlier omissions. In particular, Elliott analyzes the obstinate problem of finding an appropriate place for such oral tales, versions of which may predate colonial settlement but were transcribed much later. Though it was published in 1894, the Coyote story appears in the first volume of *The Norton Anthology of American Literature, Literature to 1820*, thus imparting to the story a colonial context and historical significance that, Elliott argues, may be misleading or altogether inappropriate.[44] In his discussion of the placement of this story, Elliott exposes the endurance of late-century literary historical parameters well into our own time, with the enduring temptation to overlook the continuing survival of Native peoples, narratives, and storytellers, and thus to exile them to a distant, prehistoric past that predates colonial settlement of North America. Despite our best efforts to overturn the nationalist customs that governed literary history, the profession has yet to find a place for Native narrative in an intellectual corpus that has long excluded it. Though contemporary Native writers have been embraced by our vision of the literary present, our versions of the American literary past may not be so different from that of our late-century forebears after all.

PART II

{ *Class, Authority, &*
Literary History

CHAPTER 3

Copyrighting American History

International Copyright and the Periodization of the Nineteenth Century

With the publication in 1930 of the third and final volume of his *Main Currents in American Thought*, Vernon Parrington gave singular shape and force to an already established literary history of the American nineteenth century, which had long been divided into two discrete eras hinged politically and culturally by the Civil War. After 1865, goes the version of the narrative he offered, the Boston Brahmins and their "love of standards" were unseated by itinerant, gritty, self-made writers based in New York.[1] For Parrington, this literary restaging of the American Revolution in which Old World aristocratic power fell at the hands of an American populism was best exemplified by Mark Twain—"a native writer thinking his own thoughts, using his own eyes, speaking his own dialect—everything European fallen away."[2] This literary history of aristocratic overthrow and democratic ascent has proved resilient, as repeated through much of the twentieth century by such esteemed scholars as William Charvat, Lewis Simpson, and Robert Spiller.[3]

This narrative of the American literary nineteenth century presumes that authorial pedigree indexes political sympathy and literary affiliation, an assumption recently debunked by the research of such critics as Michael Davitt Bell, Nancy Glazener, and Amy Kaplan, who have exposed the marked conservatism of many late-century writers bundled together with literary antielitism. Today it is more apparent that the ostensible antielitism attributed to the literary late century derives less from the conditions of postwar authorship than from the preferences of some realists, such as Howells and Twain, for texts committed to the "phrase and carriage of every-day life."[4] One has only to read Howells's columns and reviews in *Harper's* to recognize that a late-century writer's undistinguished parentage by no means indicated a diminishment in the "love of standards" attributed to antebellum New England. Similarly, one has only to reflect on the many writers both before and after the Civil War whose pedigrees fail to conform to the terms offered by this narrative to begin to wonder about the origins of this insistence on using class to organize the literary nineteenth century.[5]

The origins of Parrington's literary history emerged decades before the end of the nineteenth century, and its constituent parts were already in wide circulation by the 1880s. Writers routinely depicted themselves as home-grown literary commoners and their literary forebears as affected, snobbish aesthetes. Proponents of literary realism were especially partial to such rhetoric. A tireless draftsman of this language, Howells adapted Emerson's and Whitman's rhetoric to depict the new realist writer as one who necessarily "feels in every nerve the equality of things and the unity of men. . . . It is his business to break the images of false gods and misshapen heroes, to take away the poor silly toys that many grown people would still like to play with."[6] Similar depictions of the triumph of literary vitality over effete tradition pervade periodicals of the period, but realist oratory actually constitutes a relatively small proportion. In fact, the rhetoric of literary populist triumph instantiated in Parrington's literary history of the nineteenth century emerged less from realist rhetoric than from the extensive effort of late-century writers to generate public sympathy for a campaign to legislate the international protection of copyright. Resolutely portraying the writer as a vigorous, manly, and patriotic laborer, copyright activists attempted to alter the widespread suspicion among Americans that literature was the realm of elite, privileged intellectuals with deeper ties to Europe than to the United States. In accomplishing these ends, the international copyright movement not only helped shape one of the more enduring intellectual products of late-century literary history—that is, the periodization of the nineteenth century—but also served as an important driving force behind the production, circulation, and celebration of American literary history in the late century. Indeed, the successes of the international copyright movement can be attributed in part to its canny use of literary history to manufacture knowledge that was designed to influence public opinion but that would also long outlive the circumstances of its origination.

Between 1868 and 1891, writers across genres, aesthetics, and even —in the terms of Parrington's periodization—literary periods participated in concentrated activism in support of international copyright legislation. American domestic copyright laws, instituted in 1790, preserved authors' rights only within the nation's boundaries, and neither protected the American author from unauthorized reprinting abroad nor guarded foreign authors from piracy within the United States. Without international protection, English-language writers on both sides of the Atlantic complained of unauthorized reprintings not bound by law to pay royalties; of the frequency and license with which pirates made changes to their writings, even altering endings and adding characters; and of having their names attached to ghost-written books. After a few false starts before the Civil War, the copyright movement emerged as a fully organized campaign shortly after the war's end. Writers as diverse as Twain, Oliver Wendell Holmes, Henry James, E. P. Roe, and Edmund Stedman were active members of the American Copyright League, which counted over seven hundred members and presided over a lengthy campaign that included petitions, boycotts, and lobbying. Writers testified before Congress, contributed to public readings, signed petitions, and wrote scores of testimonials and essays describing the injustices of international piracy and detailing the moral, literary, and national benefits of international protection.

In a political movement composed largely of literary workers— writers, editors, publishers—it should come as no surprise that international copyright activists used the full range of print media at their disposal, from journalism to poetry. Sympathetic editors such as Richard Watson Gilder and R. R. Bowker made their periodicals—the *Century* and *Publisher's Weekly*, respectively—important vehicles for the international copyright movement, regularly reprinting articles published elsewhere and allotting space to open letters on the subject.

Poets such as James Russell Lowell and James Herbert Morse turned their talents to the copyright cause and produced short, pithy verses that served as literary epigraphs to countless prose works addressing copyright. Critics such as Howells and George Lathrop used their columns to denounce piracy as the single greatest impediment to an American literature, and scores of other writers contributed their writings and celebrity by participating in literary readings sponsored by the American Copyright League. The writer and Presbyterian minister Henry Van Dyke even made use of his pulpit with the 1888 sermon "The National Sin of Literary Piracy," which was issued as a pamphlet that year by Scribner's and touted as the final moral word on the matter.[7]

Copyright supporters encountered significant obstacles to their efforts, from widespread public indifference to outright hostility from printers unions that feared legislation would result in reduced book production and shrinking employment. John Tebbel has argued that the primary obstacle to both public and congressional interest was widespread suspicion of intellectual culture, and literature in particular, both of which were construed as antidemocratic traces of European aristocracy.[8] Indeed, the language used on both sides of the debate substantiates Tebbel's claim. Although the International Typographical Union of North America eventually endorsed international copyright legislation in the belief that it would increase domestic printing, it suspected the motives of American writers in waging this campaign; in its official journal, it suggested that American writers neither needed the money they claimed to have lost through pirated copies nor had any real loyalty to the United States.[9] Copyright activists bent over backward to counter this kind of suspicion. Local and national periodicals of the 1880s are replete with attempts of American writers to raise public awareness and transform themselves in the public imagination from aristocrats to literary laborers on a par with other manual workers. It is in texts published in pursuit of this mission that the limits of Parrington's literary history come into view.

Examples of these texts abound in the 1880s and can be chosen virtually at random. In 1884, the novelist J. W. De Forest signed a petition and attached a brief statement that was published, among other places, in the *New York Times*: "The American author is the only American laboring man who need not hope to live by his labor."[10] That same year the *New York Times* printed an open letter from the novelist and editor Charles Dudley Warner to George Lathrop, the *Atlantic Monthly* editor and a realist critic (as well as Nathaniel Hawthorne's son-in-law), in which he declared that writers "are producers of valuable materials and things."[11] In 1888, the Ohio Congregationalist minister and writer Washington Gladden directly compared the writer to the laborer: "The author has the same right to the product of his mind that any workman has to the product of his hands."[12] Even an opponent of international copyright, the Philadelphia printer Roger Sherman, resorted to the language of labor in making his case, writing in an open letter to the New York Congressman William Dorsheimer, which he published as a pamphlet in 1884: "If you accord to foreign authors the same right in this country that native writers possess, you tax the American citizen for something that he now possesses free, and you deprive the American artisan of the labor which he would be called to perform in the production of these books."[13] Van Dyke freely used the language of labor in his sermon "The National Sin of Literary Piracy":

> The value of any literary work depends upon the form which it gives to those ideas which belong to the common stock of truth. This form is the result of toil,—toil which is more arduous and exhausting, toil which requires more patience and self-denial, toil which costs a large outlay of time and money to prepare for it, and a greater wear and tear of vital tissue to execute it, than perhaps any other kind of labor. The disembodied ideas are no man's property; but the embodied ideas, which have been brought into shape and order by the lonely worker in the sweat of his brain, are his own, just as much as the statue carved from the marble is the sculptor's own, just as much as the wheat cultivated in the field is the farmer's own.[14]

Van Dyke's weighted language shows significant energy and persistence in trying to alter the class status of literary labor.

While copyright advocates did not succeed in dispelling the persistent public suspicion of intellectual work, their efforts overwhelmed the literary press with rhetoric depicting the writer as a laborer, an image designed to offset the lingering associations of authorship with aristocratic prerogative. The absorption of this language into literary history did not transpire because historians took at face value the claims of postwar writers to working-class kinship. If that had been the case, literary historians might have heeded the similar rhetoric of labor deployed by antebellum writers, recently documented by Michael Newbury.[15] This rhetoric of literary labor had even played an active role in the prewar copyright movement, as evidenced in John Jay's 1830 address before the House Committee on the Judiciary, in which he proclaimed that the writer "writes and he labors as assiduously as does the mechanic or husbandman."[16] The rhetoric of authorial labor, then, was by no means specific to the postwar period or even to that phase of the copyright movement; what made possible the canonization of this late-century rhetoric was an enthusiasm and appetite for historical narrative that pervaded not only the late century but also the international copyright movement itself.

The copyright movement was perhaps the most important institutional sponsor—other than the university—of literary history in the period. To substantiate their claims, copyright activists during the 1880s published countless works documenting injuries from piracy across American history. The publisher George Haven Putnam's 1891 collection, *The Question of Copyright*, contains no fewer than five separate histories of literary copyright, from antiquity to the late nineteenth century. Writers less inclined to produce full-length histories often peppered their writings on copyright with examples taken from the American literary past. Many of the era's most accomplished literary historians—including Thomas Lounsbury of Yale, Moses Coit Tyler of Cornell and the University of Michigan, and Charles Richardson of Dartmouth—were avowed sympathizers of and activists in the copyright movement. Other writers began their careers as literary historians by writing in support of international copyright. For example, Brander Matthews got his start in literary history by writing essays chronicling literary property rights. The ties between literary history and the copyright movement were so pronounced that even works of literary history with no immediate service to the movement functioned as barely disguised copyright propaganda. For example, Thomas Lounsbury's 1882 biography of James Fenimore Cooper expressly discussed Cooper's long-standing problems with piracy, a discussion whose relevance to contemporary politics was made plain when Lounsbury interrupted his historical account to editorialize: "We may hope that we have gained since his time; but even at this day we have little to boast of."[17] Similarly, Edmund Stedman and Ellen Hutchinson, editors of the extraordinary eleven-volume anthology *Library of American Literature* (1888–90), included alongside works of short fiction and poetry an essay on copyright by George Putnam, thus tacitly endorsing Putnam's argument while anointing the movement itself as an important event in American literary history. In this way, the international copyright movement provided a vehicle for the widespread production of literary history, which was thereby imbued with political and disciplinary importance.

The centrality of the production of literary history to the copyright movement merits some analysis. At the very least, historical narrative provided activists with a cover by which they were able to evade political land mines. The copyright movement was exceedingly contentious, largely due to the outrage that often met authors' appeals because of the widespread assumption that American writers either were already wealthy or came from the patrician class. The publication of any essay on authors' rights was sure to bring an outpouring of letters arguing opposing positions. Even activists in favor of international copyright were known to argue with each other, as the lengthy quarrel between Lounsbury and Henry C. Lea published in the *New-York Tribune* in 1884 attests.[18] But literary history seems to have provided copyright activists with a respite from such arguments and the threat of dueling in the press. In fact, activists quickly exhausted argument as a vehicle for the movement, and there are, in fact, relatively few solely argumentative writings in the copyright archives. Instead, the vast majority of work published on the copyright question in the 1880s is limited to the recitation of data: histories of copyright, myriad reprints of the texts of copyright bills, and bibliographies of publications on copyright. These works allowed activists to keep the copyright movement in the public eye while avoiding the inevitable disagreements that threatened to make their efforts seem subjective and morally indefinite. This is not to suggest that the many literary histories published in support of copyright are without argument; rather, as one of the strategies by which activists were able to circumvent bitter public quarrels, the medium of literary history allowed argument to pass under the radar of detractors with ready pens.

This collateral benefit aside, literary history chiefly allowed writers to circumvent the ire of a public unsympathetic to the financial pleas of a constituency they believed to be aristocratic. Literary history, that is, proved instrumental in bridging class divisions that for so long had interfered with public support of copyright protections. Brander Matthews's telling, if disingenuous, explanation for the prominence of literary history in copyright literature neatly illustrates the usefulness of historical narration in this context:

> The struggle to secure the protection of our laws for literary property produced by citizens of foreign countries has been long and wearisome. To some it may seem fruitless. An ocean of ink has been spilt and a myriad of speeches have been made; and yet there are no positive results set down in black and white in the Revised Statutes of the United States. But the best cure for pessimism is to look back down the past, and to take exact account of the progress already made. This examination reveals solid grounds for encouragement in the future. The labor spent, although often misdirected, has not been in vain. Something has been gained.[19]

Matthews attributes the rise of literary histories to the need to take stock of past successes in order to retain optimism amid unremitting obstacles. But his designation here of the "citizens of foreign countries" as the primary beneficiaries of copyright activism reveals the latent motives of such literary histories to be hiding in plain sight.

International copyright promised to protect not only American writers from piracy abroad but also foreign writers from piracy within the United States, where many imprints specialized in cheap reprints of foreign works, usually British ones. Copyright activists often discussed copyright within a moral and legal framework that allowed them to address piracy without the specificity of authorial nationality. Although the interests of foreign writers pirated in the United States did occasionally appear as terms of debate, copyright activists generally appointed American writers as unambiguous victims of a British publishing industry that belittled American literature even as it brazenly pirated it. In an interesting turn to the foreign author as the primary beneficiary of copyright law, Matthews displaces the onus of piracy—and the benefits of copyright law—away from himself and his peers. Matthews's own well-known wealth and aristocratic lineage tacitly underlie his decision to invoke the foreign writer, enabling him to deflect the criticism of self-interest leveled by skeptics and to reconstitute himself and the movement as altruists campaigning for the sake of others. It is fitting that Matthews would attempt to imbue the copyright movement with selflessness in a context that largely served that very purpose for copyright activists: literary history allowed activists to document the injuries of piracy without making themselves open to accusations of selfishness and money-grubbing.

Matthews's widely reprinted essay "American Authors and British Pirates" offers a typical example. First published in the *New Princeton Review* in 1887 and issued as a pamphlet two years later by the American Copyright League, the essay counters British protestations of innocence with a meticulous catalog of pirated American books for sale in Britain at the time. In opting for hard data over transparently motivated argument, this essay conveys the widespread desire of activists to stay above the fray by allowing evidence to stand alone and speak for itself. Before beginning this inventory, Matthews briefly offers a literary history of piracy and its affects on earlier writers such as Cooper, Hawthorne, and Longfellow, substantiating his claims with evidence culled from biographies, letters, and diaries attesting to the wrongs these writers endured. This prefatory narration of the literary past primes readers to be receptive and sympathetic to the list that will follow, for it draws on a presumed affection for writers whose status was in the process of being fortified by the very medium of literary history in which Matthews here works. Matthews uses literary history to waylay accusations of self-absorption and envelop the movement with dutiful piety and filial respect. The result is the constitution of copyright activists as literary avengers redressing the wrongs endured by those who had been unable to act.

No figure of literary history serviced this aim more frequently than Washington Irving, whose status as the nation's first internationally recognized writer made him central to any American literary history and a suitable case study of copyright infringement, as his transatlantic celebrity made him particularly vulnerable to foreign piracy. Copyright sympathizers persistently narrated Irving's experiences with British piracy, and his centrality to the copyright movement may have been facilitated by the waning reputation and aristocratic pretensions of Cooper, Irving's most famous colleague in piratical injury in early American letters. In the preface to his collection *The Question of Copyright*, Putnam interrupts his discussion of the general inadequacy of copyright law to relate the bitter circumstances surrounding Irving's patrimony after his death. The brief extension of copyright after an author's death had made Irving "unable to insure for his nieces (his adopted children) the provision which they needed, and which a continued copyright in their uncle's works would have secured for them."[20] Putnam's heartrending account of displaced bequests and disinherited daughters reduces the complex matter of copyright to a simple moral calculus: copyright is necessary to protect the vulnerable and powerless, an argument that directly counters the arguments of those critics who intertwined authorship with hereditary power and one made possible by the narration of American literary history.[21]

It is impossible to reconstruct the reception of such rhetoric, especially because copyright supporters controlled literary media and closely monitored the ways in which copyright was handled in the press. However, one must not discount the influence of literary history in imbuing copyright rhetoric with legitimacy and erudition, for the authors—or circulators—of such rhetoric were reputable writers, critics, and scholars whose reputations also helped lend it credence. But altering public perception of literary work required the proliferation of rhetoric not only about labor but also about the aristocrat, the apparition that has long stalked literary work in the West and that late-century American writers were at pains to cast off. And it is in pursuit of this aim that the rhetoric of international copyright mediated uneasily between the literary present, in its struggle to affirm authorial labor, and the literary past, in its use of literary history to construct a dethroned literary aristocracy. I do not want to suggest that this occurred with the production of literary histories that inflected the American literary past with elitism and privilege. On the contrary, literary historians—Matthews among them—take pains to depict antebellum writers such as Hawthorne as working men, establishing their character by documenting the financial burdens they endured, information that derives from the premium put on literary labor in this period. Instead, the periodization of the nineteenth century was made possible by the entanglement of literary history with political history. Indeed, the conflict at the core of the international copyright movement pitted the aristocrat against the populist, but in their struggle to divest themselves of the taint of aristocracy, copyright advocates manufactured narratives that displaced the immediate political and literary context of the copyright dispute onto the literary past, as reiterated by Parrington's literary history of the nineteenth century.

For explication, I turn to an example taken from early in the post–Civil War copyright movement, with the founding of the International Copyright Association, a precursor to the American Copyright League that disbanded after the financial panic of 1873. At the first meeting of the Association, the Presbyterian minister Samuel Irenaeus Prime—a founder and editor of the *New-York Observer* and manager of the "Editor's Drawer" column in *Harper's Magazine*—proclaimed the movement "a demand for *justice*. It is not asking for privileges; it is the assertion of rights."[22] On the heels of this announcement, Prime tells a story meant to illustrate these wider political aims:

> In the year 1784, the year after our National Independence was recognized by treaty with Great Britain, an English publisher seized upon Morse's Geography, an American copyright work of great literary and pecuniary value, and published it without recognition of the rights of the author, and without making him the least compensation. That system of piracy thus begun has been relentlessly pursued by the British, with a disregard for our rights which has justified the remonstrances of authors and publishers, and which they have bitterly and often complained of, these many years.[23]

Prime's story of the first geography published in the United States by an American, Jedidiah Moore's *Geography Made Easy* (1784), gives way to a larger narrative of British tyranny. Situated in the aftermath of the American Revolution, this story treats the piracy of Moore's *Geography* as the founding moment of a long-standing practice in which the British contravene American political as well as literary sovereignty. Within the logic of Prime's narrative, it is important that Moore's *Geography* was published in the wake of the American Revolution, for Prime regards Moore's text as the cultural fruit of that political rupture. Prime also sees in this piracy, however, a continuity of British tyranny, although it has evolved from political to cultural and literary tyranny. British oppression endures in the literary arena, and the international copyright movement emerges as a modern version of the American Revolution in its pursuit of literary independence from Britain. Prime's rendering of the current dispute as an atavistic extension of the American Revolution is designed to assure activists of the successful conclusion to this most recent quarrel.

Prime's account points to the primary vehicle by which copyright advocates were able to affix aristocracy to the American literary past: the centrality of Britain and transatlantic literary relations in the copyright movement. Despite the movement's avowed internationalism, England and Scotland were its principal targets, as shared language made piracy easy and economical for British and American publishers alike. Hostilities toward Britain overwhelmed the movement; the literary histories produced in support of copyright were, like Matthews's essay "American Authors and British Pirates," generally limited to incidents of British piracy endured by American writers. The narration of literary history enabled activists to reduce the very complicated matter of international copyright, which entangled international relations with class-based disputes within the publishing industry between workers and authors, to a transatlantic quarrel within what James Russell Lowell termed the "community of blood, of law, of language, and of books existing between Great Britain and the United States."[24] As F. A. P. Barnard, then president of Columbia University, put it, "Between Great Britain and the United States there has been a war in the literary field of a century's standing, signalized by incessant acts of pirateering on both sides."[25]

Isolating Britain as the principal villain was astute, for it allowed copyright activists to revise somewhat the terms of authorship already in circulation. Eager to relieve themselves from the freight of aristocracy, late nineteenth-century writers were able to map the populist–aristocrat dyad onto their literary grievances with Britain, whose prominent aristocracy made it an easy target. In depicting themselves in conflict with Britain, American writers were able to reposition themselves in this dyad as the abused victims of a literary aristocracy. In 1890, the *New York Times* published an editorial on copyright containing this rhetorical move:

In American communities there is a well-grounded tendency to regard a man who is merely the heir to a fortune as one who has never endured the tests of labor and hardship, in contradistinction to the feeling in Europe, which makes people ridicule and belittle the "self-made" man, whether or not his manners are such as deserve it. Authors are essentially self-made men, in the best sense of that abused term, and as such are often subject to a certain coolness on the part of fashionable folk at home and abroad, for the latter are taught to value most the descendants of ancestors raised by wealth above the struggle for existence.[26]

Britain and the United States stand in clear opposition here in their respective attitudes toward pedigree, and the article uses British reverence for aristocratic lineage as an explanation for their ill-treatment of American authors, especially in copyright matters. With the disingenuous announcement that "authors are essentially self-made men," the article is able to make writers the apotheosis of the American values of self-reliance and self-invention, and Britain the center of aristocratic operations. And this move leads inexorably to the alignment of copyright with democracy, as with Matthews's observation that "it is pleasant for us Americans to know that this first feeble acknowledgment of copyright was made by a republic": namely, Venice in 1469.[27] Matthews saw more than coincidence in the simultaneous emergence of copyright and the rise of democracy in the English-speaking world, for, he argued, the legal protection of authorship is an indispensable step in the legal enfranchisement of all people. Twain, an avid copyright activist, concurred in *A Connecticut Yankee in King Arthur's Court* (1889), in which Hank Morgan, a Connecticut foreman displaced to the sixth century, begins his campaign to dismantle Camelot's aristocracy by establishing intellectual property laws: "For I knew that a country without a patent office and good patent laws was just a crab, and couldn't travel any way but sideways and backwards."[28]

High-profile tours of the United States by British writers complicated Britain's public image within the copyright movement. Matthew Arnold, Charles Dickens, and Anthony Trollope were among the outspoken advocates of an Anglo-American international copyright agreement, and all used their tours of the United States to generate interest among Americans.[29] Dickens undertook two tours, the first in 1842 and the second immediately following the American Civil War in 1867; both tours have been credited with invigorating the American copyright movement through his explicit, if awkwardly received, exhortation on the matter.[30] These tours produced mixed feelings among Americans, who were disappointed by what they perceived as ingratitude, rudeness, and explicit cultural criticism from their guests. When Dickens famously addressed international copyright, he outraged Americans with his accusations of piracy and requests for remuneration, thereby consolidating copyright activism with greed, ingratitude, and anti-Americanism in the American consciousness, associations that thwarted later American copyright enthusiasts.

Although Dickens has been credited with launching the postwar copyright movement, Arnold cast the longer shadow in providing an unwitting vehicle by which late nineteenth-century activists were able to define themselves as populists and defenders of American democracy against British cultural elitism. In advocating literature as "simply trying to see things as they are," Arnold found a receptive audience among post–Civil War American writers sympathetic to the realist idiom, among them Matthews, Howells, and Sarah Orne Jewett.[31] Although he frequently criticized the British hereditary aristocracy, Arnold advocated instead a kind of cultural aristocracy composed of writers and other intellectuals in the hope that it would elevate the national tone, a vision that comported with the ambitions of American realists such as Howells and Frank Norris. At times, Arnold sounded virtually Emersonian in decrying the desiccation of literary culture and the ascendance of "something bookish, pedantic, and futile" in the public perception of "the word culture." Culture, he continued, is "great help out of our present difficulties . . . through this knowledge, turning a stream of fresh and free thought upon our stock notions and habits, which we now follow staunchly but mechanically."[32] Although a similar belief led Emerson to anticipate a new age in American life and to elevate the plebeian as fit aesthetic and philosophical material, it caused Arnold to criticize the United States for the dominance of the very element that Emerson had exalted. Arnold frowned on the American emphasis on work and its accompanying anti-intellectualism, and although he reified the terms that were at the center of international copyright rhetoric, Arnold indirectly cast aspersions on authorial efforts to pander to these aspects of American culture. It is no surprise, then, that despite the fact that many American writers were sympathetic to some of Arnold's beliefs, they turned against him during his tour, taken during the peak of copyright activism in 1883 and 1884, portraying him as the embodiment of British aristocratic elitism.

Arnold's fraught relationship with the United States was propelled by numerous missteps in which his remarks about American anti-intellectualism were roundly denounced by those American writers who most suffered from this insularity. His position on copyright didn't help matters, as he interpreted the national apathy toward international copyright as evidence of American philistinism, thus sparking the ire of copyright activists intent on aligning themselves with the very population sector he denounced.[33] American writers of varying social positions recoiled at Arnold's manner, which was perceived as anti-American and condescending. Just as the self-made writers Howells, Twain, and Whitman flexed their populist muscles in response to Arnold's behavioral signifiers of aristocracy, so Lowell and Thomas Wentworth Higginson charged Arnold with an aristocratic bias in his criticisms of the United States. Coming from two Boston Brahmins with elite lineage and concerted ties to England (Lowell was at that time the American diplomatic liaison to Britain), such claims seem like conspicuous attempts to transfer the onus of Anglophilic snobbery from themselves to Arnold.[34] In fact, Higginson and Lowell exaggerated Arnold's aristocratic sympathies, as he had consistently lamented the power and influence of the British aristocratic classes, which in 1869 he characterized as "unintelligent" and out of touch.[35] Arnold responded to Higginson and Lowell with the 1882 essay "A Word About America," in which he claimed to share Lowell's hopes that American culture might produce an environment receptive to "culture" and populated by judicious consumers. He disavowed aristocratic biases, claiming that "if American democracy gives this, Mr. Lowell may rely upon it that no narrow Anglicism shall prevent my doing homage to American democracy."[36]

Arnold made several more awkward missteps that allowed American writers to regard him as the embodiment of aristocratic snobbery and themselves as injured populists. In 1884, he unwisely delivered a lecture in which he announced that Emerson lacked greatness as a poet, writer, and philosopher. Outrage and controversy immediately followed, especially in the Boston press, and his criticisms were widely distorted to constitute evidence of Arnold's anti-American irreverence and snobbery.[37] Upon his return from the U.S. tour, Arnold published several more pieces that aggravated already hostile relations, including "A Word More About America" (1885), composed in direct response to his trip, and "Civilisation in the United States" (1888), which was published shortly before his death and became infamous for his statement that the United States failed to hold his interest. One reader, Civil War general James Fry, responded in the *North American Review*: "Surely we have been interesting to British Sovereigns from Victoria all the way back to George the Third, and to British statesmen from Gladstone to Pitt; and it is beyond dispute that we have proved interesting to the British Army and Navy whenever we have met them."[38] Like copyright advocates such as Samuel Prime, Fry narrated past American military engagements with Britain to resolve present transatlantic difficulties. But the episode that caused the greatest outcry against Arnold occurred in 1887, when he gave Ulysses S. Grant's memoir an unfavorable review and took potshots at Grant's grammar, which inflamed American indignation at seeing their Civil War hero humiliated by a critic they already regarded as an aristocratic snob. Fry again resorted to military language in the *North American Review*, pronouncing Arnold an "enemy."[39] As the publisher of Grant's enormously successful memoir, Twain went immediately on the defensive with an address given to a military audience, Connecticut's Army and Navy Club, in which he subjected Arnold's review to the same grammatical scrutiny.[40]

It is plain that the centrality of Britain in the American literary imagination of the 1880s allowed copyright enthusiasts to position themselves as populists locked in a struggle with British hegemony. However, what has proved to be especially important and enduring is the incorporation of this ploy into a literary historical narrative of the nineteenth century promoted by Parrington and others. Indeed, the narration and reperformance of American victory over Britain circulated by copyright activists is, at its core, the same story as Parrington's literary history. Both narratives position a culture predicated on pedigree and Old World sympathies in conflict with a culture characterized by self-invention and self-creation, and both narrate the demise of lineage in favor of meritocracy, the decline of aristocracy in favor of populism. The discourse of Anglo-American political history that made the dyad of populist-aristocrat particularly weighty in the late century figures as an early avatar of the narrative of democratic ascendancy at the core of the literary history of the nineteenth century. Vital to the imbrication of these two narratives is a consciousness of the past, which offered a rubric for disentangling the untidy relations within the literary circumatlantic and leaving late nineteenth-century American writers free to define themselves as independent of these transnational, transhistorical relationships. Despite the martial rhetoric freely bandied about, Britain and the United States enjoyed stable political relations in the late nineteenth century and were mutually dependent trade partners; the late eighteenth-century military engagements that figured in metaphors of the literary transatlantic were already swaddled in nostalgia and remoteness.[41] The pastness that encircled this metaphorical conceit became the vessel that contained the anglicized Old World, which had long fueled American suspicions of authorship. To the advantage of late-century writers, the past became the site onto which a literary aristocracy was displaced, as narrated by Parrington's periodization of the nineteenth century.

Coiled beneath the depiction of the past as a ferment of aristocratic sensibilities and sympathies lies one of the central arguments used by copyright activists. Attempting to communicate the wider consequences of pervasive transatlantic piracy, writers contended that the surfeit of cheap pirated editions of British literature had overwhelmed American literature, making it impossible for American writers to compete with lower-priced texts by better-known British writers. In an 1890 report to the House Committee on Patents, Congressman W. E. Simonds of Connecticut argued, "American authors are subjected to untrammeled competition with English authors who do not receive a farthing for their labor."[42] If it weren't bad enough that Britons had shamelessly pirated American writers, those writers' victimization at the hands of American publishers had led to their being squeezed out of their own literary home market. "The system is dwarfing American literature," wrote the journalist and minister Lyman Abbott. The publisher Henry Holt, in testimony before the Senate, concurred: "It is the question whether we are to continue to have an American literature—for, as you all know, American literature is languishing even now—the question whether . . . we are to derive our ways of thinking, our ideal of life and politics, from alien, unsympathetic sources."[43] That same year, Holt responded to the Philadelphia printer and copyright opponent Roger Sherman by arguing that "the competition of foreign literature whose authors are not paid is making it impossible for new authors to get a foothold, or for old ones to get proper pay."[44]

Copyright prose is replete with testimonies and arguments declaring that the wide circulation of cheap British editions had instilled in readers an appetite for British literature and, in Twain's words, "an unhealthy fascination for foreign life, with its dukes and earls and kings, its fuss and feathers, its graceful immoralities, its sugar-coated injustice and oppressions."[45] Copyright activists depicted the popularity of pirated novels among American readers as the initial step in a retrogressive return of the United States to a British colony, in which American citizens absorb and imitate the manners culled from British literature, and as an imminent reversal of the circulating narrative of democratic ascendancy. "It is not wholesome," Matthews writes, "nor a good augury for the future of the American people, that the books easiest to get, and therefore most widely read, should be written wholly by foreigners, and chiefly by Englishmen, who cannot help accepting and describing the surviving results of feudalism and the social inequalities we tried to do away with one hundred and twelve years ago."[46] While realists such as Howells deployed similar rhetoric in an attempt to stir public interest in realist and local-color fiction, the immediate political context of such language posited international copyright as a bureau of cultural immigration barring unwanted foreign influences at the border and protecting the integrity of American culture and literature.

The literary history of the first half of the nineteenth century depends upon this narrative of imitation and assimilation. Unidirectional transatlantic influence has come to be a mainstay of American literary history in the works of critics such as Aubert Clark and Robert Weisbuch, who have verified copyright activists' claim that the absence of international protection produced widespread imitation among American writers, if not readers. In the words of Henry Van Dyke, free literary piracy across the Atlantic produced American literary "mimicry of English models" and a culture of literary imitativeness among writers desperate to compete with the cheap, pirated British novels favored by readers.[47] The belief that American writers had to beat British writers by joining (and imitating) them was so central to the copyright debate that even opponents of copyright, such as Henry Carey, put the lack of originality in American literature at the center of their argument to claim the inevitability of imitation, and therefore the injustice of copyrighting ideas. The presumed imitativeness of American literature has long been believed to be a condition of the piratical waters of nineteenth-century, English-language literature, but what's especially important about this claim is its legacy in the literary history of the century. While we may debate the legitimacy of the characterization of the first half of the century as aristocratic in its allegiances, the influence of British literature on that time period endures as accepted wisdom, an influence made possible by copyright loopholes. Underlying the narration of an aristocratic literary past are the consequences of piracy for struggling American writers forced to compete with unpaid British labor. The detection of an anglicized Old World in the American literary past may describe less the dominance of pedigreed Boston Brahmins than the conditions of literary success in a market that necessitated the imitation of British fiction.

An additional variable in the construction of an aristocratic American literary past is the strong presence of James Russell Lowell in the copyright movement. Although he continued to publish after the war, Lowell found his greatest success in the antebellum era with *The Biglow Papers* and *A Fable for Critics* (both 1848), and was an important member of the popular grouping of Boston-area writers known as the Fireside Poets. A descendant of an illustrious Puritan family, a Harvard graduate, and holder of the Smith professorship of modern languages at Harvard, as well as American ambassador to England during the first half of the 1880s, Lowell typified the pedigreed Boston gentleman firmly associated by literary historians with the antebellum period. Lowell's language reveals the depth of his own literary elitism: he dubbed literary achievement the "American Parnassus" and called the literati the "Elect," a term taken directly from the religious doctrine of his Puritan ancestors and one that suggests the preordination of literary success.[48] In a letter to Howells, Lowell voiced anxiety about the decline of the literary gentility with which he and his cohort would be so firmly associated: "The danger of our literature . . . seems to me to be lawlessness & want of scholarly refinement. This is the rock I see ahead just now, & I fear we may go to pieces on it if we don't look sharp."[49]

Part of Lowell's importance in the copyright movement stemmed from his venerability and his association with the Puritans and the antebellum era, which made him a cynosure of the copyright movement and guardian of its respectability. His august status led to his appointment to the post of American minister to England, a position that lacked genuine diplomatic importance but allowed him to serve as the respectable face of American literature before British writers hostile toward the copyright-resistant American government and the brazenly piratical publishing industry.[50] Lowell was an important weapon in helping the movement retain its tone of civility. An offhand quatrain sent to the *Century* in response to a questionnaire from the editor Richard Watson Gilder was widely reprinted, as was his testimony before Congress. In particular, one pithy comment from that testimony—"There is one book better than a cheap book, and that is a book honestly come by"—became a veritable maxim of the movement, and his words were received like the wisdom of a sage or church elder.[51]

It is important that Lowell was president of the American Copyright League when the copyright law was finally passed in 1891. He had been unable to attend any of the celebrations held by the League and died shortly thereafter. Despite his absence, however, Lowell hovered over the League's 1891 banquet through numerous toasts to his health and readings of his various epigrammatic remarks as well as his apologetic letter explaining his absence. Transcripts and published accounts of the banquet communicate a solemn tone, as if the gathered party sensed Lowell's imminent death. The celebration of the passing of the law doubled as a commemoration of the rapidly passing life of Lowell; in effect, the celebration of this event in American legislative history solidified the passing of Lowell's generation and concluded the movement that produced the literary history by which Lowell and his peers would be remembered. With his death, the American aristocratic literary regime receded decisively into the past, in conformity with the periodized narrative already in circulation and at the end of the movement that produced that literary history.

It bears remarking that the subterranean currents of the aristocratic literary past delimited by American literary history were by no means confined to Anglo-American relations; rather, the very concept of an aristocratic American past summoned not only transatlantic literary traffic but also the more recent struggles with another aristocratic opponent, albeit one internal to the United States. In short, superimposed on the periodized literary history of the nineteenth century are the political and cultural conflicts that resulted in the American Civil War, and Arnold's comments about Grant and the response they elicited laid bare the interconnection between the recent and the more distant pasts. His comments rekindled American memories of the British position in the Civil War, which had been decidedly pro-South and aristocratic. The cultural similarities between the American South and Europe were already common knowledge. As early as 1835, Alexis de Tocqueville had commented on the resemblance, and in 1883, the same year as Arnold's tour, Twain expounded on Southern aristocratic pretensions in *Life on the Mississippi*. Twain's famous belief that the popularity of Walter Scott's novels in the American South had fueled aristocratic sensibilities and indirectly led to the Civil War merits a reconsideration within the context of international copyright, for the wide circulation of these British novels can be attributed to ubiquitous piracy and cheap editions.

In criticizing Grant's grammar, Arnold became a representative of two different enemies of New England and the Mid-Atlantic, the geographical regions that, in producing the nation's principal literary historians, became the nominal representatives of the nation as a whole. Arnold became, that is, a representative of two aristocratic foes, Britain and the American South. Howells's reflections on Arnold's death in 1888 illustrate the unconscious intermingling of the two in the late nineteenth century. Though Howells reluctantly conceded the legitimacy of Arnold's criticisms of American culture, he countered with a list of American accomplishments, among them the names of numerous Americans he regarded as exemplars of national character: Lincoln, Grant, Stowe, and John Brown.[52] This is an important and telling list of Americans, as they all played central roles in determining Northern beliefs and goals in the Civil War. Howells's list of great Americans indirectly communicates the spectral presence of the American Civil War—and the North's position in it—in his thinking about Arnold and the turmoil with Britain that Arnold came to represent. A British attack leads him to a retort more appropriate for a different historical event.

The entanglement of the American Revolution and the Civil War was enabled by the concerted cultural and political ties between both enemies of the American North—Britain and the South. British support of the Confederacy resonated with late-century writers. Just four years after the close of the war, Lowell published the suggestively titled essay "On a Certain Condescension in Foreigners," in which he made sense of British support for the South. He recounted a conversation during the war with an English "gentleman of the highest description" who paid him a visit to communicate "how entirely he sympathized with the Confederates, and how sure he felt that we could never subdue them,—'they were the *gentlemen* of the country, you know.' "[53] In his analysis of Anglo-American literary relations during the nineteenth century, Clarence Gohdes attests to the shared class interests and sympathies that led to widespread support for the American South among upper-class Britons, who saw the imminent demolition of the feudal economy and aristocratic social structures from which they had benefited in their own country.[54] Cultural ties, that is, produced political ties.

Copyright activists also compared their campaign to the Civil War, a rhetorical comparison made possible in part by the reappearance of discussion about tariffs in copyright debate. Popularly called the "knowledge tax" on transported books, the tariff figured prominently in copyright discussion, even though it had no direct connection to international copyright. Putnam even explicitly stated that the debate about the tariff had sufficiently "hampered" the copyright movement and distracted it from its stated purpose.[55] Regardless, the revival of discussion about tariffs and protectionists in this context generated a readiness to compare this literary struggle to the Civil War, specifically in the explicit comparison of piracy to slavery on the grounds that both enterprises involved protested transport of commodities across the Atlantic.[56] In an 1887 address, Lowell directly compared the pirated book to the smuggled slave, and that same year Howells wrote, "The American nation . . . willfully perpetuates an abuse which in a small way is morally worse than slavery. . . . Slavery compelled a man's labor, but it gave him in return food, shelter, and clothing, such as they were; literary piracy seizes the fruits of a man's labor, and gives him absolutely nothing in return."[57] Although offensive in its description of slavery and amplification of piracy, this passage condenses and concentrates the terms central to the periodized literary history of the nineteenth century, for it uses the slave both to allude to the aristocratic economy of the past and to depict the late-century writer as a laborer.[58]

With the passage of the copyright bill, activists celebrated not only the legal dismantling of transatlantic piracy but also the fulfillment of literary historical narratives of democratic ascent over Old World aristocracies. During the 1880s, copyright enthusiasts pointed toward the vast popularity of pirated British texts and the imitativeness of American fiction to proclaim the imminent collapse of American cultural, if not political, independence from Britain; the absence of copyright law threatened to return the United States to a British cultural colony, if not a political one. Matthews pointed to the Britannia series in England, composed entirely of American pirated texts, to show the imminence of this cultural hostile takeover.[59] Once the bill was passed, however, its supporters exchanged the places of the two nations to announce the triumphant success of democracy. During his toast at the celebratory banquet, Stedman, then vice president of the American Copyright League, proclaimed, "All British authors are now American authors. The old toast about the commonwealth of those who inherit the language of Shakespeare and Bacon and Milton at last means something."[60] Although the United States lagged considerably behind Britain, and Europe more generally, in its enactment of international copyright laws, its supporters interpreted the passage of the 1891 law as the spread of American values eastward across the Atlantic. In being forced to honor the property rights of American literary laborers, the aristocrat had been vanquished and Americanized. Stedman described the successes of the law in language that exposes the latent motives of the copyright movement and the literary histories it sponsored: "All will now compete on nearly equal terms."[61] American writers, that is, will now have a fair position in the English-language literary market. And this drive for position in the transatlantic market is the hidden incentive behind the enduring periodized literary history of the nineteenth century.

{ *A Higher Function*

Literary History and the
Advent of Professionalism

Professionalism is recognizable, both today
and a century ago, by the command of a body of knowledge constituted as inaccessible to the wider public. The advent of professionalism in the second half of the nineteenth century has a decidedly
mixed legacy. On the one hand, it enabled practitioners of various
fields—medicine, law, architecture—who had once had to improvise
their own training and devise their own procedures to form new con-
sortiums for the sharing and refinement of knowledge, the regulariza-
tion of training, and the creation of quality control standards, all of
which doubtless contributed to the public welfare. On the other hand,
however, professionalism participated in a decisive reorganization of
knowledge that enabled the elevation of this new elite class at the
expense of a now-dependent public whose own knowledge of such
fields was henceforth regarded with skepticism and suspicion. Knowledge that had once been common became inaccessible through its
reallocation to a small, select body of initiates who had sufficiently
satisfied such requirements as graduate training and qualifying examinations. To safeguard this now restricted knowledge, professionalism
entailed the creation of supervisory bodies such as the American Medical Association, which were created primarily to oversee such regula-
tory tools as educational standards, accreditation exams, and licensing
but that also functioned secondarily to restrict claimants to professional expertise. In granting now-restricted knowledge to a small
number of people, professionalism cast this redistribution to signify
public protection instead of public disempowerment.[1] It is only in the
late twentieth and early twenty-first centuries that Americans have
begun to challenge the intellectual restrictions of professionalism,
visible in such varied activities as the women's health movement of

the 1970s, the revival in the 1990s of herbal folk remedies, and the rise in the 2000s of do-it-yourself bloggers often deemed more credible than mainstream journalists.

This negotiation between the laudable and less savory outcomes of professionalism was of immediate consequence to the rise of American literary history in the late nineteenth century, for this newly popular genre offered late-century writers and teachers of literature a vehicle by which they could comply with professionalism. The history of professionalism's absorption in the literary marketplace is well known, thanks to the wealth of recent work examining the often salutary material consequences of professionalism on literary labor in the late nineteenth and early twentieth centuries, as with the creation of such modern amenities as the literary agent, the literary contract, the byline, and standardized pay scales.[2] While professionalism did make genuine changes in some of the practices of literary work, professionalism was for the most part a freely chosen affect for turn-of-the-century writers, who imitated the protocol institutionalized by other vocations in the hopes that it would legitimize literary work, a project also undertaken by the international copyright movement, discussed earlier. Texts such as William Dean Howells's "The Man of Letters as a Man of Business" (1893) and Frank Norris's *Responsibilities of the Novelist* (1903) are recognizable attempts to shape literary work in the mold of professionalism and to position writers in the professional pantheon of doctors, lawyers, and engineers. The professionalist aspirations of turn-of-the-century writers were by no means incompatible with the populist class sympathies of copyright reform, for both attempted to dismantle lingering public suspicions of literary work and to constitute the writer as a protector of the national welfare. The successes of the copyright movement can be attributed in part to its enlistment of many of the structures of professionalism, such as the supervisory organization, the annual convention, and the rhetoric of expertise. And like the copyright movement, the rise of literary professionalism directly contributed to the flowering of American literary history in the late century, both creating an institutional climate amenable to such work and seeping into the contents of texts written and published under such conditions.

Literary workers in the late nineteenth century encountered several obstacles to their efforts to professionalize. The heavily publicized antielitism of both the international copyright movement and literary realism posed problems for the professional requirement of expertise and specialized training. What select bodies of knowledge could literary workers claim once they had already depicted themselves as common folk interested chiefly in living and representing common life? William Dean Howells—advocate at once of professionalism, realism, and copyright reform and one of the most prominent writers to straddle successfully this gulf between the literary professional and the literary populist—resolved this dilemma by alighting on the power of the literary professional to adjudicate and supervise public literary taste. In this highly influential formulation, Howells made the writer's own judgment, honed after years of work, into a professional asset available only to the literary initiate, and gave the literary expert the task of assessing the aesthetic, moral, and social value of a text. While this position was by no means a new one, Howells committed considerable energy to its revivification and propagation.[3]

In both his fiction and his *Harper's* columns, Howells circulated story after story of the social dangers posed by uneducated taste and the need for literary supervision. For example, in an 1891 *Harper's* column, Howells lamented the availability of potentially hazardous reading material. He observed, "The novels which so abounded at [the] news-stand were, upon closer inspection, such as might be supposed to amuse men of different ages, but if they were to amuse ladies of any age, they could hardly edify them; and whatever is to be said of the reading of men, men all feel that the reading of ladies ought to be edifying, or, at least, ought not to be offensive or deleterious."[4] In this passage, Howells construes reading as potentially harmful to women in particular, a conviction that presumes women's inability to read critically and their inclination to regard all texts as potential conduct manuals. In denouncing the freedom with which women could gain access to "offensive or deleterious" texts, Howells presumes that free access is neither appropriate nor desirable, and he implicitly advocates the professionalist presumption that knowledge ought to be restricted for the public welfare. To preserve women from the presumably salacious narratives that "might amuse men," inequity of knowledge and access is socially desirable and beneficial, and his outrage tacitly endorses the establishment of some kind of supervisory structure to prevent women from gaining access to this kind of material.[5]

That same year, Howells put that same belief at the center of "Criticism and Fiction," his famous literary manifesto cobbled together from excerpts of previously published essays. In displacing his own beliefs onto the American reading public, Howells correlates the morality of texts with public morality. Central in this mission statement is a call for literary supervision, a service that ought to be performed by the most astute and judgmental readers—literary writers themselves. American readers, he asserted, want literary stewardship; they want a literary public servant to exercise judgment and discretion. Readers "require of a novelist whom they respect unquestionable proof of his seriousness. . . . [T]hey require a sort of scientific decorum. He can no longer expect to be received on the ground of entertainment only; he assumes a higher function, something like that of a physician or a priest, and they expect him to be bound by laws as sacred of those professions."[6] According to Howells, readers want literary supervision in accordance with the "seriousness" and authority of other professional guardians of the public well-being. The characteristics that Howells itemizes here—"scientific decorum," "higher function," commitment to "sacred" laws, solemnity—clearly invoke professionalism and the increasing expectation that the professional practitioner will conduct business with emotional dispassion, gravity, and full awareness of the social consequences of his labors. Like the priest and the doctor, the literary supervisor has a "higher function," the commitment to public service, and Howells appoints the writer with the task of protecting the reader.

The crisis to which Howells responded, as well as his resolution of it, proved highly influential to the formation and creation of literary history in the late nineteenth century. Unlike their peers who earned a living by their pens, literary men employed by universities experienced professionalism not as a simulation but as a very real vocational ethos, a set of disciplinary demands they were expected to adapt to and that posed considerable problems for them.[7] Before the advent of professionalism, literature professors had typically been literary writers hired on the basis of their literary reputations, social contacts, and literary enthusiasms. Professionalism, however, made the university increasingly inhospitable to literary men moonlighting as professors, though universities continued to offer prestigious positions to such brand-name writers as Howells himself, who, though he quit school at a young age, received offers of endowed chairs from both Harvard and Johns Hopkins. The divisiveness wrought by professionalism in that arena is now widely known, as it polarized the literary academy into two camps: the largely untrained, generalist literary men whose work emphasized teaching and belletristic aesthetics, and the research-minded professionals who typically held doctorates, specialized in philology, and directed their researches to a small body of like-minded colleagues.[8] As American colleges and universities began implementing professional protocols, generalist literary men found themselves struggling to adapt to new demands that they focus their energies on specialized research; doctorates became increasingly required for hiring; and publications demonstrating expertise became necessary for promotion and tenure. In accordance with these changes, the Modern Language Association, a genuine professional organization, was established in 1883. Like the supervisory bodies of other professional fields, it organized conferences, collected data on such matters as number of doctorates conferred and publications, oversaw curricula, and supervised hirings. It also published a professional journal, the *PMLA*, which, in publishing the specialized research findings of its members, emphasized highly specialized, semiscientific philological research and in this way put increasing pressure on belletristic generalists.

It was in this climate that literary history arose as a viable option for English professors suddenly required to publish scholarship. As the Princeton and Harvard professor Bliss Perry attested in his autobiography, these literary men were unable, whether because of their advanced age or familial obligations, to uproot themselves for professional retraining at the German universities that offered philological instruction.[9] Unable to command the abstruse domain of medieval philology that became the benchmark of literary academic professionalism, they often turned to the new field of American literary history, which allowed them to produce knowledge without having to learn medieval languages or embark on lengthy graduate training at this late stage in their lives. One illustrative professional trajectory is that of Columbia University professor Brander Matthews, who began his career as a literary writer, publishing fiction, plays, and numerous volumes of theatrical and literary criticism. Though he had secured a respectable name for himself, he turned to teaching as a financial precaution against the vicissitudes of the literary and theatrical marketplaces that occupied his attention throughout his life. Parlaying his social contacts and gentlemanly knowledge of literature into a teaching post at his own alma mater, Columbia University, he by no means expected to coast on the basis of his social connections, but instead adapted to the emerging culture of professionalism at Columbia by publishing literary history. The success of his 1896 *Introduction to the Study of American Literature* helped him overcome his lack of a doctorate as an impediment to professional advancement, a feat many of his peers had been unable to pull off, and he rose through the ranks there, landing a full professorship in 1899.[10] His prominence became such that in 1910 he was elected president of the Modern Language Association, serving as the nominal head of the leading professional organ of the literary academy.

Similarly, the Harvard English professor Barrett Wendell began teaching at Harvard in order to finance his own writing career, but found that his two published novels failed to find favor with Harvard president Charles. W. Eliot. After ten years of teaching without promotion, in 1891 Wendell published a biography of the late-Puritan cleric Cotton Mather, a publication whose success led him to a reputable career as a literary historian and to greater prominence at Harvard. Shortly after the publication of this first excursion into literary history, Wendell wrote to the poet and fellow literary history enthusiast Edmund Stedman, "The book has done for me what my novels never began to do, in making people take what I do seriously. I am conscious of this in numberless ways."[11]

The pressures exerted by professionalism visibly made their way into literary histories, shaping their contents, methods, and arguments. For example, literary histories published between 1875 and 1910 typically contain a wealth of data: significant dates, charts and graphs, biographical information, income, print runs, sales figures. This emphasis works to exhibit their writers' scholarly research, legitimacy, and compliance with the new culture of professionalism. Barrett Wendell's 1891 biography of Cotton Mather is typical in this respect, for its total reliance on excerpts of Mather's own writings conspicuously flaunts Wendell's extensive archival research. At the same time, Wendell's synthesis of Mather's writings also showcased the taste and judgment Howells had touted as the trademark of literary professionalism. This integration of the scholarly with the curatorial was indeed characteristic of literary histories of the late century, which folded together a wealth of data with assessments of literary value. More recent literary histories, such as the *Columbia Literary History of the United States*, edited by Emory Elliott (1988), frequently regard aesthetic evaluation with suspicion because it has so often served as a pretext for the dismissal or total omission of female and minority writers from the canon and literary history.[12] For turn-of-the-century literary historians, however, the construction of literary history entailed the practice of literary criticism through the discernment of literary quality, an endeavor that complied at once with the Howellsian expectations of the literary cognoscenti and the institutional expectations of university administrators. Though aesthetic evaluation and historical research were performed alongside one another in these texts, they were essentially separate activities, with one seldom illuminating or spilling over into the other.[13] For example, in his 1888 literary history, the Dartmouth professor Charles F. Richardson proclaimed the Bay Psalm Book "the worst volume of verse ever produced in America."[14] Though published in a well-regarded and influential work of literary history, his consideration of this Puritan translation of the Psalms is largely aesthetic and moralistic, and overlooks altogether its wider function or position in Puritan literary history. In this way, Richardson was able to produce knowledge about the American literary past while urging his readers to stay away from texts and writers he found diminished by turn-of-the-century tastes and standards.

The investment in these two markers of professionalism in literary history—evaluative appraisal and the production of historical knowledge—was so pronounced that in 1886 several controversies about their execution produced a public discussion about the function and primary loyalties of American literary history as a whole. These two episodes helped formalize the emerging generic features of American literary history, and the debates that greeted the publication of two high-profile, heavily publicized literary histories—Edmund Gosse's *From Shakespeare to Pope* (1885) and Edmund Stedman's *Poets of America* (1885)—reveal the deep influence of professionalism on the genre's developing form. Both literary histories were received unfavorably because of their respective failures to execute both tasks satisfactorily. Whereas one literary history was reprimanded for its faulty, visibly amateurish research, the other was attacked for its inattention to aesthetic, evaluative matters. The acrimony heaped upon both texts communicates the very high hopes for literary histories in the late century, to a degree that any chinks in their professionalist armor were greeted as embarrassments, scandals, and signs of an imminent literary catastrophe. Responses to both texts position literary history as the flagship of late nineteenth-century literary professionalism, accorded special respect even by Howells himself, the period's leading advocate of market-based literary professionalism.

Though a history of British literature, Edmund Gosse's *From Shakespeare to Pope* received considerable attention amid the American appetite for literary history in the wake of the nation's centennial celebrations and served as a warning to aspiring Americans hoping to write similar texts. Best known today for his autobiography, *Father and Son* (1907), Edmund Gosse was an enormously prolific English writer of poetry, literary biography, and criticism. In the 1880s, he contributed to the growing currency of literary history by publishing several works on such topics as seventeenth-century poetry, Thomas Gray, and William Congreve. Gosse's researches profited from American patronage, as with the sponsorship of Howells, who helped him secure an appointment at the Lowell Institute in Massachusetts in 1884 and 1885. During this appointment Gosse delivered a series of lectures on British literary history that he then collected in the 1885 volume *From Shakespeare to Pope*. Gosse repaid this debt by dedicating his literary history to Howells in a poem that took up two full pages and paid special homage to the Boston literary culture that had fostered his book. Howells returned the favor by puffing his friend's various contributions to literary history in his *Harper's Monthly* column in March 1886, praising Gosse's cordial, graceful style.

Six months later, however, John Churton Collins, a former friend of Gosse's and a colleague in London literary circles, published a scathing, abusive review in the pages of the *Quarterly Review* of London.[15] Collins began his review by situating Gosse's book in the context of the changes that had overtaken Anglo-American universities. He wrote, "That such a book as this should have been permitted to go forth with the *imprimatur* of the University of Cambridge, affords matter for very grave reflection. But it is a confirmation of what we have long suspected. It is more proof that those rapid and reckless innovations, which have during the last few years completely changed the faces of our Universities have not been made with impunity."[16] He continued with the assertion that "a book so unworthy, in everything but externals, of a great University has never been given to the world; and secondly, that it is the bounden duty of all friends of learning to join in discountenancing so evil a precedent" (295). In a review spanning thirty pages, Collins itemized in painstaking detail dozens of Gosse's factual mistakes, from erroneous dates to faulty historical allegations, to support his claim that the "ignorance which Mr. Gosse displays of the simplest facts of Literature and History is sufficiently extraordinary, but the recklessness with which he exposes that igno-rance transcends belief" (300). Collins in this way exposes Gosse as an impostor feigning professional expertise he simply did not have.[17] He concluded his review by calling for the elevation of intellectual stan-dards for such research, and recommended that literary editors emu-late the greater rigor of science in maintaining scholarly integrity. Because of the vast wealth of data mustered against Gosse and the sheer ugliness of Collins's attack, the review was dubbed the "scandal of the year" and was so widely talked about that everyone from Mat-thew Arnold to Prime Minister Gladstone to the archbishop of Can-terbury weighed in.[18] According to the London correspondent of the *Critic,* "People—literary people—talk of nothing else. It has generated such rumors as are not to be stated; it has split the town into camps, and by many it is opined that it will cause the death of two men—the assailant and the assailed: the one for his animosity and the suspicion of *mala fides* which is discovered in his work; the other for the ingenu-ous poverty of his defense against so brilliant, so determined, so irre-sistible an attack."[19]

Scholars have long recognized that the widely varying professional fortunes of Gosse and Collins were central to the acrimony of Col-lins's attack. Gosse and Collins had been friends and literary col-leagues early in their careers, and both attempted to find employment in the British literary academy, which at that time resembled the United States in its function as a refuge for struggling writers. The hiring practices of the British literary academy resembled those of the United States in their chief reliance upon social contacts and personal favors rather than upon scholarly credentials. Gosse's academic career up to the publication of his 1885 literary history had been the product of such practices. Though Gosse lacked an undergraduate education altogether, he parlayed his many powerful social allies to his advan-tage and landed several academic positions: Howells's patronage in the United States had helped him gain a foothold in the academy, and, in England, Matthew Arnold, Leslie Stephen, and Alfred Lord Tenny-son helped Gosse become Stephen's successor as the prestigious Clark lecturer in English literature at Trinity College, Cambridge—despite never having graduated from college. Collins, on the other hand, had a more solid academic background: a graduate of Oxford, he had already established his credentials for the professionalized academy by having produced several respectable scholarly editions. A stickler for detail and historical data, Collins had already published numerous works protesting the condition of the literary academy and advocated the implementation of more rigorous techniques for the study of British literature, especially medieval literature. Perhaps because of his unpleasant reputation as a literary crank with a cutting review always at the ready, Collins failed to land an academic position, and at the time of the review was scrambling to support a sizable family by teaching literature to aspiring British civil servants. His 1886 review expressly took aim at Gosse, one very high-profile product of these long-standing hiring practices, to expose before the transatlantic literary world the dangers of hiring the unqualified. In this way, it directly contributed to the professionalist tightening of academic standards, the imperilment of untrained literary men employed by universities, and the absorption of professionalism into literary history.

Collins's review had multiple consequences. Upon its publication, Gosse's academic career ground to a halt. Though numerous students wrote letters on his behalf, Gosse resigned from his position at Cambridge in 1889. In the United States, Collins's review generated considerable attention and embarrassment. In the wake of this boisterous literary scandal, Howells conspicuously neglected to write to his friend and offer comfort. He addressed the matter only after Gosse had sent him a copy of his published rebuttal, a move ostensibly designed to elicit words of consolation and solidarity. Howells's reply fell far short of the mark Gosse must have hoped for, and Howells's embarrassment is marked, which is not surprising, considering his own involvement in this now embattled book: not only had he sponsored the lecture tour that produced this book, but Gosse had also prominently dedicated the book to him. Howells was tacitly implicated in this humiliating public exposure of faulty scholarship, and his indignation is visible in his tepid correspondence with Gosse. "Thank you for sending me your defence [sic] against the Quarterly," he wrote in November 1886.

"You needed none with this family, but we all thought your answer to the brutal assault which we've not yet read, admirable. I know the assault from hearsay, [Thomas Sargeant] Perry having told me how foolish and dishonest it was. The feeling here is all one way. [Thomas Bailey] Aldrich says the close of your reply—the last two paragraphs—is most masterly, and I think so, too."[20]

In these few words of consolation, Howells obliquely admits to having taken the reception of Gosse's book personally; in his claim that Gosse hadn't needed to defend himself "with this family," Howells admits to, and disavows, having thought that Gosse did in fact owe him an explanation for the shoddiness of a book that Howells had sponsored. In deflecting attention from Gosse's mistakes and turning instead to Collins's "brutal" review, he thoughtlessly admits that it has been the talk of American literary circles, a fact that Gosse probably did not want to hear. The garbled syntax of the second sentence of this letter perhaps intimates Howells's mixed feelings about Collins's review: the misplacement of the word "admirable," though ostensibly intended to modify Gosse's "answer," actually describes Collins's "brutal assault," and one wonders whether Howells's misplacement communicates tacit agreement with Collins; after all, his own review of Gosse's *From Shakespeare to Pope* had shied away from a commendation of his erudition and scholarship.

Until this review, American attitudes toward literary history had been trusting and unquestioning. With scores of literary men turning their attention to this new genre, standards had been lax, as no one other than Thomas Wentworth Higginson had been really regarded as a specialist or noticed factual mistakes.[21] Indeed, Gosse's literary history had been warmly received by the American press—Howells included—without notice of what Ann Thwaite described as its "more glaring errors."[22] John Churton Collins, however, communicated to the literary transatlantic that one could not do literary history casually, that it required exactitude and very high standards. According to Collins, literary history ought not to be the work of untrained amateurs, men of letters attempting to make a place for themselves in the rapidly professionalizing literary academy; rather than safeguard-

Class, Authority, & Literary History

ing the public welfare like true professionals, such pretenders, Collins argued, only damage public knowledge through the circulation of misinformation. Though literary history remained popular among this constituency, Collins's review raised standards of factual accuracy and, in so doing, helped literary history acquire the exacting criteria and reputation requisite for professional status. Not surprisingly, after Collins's review, Howells seems to have taken greater pains to ensure the exactitude of his own work, sending it to literary historians to proofread for errors; as he wrote to Edmund Stedman in 1894, "The dead cannot help themselves, but I give the quick a chance."[23] At the same time, this scandal exposed the difficulty of demanding literary professionals to execute both tasks attributed to literary history— scholarship and aesthetic evaluation—for qualification for one enterprise by no means imparted legitimacy in the other. As Ian Small puts it, the "authority of the critic resided in the nature of his reactions, or in the quality of his judgements and his sensibilities. . . . Factual accuracy, the domain of the scholar, could neither confirm nor refute such judgements."[24]

The Gosse-Collins affair made visible the unfortunate consequences of untrained literary men trying their hands at the kind of scholarly research now required for promotion and tenure but for which they were unprepared. In the same March 1886 column in *Harper's Monthly* in which Howells praised Gosse's beleaguered literary history, he also made a pitch for aesthetic evaluation, the other trademark of professionalism in turn-of-the-century literary history and one just as fraught with controversy as the production of accurate historical knowledge.[25] In his review of Edmund Stedman's *Poets of America* (1885), Howells complained about the absence of rigorous criticism from Stedman's literary history and his abundant critical generosity toward poetry in an era in which narrative fiction was rapidly replacing poetry as the nation's leading literary genre. An accomplished and renowned poet, Stedman had become by the time of Howells's review an important and well-regarded literary historian with a special expertise in poetry. Between 1875 and 1900, Stedman published four separate works of literary history and several anthologies, including the mammoth eleven-volume *Library of American Literature* (1888–90), the 1895 *Victorian Anthology*, and the 1900 *American Anthology*. The 1885 work reviewed by Howells, *Poets of America*, was conceived as a companion volume to his 1875 *Victorian Poets* and related the history of American poetry with special emphasis on the nineteenth century.

Though Howells and Stedman had been friendly colleagues and correspondents throughout their lives, Howells's review criticized with uncharacteristic force the liberality with which Stedman seemed to pronounce every other American poet a genius. Howells turned this critical negligence into evidence supporting the need for literary professionals to take a more active role in assaying literary quality. In a recommendation that augurs the emergence of peer review, that mainstay of the professionalized academy, Howells used Stedman's literary history to argue that writers need to use their special expertise in evaluating literary quality. Because literary history essentially functions as the final word on a writer's worth, retrospectively assigning judgment on writers of the past, Howells designated literary history as a form of literary criticism entrusted with the task of appraising value and supervising the reader. Without such assistance, the reader interested in the American literary past would be left without direction, a freedom that Howells had depicted throughout his career as rife with danger.

Howells expressed particular annoyance at Stedman's inclination to depict writing less as serious and arduous labor than as the passive channeling of divine inspiration, a representation at odds with the late-century emphasis on literary labor propounded by copyright activists, would-be literary professionals, and realists. At stake in Howells's review is the very status of the literary professional, for Stedman's lack of stringent standards seemed poised to erode the office and authority of the literary professional. He wrote, "[I lament] the lack of good old-fashioned criticism which we once had. We can remember the day when every quarterly, monthly, weekly, had its gridiron well heated, and its tender young poet or poetess always grilling on the coals for the amusement of the spectators. . . . In this state of things, we leave all anxiety for the poetic future to Mr. Stedman; we forebode not a famine, but a gross surfeit of poets, and great ones at that, all of the most unmistakable 'genius,' unless the sort of criticism which we lament can be restored."[26] If we don't make writers afraid of our judgment, Howells suggests, then every man, woman, and child will publish books, thereby diluting the literary market and mitigating the status of literary professionals. In adjudicating quality, Howells suggests, the critic serves as kind of gatekeeper, discouraging amateurs and upholding high standards for admission.

Stedman responded several months later with the publication of the essay "Genius" in the *New Princeton Review*. Though Stedman didn't directly respond to Howells's remarks about the responsibilities of the critic, his later works of literary history did. Despite Howells's complaints, *Poets of America* did indeed include aesthetic, evaluative criticism, though not of the directive, supervisory stripe urged by Howells. Stedman's later literary histories seem deliberately designed to irk Howells with the excision of all explicit literary criticism and chief reliance on biographical data and long literary excerpts. In withholding expert opinion on the relative merits of the many writers and texts included there, his later works such as the *American Anthology* (1900) invited readers to evaluate the texts for themselves. In his review of that later work, Howells expressed his annoyance at such an omission and his desire for greater literary direction, describing himself as so overwhelmed by the wealth of unvetted material as to be paralyzed.[27] In soliciting reader interpretation and appraisal, Stedman's later literary histories indirectly communicated high regard for reader response and skepticism about the office of the literary critic. Stedman explicitly expressed these opinions during his celebrated 1891 lectures on poetry at Johns Hopkins University: "One must in the end make his own acquaintance with [poetry's] best examples and form his judgment of them. . . . The poet's verse is more than all the learned scholia upon it. He makes it by direct warrant."[28] For Stedman, readers ought to form their own judgments about literature and reject the critic as unnecessary interference preventing the reader's direct access to the text. This enthusiasm for reader self-education led him to edit the first anthology of American literature, the *Library of American Literature*, which was composed exclusively of literary excerpts and explicitly marketed for autodidactic use in the home.

Stedman's unusual disregard for literary criticism may be due to his career path. Like many of his literary peers employed by universities, he attended college (though he did not graduate), hoped to earn a living by writing, and began his career promisingly with several popular works such as the poem "The Diamond Wedding" (1859). And like his peers, financial need drove him to find employment elsewhere; Stedman found work as a stockbroker, continuing to publish as a poet and critic while working on Wall Street (an arrangement he depicted in his 1869 poem "Pan on Wall Street"). Stedman's kinship with his academic literary peers was such that he nearly became one of them when he was offered the Billings professorship of English at Yale, a position he declined because he believed himself too old for the job at the age of sixty-two. However, his similarity to his peers ends there, for when Stedman began contributing to literary history, he already had the status, reputation, and legitimacy his peers sought in writing their histories. This is a vital difference, for Stedman is the only foundational literary historian of any importance in the 1880s who worked outside the academy, though numerous nonacademic writers such as Julian Hawthorne and Donald Mitchell would pen literary histories in later years. Though Stedman knew and was friendly with many of these other literary historians, he remained immune to the problems they faced in the changing academy: as a financial professional, he never had to adapt to *literary* professionalism to compete with ambitious colleagues, nor did he ever have to prove his scholarly credentials. Consequently, the contents of his later literary histories noticeably lack the incisive evaluations that dominate literary histories of the period and that evidence their writers' compliance with changing institutional demands.

Published just as literary histories were beginning to flourish at the turn of the century, this exchange between Howells and Stedman generated considerable buzz, with such periodicals as *The Critic*, the *Boston Gazette*, and the *Penny Post*, among others, publishing articles that summarized and commented on the arguments presented by both men.[29] This broad circulation helped consolidate and establish the formal qualities of this new literary genre: it educated and implanted expectations in readers and circulated both a blueprint for the literary history and a manifesto on the importance of including criticism in literary history. Certainly, the review communicated to the literary community the high stakes of failing to adhere to Howells's demands that literary histories assume the task of winnowing out the quality texts from the inferior ones. Expectation became such that, by 1903, Thomas Wentworth Higginson, the period's premier expert on literary history, admitted to sacrificing the historical range and depth of his *Reader's History of American Literature* to satisfy this aesthetic requirement. His book, he acknowledged, "will not assume to be in any sense a minute literary encyclopaedia of this work, but will rather attempt to select, as time selects, the best or representative names of each period in its course. The intrinsic literary importance of these writers will be considered, rather than their merely historical importance. Many minor names, therefore, which might properly be included in a summary of respectable books hitherto produced in America are here omitted altogether; and others are given minor mention as their literary merit appears to warrant."[30] Though Higginson did not have a university appointment and did not need to prove to anyone the legitimacy of his erudition or compliance with professionalism, the generic features of literary history were already so well established that even the venerable Higginson announced the discernment of literary quality as the prime criterion of selection.

While professionalism may have instituted scholarly quality control and caused the implementation of rigorous standards, it also left some unfortunate blemishes on the literary histories produced in its wake. Literary historians often manipulated the data at their disposal to legitimize the membership of literary scholars and critics in the ranks of professionals committed to the public welfare. This is especially visible in the frequency with which literary histories incorporated Howells's formulation of literary professionalism in the narratives they told about the American literary past. Just as some literary

historians told stories about Irving and Longfellow designed to cultivate popular sympathy for copyright reform, so others often incorporated a narrative in wide circulation in the late century about the
dangers of unsupervised reading and the importance of literary professionals in protecting such vulnerable readers. Stories about the
dangers of reading were by no means a new phenomenon, as evidenced by such texts as Cervantes's *Don Quixote* (1605 and 1615), Charlotte Lennox's *Female Quixote* (1752), and Jane Austen's *Northhanger
Abbey* (1817), all of which narrate the pitfalls of readers' inability to
differentiate fiction from reality and their foolish attempts to reproduce literary inventions in their own lives.[31] In the 1880s and 1890s,
however, Howells published a series of novels that reactivated and
revised this enduring narrative about the consequences faced by readers whose poor judgment leads them to ill-advised books that they
then imitate. As several of his novels suggest, poor literary judgment
may result in the confusion of particularly vulnerable readers, such as
the uneducated and the young, and lead them to make foolish choices.
According to Howells's alarmist rhetoric and narratives, at stake in
professional literary judgment was the very future of American youth.

Beginning as early as 1881 with *A Modern Instance*, a novel that
received a wealth of attention because of its depiction of divorce,
Howells used the medium of fiction to dramatize the importance
of literary supervision on behalf of those lacking sound judgment.
Though not a novel about reading per se, *A Modern Instance* inter-
twines a narrative about the consequences of an imprudent marriage
with a narrative about the professionalizing literary marketplace, as
it begins to regulate quality control, institute ethical standards, and
weed out those practitioners who fail to honor these protocols. At the
center of both narratives is Bartley Hubbard, an unhappily married
journalist unable to adapt to the culture of professionalism growing
up around him. His values, work habits, and relationships, both business and personal, become ever more problematic and unacceptable:
he plagiarizes a story, breaks a promise made to a source, conducts
himself immorally in the workplace, and falsifies an article. He gradu-
ally comes to be snubbed by those colleagues who adhere to the pro-

fessionalist credo Hubbard shamelessly flouts, and is eventually expelled from the Boston literary marketplace. Fleeing this professional disgrace, he abandons his young child and his wife, who foolishly married Hubbard despite ample evidence attesting to his weak character and shady morals, such as his taking liberties with her before proposing marriage and his ill-treatment of another woman, who consequently becomes a prostitute.

Though this domestic narrative does not explicitly address the changing literary scene that finds Hubbard so unmanageable, it is nevertheless of direct relevance to Howells's oblique portrait of the turn-of-the-century literary marketplace, for it illustrates the stakes of professionalism: without it, humbug practitioners like Hubbard may prey upon those who are most vulnerable and least equipped to recognize them for what they really are. In describing the obligations of the literary professional, the character Dicker, the ostensible leader of the nascent consortium of professionalized journalists, precisely articulates the connection between these two narrative strains. He remarks, "I consider a newspaper a public enterprise, with certain distinct duties to the public. It's sacredly bound not to do anything to deprave or debauch its readers; and it's sacredly bound not to mislead or betray them, not merely as to questions of morals and politics, but as to questions of what we may lump as 'advertising.' "[32] In this passage, Howells offers a narrative of reader corruption, in which a misleading or specious text has the power to "deprave or debauch," which is precisely what Hubbard does to the two trusting women who lack the incisive judgment of the literary professionals who root him out. In this way, Hubbard's inability to abide by professionalism indexes his power to corrupt the vulnerable and gullible.

The power of the text to injure is also at the center of Howells's 1885 novel, *The Rise of Silas Lapham*, which adheres to the same narrative structure as *A Modern Instance*. It, too, contains two interlocking narratives divided along the axis of gender. The first narrative follows the career trajectory of a Boston man, the paint magnate Silas Lapham, from his beginnings in a small New England town to his eventual bankruptcy and decline. The second narrative follows the romantic decisions of his daughter Penelope Lapham, as she falls prey to specious influences and seems poised to make a disastrous marital decision. The parallels between *The Rise of Silas Lapham* and *A Modern Instance* are plain, but in the 1885 novel Howells brought to the fore the literary context implicit in *A Modern Instance*. The novel recounts the socially awkward courtship and engagement of Penelope Lapham to Tom Corey, an aristocratic employee of her father's. Penelope's romantic difficulties are aggravated by the reading of a sentimental novel that inspires her to break off her engagement in solidarity with her heartbroken sister, Irene, whose love for Tom goes unrequited. This narrative allowed Howells to depart from the cloaked suggestions of *A Modern Instance* to tell a story about the necessity of professional literary criticism: just as *A Modern Instance* hinges on the inability of overly trusting characters to interpret correctly, so *The Rise of Silas Lapham* has at its center a highly impressionable, unskilled reader whose inability to interpret leads her to make rash decisions that jeopardize her respectability and sexuality. And like the professional men of *A Modern Instance* who defend and protect Hubbard's hapless wife, the plot of *The Rise of Silas Lapham* is resolved with the intervention of the professional man Minister Sewell, whose literary opinions restore order and undo the damage caused by poor literary choices and even worse reading skills.

Two years after the publication of *The Rise of Silas Lapham*, Howells published *The Minister's Charge* (1887), a novel that more fully developed Sewell's conjoined role as literary critic and protector of the young and foolish. The novel begins after Sewell thoughtlessly offers encouragement to an untalented young poet, Lemuel Barker, whose inability as a writer is outmatched only by his faults as an interpreter, for he fails to recognize Sewell's polite insincerity and embarks on a fruitless attempt to become a professional writer. The novel follows the consequences of this dishonest literary criticism and Sewell's failure to weed out literary pretenders. In showing the upshot of Sewell's well-meaning politeness, Howells reaffirms the acumen of literary professionalism, which recognizes inability when it sees it, and is therefore obliged to reject those who fail to meet its standards.

Narrative fiction allowed Howells to repackage and recirculate the same theories and beliefs he had articulated in reviews and essays, but in a less blatantly didactic form. Moreover, such fiction could do what he could not do in reviews and essays—that is, dramatize the far-reaching social benefits of literary criticism and perform the professionalism of its practitioners. It is one thing simply to assert that literary criticism is necessary and important, as Howells did in the 1886 review of Stedman's literary history, but it is altogether another thing to *show* this necessity in narrative fiction, to use the behavior and inner lives of characters to demonstrate the vital social service performed by literary critics and the consequences of failing to fulfill the responsibilities of professionalism. And in masking these beliefs in the guise of narrative fiction, Howells was able to conceal their constructedness and imbue them with inevitability.

The stories Howells told to develop and substantiate his literary critical ideas found their way into the literary histories of the era, such as Henry A. Beers's *Initial Studies in American Letters* (1891), Julian Hawthorne's *American Literature* (1892), and Barrett Wendell's *Literary History of America* (1900), which absorbed and retold these stories as a response to the crisis of professionalism. This narrative is visible in their treatment of one of the most renowned literary critics of the nineteenth century, Margaret Fuller. In the hands of turn-of-the-century literary historians at pains to affirm their adherence to professionalism and suitability for promotion and tenure, Fuller's life story was crafted after the pattern of such narratives of faulty reading as *The Rise of Silas Lapham*. In literary histories published over a thirty-year span, Margaret Fuller's biography was used to evidence the civic importance of literary professionalism. Thus, the institutional climate that promoted literary history made its way into the contents of these texts, taking as its quarry one of the most renowned and controversial literary critics of the nineteenth century. It was only with the work of feminist scholars in the 1970s and 1980s that Margaret Fuller's full importance began to be restored and the damage of late-century professionalist literary histories undone.

Despite their numbers, popularity, and influence, American women writers typically receive short shrift from late-century literary histories. This willful omission can be attributed to the professionalist purge, specifically in its attempts to dismantle the lingering public perception of literary work as a feminized avocation of the leisured. The company of women writers discussed in these texts is quite small and selective: Anne Bradstreet receives regular attention, and the vast popularity and political import of *Uncle Tom's Cabin* (1852) afforded Harriet Beecher Stowe an occasional entry. However, in histories that often expunge altogether women writers of the nineteenth century, Margaret Fuller appears consistently and with a striking uniformity. Her status as Emerson's favored interlocutor and collaborator, as well as her celebrated reputation as a child prodigy, imparted an intellectual credibility and distinction that set her apart from the legion of nineteenth-century women writers typically ignored by literary historians. The occasional ungainliness and difficulty of Fuller's prose made her a slow-moving target for historians expected to discern literary excellence and shape readers' tastes. However, literary histories instead typically evaded Fuller's work, dubbing it altogether unworthy of discussion. For example, in 1896, Fred Louis Pattee noted, "If judged alone by her actual literary product, she would deserve but a passing notice."[33] Though literary historians judged her work undeserving of inclusion, her biography alone explains her unlikely presence in turn-of-the-century literary histories.

The attention literary historians pay to Fuller typically involves a recitation of Fuller's life story, and the narrative they tell about her has little variance: Fuller received an unusual, ambitious education at the hands of her father, Timothy Fuller, who encouraged her to read widely and deeply, and she consequently became bookish, highly opinionated, and often disagreeable. She taught school briefly, worked as a writer and literary critic (an episode conspicuously ignored by literary histories), and then traveled to Italy, where she met and married a poor Italian aristocrat some years younger, whom she bore a son. Some historians allude to the lingering rumors that Fuller had become pregnant out of wedlock, and nearly all communicate their disapproval of Fuller's choice of mate. On her return passage to the

United States in 1850, the ship was overrun with an outbreak of small-pox, which killed the ship's captain and which Fuller's son narrowly survived. However, just miles off the shore of Fire Island, New York, the ship sank, killing Fuller and her family. Her life story is not without interest or drama, but the recitation of the story in literary histories takes the place of a substantive consideration of a celebrated writer and her work. Howells himself contributed to this climate of opinion in 1903 with his comments that Fuller "as a literary force was spent long ago; but her tragical fate, in returning home to be shipwrecked with her young husband and child on her native shores, has given a lasting pathos to her memory, and this is what appeals to the student of literature rather than anything she said; and she said a great many things."[34] Fuller is noteworthy because of her life story and death, not because of her work. Literary historians have always used select details of author biographies—such as Emerson's decision to leave the pulpit or Poe's financial struggles—to betoken events or trends of wider historical significance.[35] However, Margaret Fuller is the only figure to receive attention in late-century literary history solely on the basis of author biography, her life history packaged as an event of historical significance.

Fuller had not always been so treated by critics and literary historians. In their 1855 *Cyclopaedia of American Literature*, the first work of its kind, Evert and George Duyckinck solidly asserted her centrality to antebellum letters. Published about twenty-five years before the wide proliferation of literary history, this expansive two-volume work included biographical entries and literary excerpts of even the most minor contributors to American literature up to that time. Though this book is today seldom read or cited, it offered turn-of-the-century founders of literary history an invaluable resource, often strip-mined for data, and its tracks are visible either in cited bibliographic entries or in unattributed passages lifted practically verbatim. Just five years after Fuller's death, the Duyckinck brothers offered a foundational account of Fuller's life and work, and their discussion was clearly the genetic antecedent of later versions that would appear in literary histories. The Duyckincks had known Fuller—Evert Duyckinck had been a keen supporter of her work during her stay in New York—and the entry devoted to her is extensively detailed, personal, and heartfelt.[36] Especially affecting is the Duyckinck brothers' inadvertent contribution to Fuller's diminution of reputation, for, in their attempts to glorify and elevate her, they unwittingly offered a vocabulary and template for her detractors, who co-opted and manipulated the Duyckincks' narrative and language.

The Duyckincks' method of framing a writer's work within the context of his or her life was of especial significance in their handling of Fuller, who had been so celebrated by her prominent circle of supporters but whose body of work and life story had been so out of step with the time.[37] Fuller's postmortem reputation was complicated by the whiff of unwholesomeness that lingered in her life story and a body of work that confounded and alienated readers who'd heard reports of her brilliance. As was their usual method, the Duyckincks recounted Fuller's life story and, in so doing, produced a narrative of her life that has been repeated ad infinitum and would provide turn-of-the-century literary historians with grounds for dismissing Fuller altogether. As would become typical of these accounts of her, the Duyckincks began with a description of Fuller's famously prodigious education:

> During her early years the whole attention of Margaret was confined to books. She was taught the Latin and English grammar at the same time, and began to read the former language at six years of age. Her father set her this task-work of study, which soon grew into a necessity. At fifteen she describes her days' performance to a friend. She was studying Greek, French, and Italian literature, Scottish metaphysics—we may be sure a full share of English reading—and writing a critical journal of the whole at night. The result of this was a forced product of the parental discipline; but it would have been no product at all without a vigorous, generous nature. This the pupil possessed. Her temperament, bold and confident, assimilated this compulsory education.[38]

The Duyckincks follow a detailed list of Fuller's impressive intellectual pursuits with two important, mitigating variables: the impact of this education on her unusual character and her father's ultimate responsibility both for her education and for her character. These two details would prove invaluable to the narratives about Fuller that would surface in later literary histories, but what bolstered their discussion of Fuller's father is the belief, offered by the Duyckincks in this early version, that her education was at the root of her unusual personality. They presumed an incongruity between her highly developed cerebral training and her "vigorous, generous nature"; according to the Duyckincks, her education proved a success because it had been attached to such a vibrant, affectionate character. Later, they offer a somewhat different picture: "This education acting upon a sensitive nature made excitement a necessity. Her school life . . . appears a constant effort to secure activity for herself and the notice of others" (525). Here, her education services a wider desire to attain public attention, a claim that later historians would embellish.

In representing the wide range of Fuller's writings, the Duyckincks paid particular attention to her work as a literary critic under Horace Greeley at the *New-York Tribune* and dubbed literary criticism "her chief province; and criticism as exhibited by her pen or words, whether antagonistic or otherwise, is but another name for sympathy" (525). In their effort to constitute her first and foremost a literary critic, the Duyckincks append to their account of Fuller's life and work a reprint of an undated dialogue in which Fuller staged a contentious debate between the Poet and the Critic, in which she defends the office and dignity of the literary critic. The Critic states, "I am the rock which gives you back the echo. I am the tuning-key, which harmonizes your instrument, the regulator to your watch. Who would speak if no ear heard? Nay, if no mind knew what the ear heard?" (527). In a position evocative of Howells's, Fuller constitutes the critic as a literary "tuning-key" that establishes standards for literary quality and evaluation.

In relating Fuller's life story and tragic death, the Duyckincks break off their historical account with a brief, affecting epitaph: "So perished this intellectual, sympathetic, kind, generous, noble-hearted woman" (527). The proliferation of adjectives here communicates a wealth of unchecked, unambiguous affection for Fuller, "whose native disposition, studies, association with her contemporaries, and remarkable fate, will secure her a permanent place among the biographies of literary women" (524). Their affirmation of her presence in literary history is poignant, for they proved correct only insofar as Fuller's life story occupied a fixed presence in early American literary histories—though not on account of her literary merits or contributions but because of the lessons literary historians extracted from her life story and sad end. The affection the Duyckincks lavished on Fuller did not endure in the literary record, nor did the published sentiment expressed by Ralph Waldo Emerson, Thomas Wentworth Higginson, Julia Ward Howe, and others, who in print celebrated her life and work. Rather, late-century literary histories cultivated an image of her as obstreperous, underachieving, and improper, a portrait that quickly surpassed the affectionate published accounts of some of the most prominent writers of the era.[39] Though she was a literary critic and therefore a peer of later literary historians, her disordered personal life rendered her the anti-type of later critics, who conflated literary expertise with good sense about other quarters of life. The failures of her literary judgment to provide guidance in such matters as marriage and sexuality automatically rendered her suspect and a potential threat to the model of the professional literary critic in circulation in the period. In this way, literary historians under pressure to professionalize used her life story to remove her as a potential liability and to reaffirm their own professionalism.

In 1879, just as literary histories began to proliferate, Henry James published a monograph on Hawthorne that devoted ample attention to Fuller because of his famous suspicion that Hawthorne had modeled the character Zenobia in *A Blithedale Romance* (1852) after her. Though James mistakenly asserts that Hawthorne and Fuller had not known each other, he nevertheless digresses in his monograph for an extended exposition on Fuller, whom he treats with mild respect.[40] Though it received only moderate attention at the time of its publication, including a complimentary 1880 review by Howells in the *Atlantic Monthly*, *Hawthorne* was widely consulted by late-century literary historians researching Hawthorne and regularly appeared in the bibliographies of their published histories. In this way, James's monograph plays an important role not only in the history of Hawthorne scholarship but also in the history of Margaret Fuller's literary repute. In the evolution of Fuller's literary stature and the collection of narratives about her, James's contribution is worth discussing here because, in drawing attention to the cult of Margaret Fuller that had grown up around her since her death, it made very specific recommendations about how best to evaluate and assess her place in American literary history, recommendations that seem to have been heeded. In effect, James offered a methodology of interpreting and evaluating Fuller, and in so doing, altered in lasting ways the language and narrative tendered by the Duyckincks.

Like all critics after her death, James was compelled to relate the details of her life story, though he attends to the aspects that appealed to him most. James's account of Fuller's life does not touch on her prodigious education—which would obsess later historians—but is instead characteristically interested in her European travel. The story that he tells about her is worth quoting in full:

> Some of her writing has extreme beauty, almost all of it has a real interest; but her value, her activity, her sway (I am not sure one can say her charm), were personal and practical. She went to Europe, expanded to new desires and interests, and, very poor herself, married an impoverished Italian nobleman. Then, with her husband and child, she embarked to return to her own country, and was lost at sea in a terrible storm, within sight of its coasts. Her tragical death combined with many of the elements of her life to convert her memory into a sort of legend, so that the people who had known her well grew at last to be envied by later comers.[41]

James's interest in recounting the conditions of Fuller's death is motivated not by an investment in using Fuller as an object lesson, as would be typical of later literary histories, but by his lifelong interest in telling stories about relations between Americans and Europeans and the consequences of European travel. Regardless of the reasons that rendered Fuller appealing to him, James offers here a method of engaging with her. Though her work may be of interest, it is secondary to her life story. Equally important, James's recommendation transforms Fuller from a critic and producer of narratives—as the Duyckincks characterized her—to a narrative herself, to a curiosity of chronology and fortune.

Amid his slight appreciation for her work, James maintains that Fuller's legacy is not a literary one. Though she "occupied so large a place in the thoughts, the lives, the affections of an intelligent and appreciative society, [she] left behind her nothing but the memory of a memory" (62). James attributes Fuller's spectral presence in literary history to the medium in which she did her best work but that eluded documentation. Without the weighty ballast of historical record, Fuller's most significant works have survived only anecdotally: "Her function, her reputation, were singular, and not altogether reassuring: she was a talker; she was *the* talker; she was the genius of talk."[42] In a series of clauses that escalate in emphasis and hyperbole, James reiterates what had already been central to the cult of Margaret Fuller, an acclaimed conversational genius heard and remembered by a dwindling audience and whose nearly complete absence from the historical record only helped contribute to her cult.[43] If the homologies between James's and the Duyckincks' accounts can show us anything, it is the recurring impulse of commentators to select, among Fuller's vast and diverse corpus, her primary literary medium. But whereas the Duyckincks attempt to substantiate the importance of her contribution to American letters by designating her first and foremost a literary critic, James's emphasis on speech throws her status into question, to dematerialize, as it were, her work and influence. Especially important is James's revision of the Duyckincks' formulation of Fuller as literary critic; in exercising his own abilities in that same office, he downplays her contribution to the very medium in which he works and instead relocates her to the frivolous, feminized domain of the talker. Though James perpetuates enduring myths about Fuller, his affirmation that she was chiefly a talker is by no means a neutral claim, for it accesses enduring stereotypes of the woman as chatterbox, who cannot exercise restraint or listen, who unthinkingly repeats and passes on information.[44] The talker, moreover, has long been in stark opposition to the doer, and James reproduces this dyad by intimating that, despite her many writings, Fuller didn't really *do* anything but talk; after all, she "left behind her nothing but the memory of a memory."

Literary histories published soon after James's monograph tend, with few exceptions, to adhere to his method of evaluating Fuller: they discount her writing and treat her life story as her sole literary or narrative artifact meriting discussion. Central to these accounts of Fuller is an avid interest in her early education, which the Duyckincks had described in detail but that failed to interest James. Fred Louis Pattee's handling is an exemplary case in point. "Before criticizing Margaret Fuller's life and character," he wrote, "one must take into consideration her early education. Her father, a scholarly man, spared no efforts to make her a youthful prodigy. Her brain was terribly stimulated. At the age of six she was poring over Latin verbs; at eight she was eagerly reading Shakespeare, Cervantes, and Molière, and before she was twelve she had become familiar with the leading masterpieces of the Greek, Latin, French, Italian, and English."[45] This condensation of the Duyckinck biography warrants some analysis. The effectiveness of this narrative is due in part to the calculated enumeration of Fuller's impressive and highly unusual intellectual achievements, which are intimidating for the depth of their engagement in the humanistic tradition and for the stark disparity between these accomplishments and the young age at which she achieved them. The excesses of this account—its level of detail, its apparent interest in astounding the reader—bespeak the particular interest Pattee and his contemporaries took in Fuller's education. In its unusual scope and disregard for convention, her education would have been of especial significance to literary historians of the turn of the century, who were typically employed by those educational institutions from whose protocol and methods Fuller's education had so roundly departed. Fuller's education was conspicuously out of step with the culture of professionalism that had been growing up around these literary historians and that had underwritten these histories, as she overrode existing educational limits and laid claim to fields of knowledge that had long been the sole province of men of the elite classes. In this context, Fuller's wide education profoundly countermanded a core precept of the very academic culture that had compelled the writing of these literary histories, and Fuller is constituted by these accounts as a freak not just because of her unorthodox life and death but also because of the intellectual regulations that she so aggressively flouted.

In this light, James's earlier indifference to Fuller's education is particularly telling, for, like Stedman, he never worked in a university and therefore had no particular investment in demonstrating his compliance with professionalism. The pronounced disparity between James's handling of Fuller's education and that of other literary historians at the turn of the century suggests that these later accounts are cloaked defenses of professionalism and the redistribution of knowledge it enforced. While professionalism posed significant problems to literary men of the era who found themselves outpaced by their professionalized, philologist colleagues, they here tell a story about Fuller that affirms the value of this redistribution.

After all, Fuller's life story is not a happy one, and these accounts, Pattee's among them, blame her early education for her difficult life and tragic death, and suggest that adequate supervision might have prevented both. The narrative structure of these accounts bears some consideration, for they are generally confined only to the beginning and end of Fuller's life: her childhood education and her controversial final years. The events in between—her experience as a teacher, her collaboration with Emerson in editing *The Dial*, her voluminous writings, her work as a critic and book reviewer for the *New-York Tribune*, her famous "conversations"—receive minimal attention and are often dismissed as ineffectual, perplexing, and wanting in historical documentation. This reduction of Fuller's life to bookends that frame and ultimately overshadow the life they contain works to construct a new narrative of her life that sees a clear, unambiguous trajectory from her early education to the events of the last years of her life—her premarital pregnancy, marriage, and death. Pattee, for example, states that her education rendered Fuller nearsighted and badly socialized, implying that her education rendered her unattractive and unmarriageable. The embedded subtext here presumes that her education directly affected her later marital decisions; having been rendered unattractive to men, Fuller made unfortunate, rash decisions when she found herself faced with a rare suitor, however inappropriate he may have been. Pattee's account is typical, especially in his description of Fuller as excessively "stimulated," a term that reappears persistently throughout these literary histories and may have derived from Fuller's own posthumously published memoirs. Describing the unorthodox education that so interested these later literary historians, she wrote, "Thus, frequently, I was sent to bed several hours too late, with nerves unnaturally stimulated," a comment with unmistakable sexual overtones and that gives voice to the sexual yearnings late-century literary historians attributed to her.[46] Turning Fuller's own words against her, literary men of the era, Howells and Pattee among them, intertwined the intellectual with the conjugal.

Implicit in this criticism of Fuller's overstimulation is the germ of Howellsian literary professionalism. Unchecked reading may culminate in the disarray of domestic matters: improper sexual relations, an ill-chosen marriage, social estrangement, or spinsterhood. Decades after the initial flowering of literary history, Vernon Parrington made explicit what had been implicit in late-century literary histories when he wrote in 1927 that Fuller's "ardent nature was the victim of disastrous frustrations, rendered the more acute by premature development. If she had been married early, as Harriet Beecher did, and her excessive energy had been turned into domestic channels, her life might have been less tragic, whatever the effect might have been on her intellectual development."[47] In Parrington's logic, Fuller's excessive intellectual stimulation engendered premature sexual stimulation without an appropriate outlet, her education having rendered her unmarriageable. Her undirected sexual energy resulted in impulsive, imprudent behavior that led her to an ill-advised marriage and to her death, though the precise relation between her marriage and her death remains unstated.[48]

Just as Howells used a similar narrative in *The Rise of Silas Lapham* to illustrate the value of men such as Minister Sewell, so these accounts of Margaret Fuller's education communicate the value of professional literary supervision. Fuller's life confirms in narrative terms the importance of redrawing and protecting fields of knowledge from wide consumption, but literary historians also used this narrative to affirm their own role in this new literary economy. While these accounts often express contempt for Fuller and her Italian husband, the villain of these accounts is plainly her father, Timothy Fuller, whose mismanagement of Fuller's education receives harsh censure from historians who visibly value the imposition of literary limits and the exercise of literary judgment. As Barrett Wendell put it in 1900, Fuller was the "daughter of an eccentric but very assertive citizen of Cambridge. . . . Educated by her father according to his own ideas, she was much overstimulated in youth, and grew into something which impressed people who disliked her as an intellectual monstrosity."[49] It is one thing for Fuller to contravene the precepts of professionalism and make ill-advised literary decisions, but it is altogether another matter for her father to administer such an unorthodox and fatal education, which left her undesirable and socially incongruous. Timothy Fuller's explicit interest in breaching literary limits flies in the face of the patriarchal rhetoric and imagery that suffuse literary criticism at the turn of the century, which consistently appoints the father as both a model of the literary critic and the ultimate literary overseer of female reading. For example, in the 1902 article "What Should Girls Read?" Howells appointed the father the ultimate protector and literary supervisor of young girls and women.[50] In failing to exercise paternal responsibility, Timothy Fuller abdicated the office of the patriarchal literary critic by refusing to referee literary texts and offering his daughter unlimited literary access. Lingering in these accounts of

Timothy Fuller's disastrously ill-fated curriculum is the clear endorsement of literary management at the hands of responsible patriarchal authority—the father or his surrogate, the literary critic—lest readers gain unrestricted access to specious influences and make regrettable decisions.

Howells's narrative of the imperiled female reader came full circle in a 1903 review, his only published discussion of Fuller. In his column in *Harper's Weekly*—whose title, "Diversions of the Higher Journalist," allowed him to announce his own professionalist leanings—Howells reviewed several recently published collections of private letters, including a compilation of Fuller's love letters written between 1845 and 1846 to a "German Jew," a love object Howells was not above skewering.[51] While this review—as well as the publication of these letters—is certainly another major contribution to the depreciation of Fuller's literary standing, this review allowed Howells, in a moment of marked circularity, to reiterate and endorse the narrative of Fuller's life, whose core narrative structure he had in effect authored and popularized in such narratives as *The Rise of Silas Lapham*. While this review communicates the consistency of Howells's convictions throughout his life, it also illustrates how his own narrative of the endangered female reader had been absorbed, revised, and circulated by the literary culture in which he wrote—to a degree that Howells's own work as a literary critic enabled him to review literary texts that adapted his own narrative. Howells failed to recognize his own narrative when he encountered it in this form, but he nevertheless responded to it precisely as his literary historian peers had: with outrage and a desire to implement institutional structures to prevent women from behaving in the future as Fuller had.

In reviewing documentary evidence of Fuller's literary and sexual imprudence, Howells, like his literary historical peers, used her life story as an opportunity to reaffirm the importance of literary professionalism. The premise of such epistolary collections is from the outset offensive to Howells's sensibilities, as they publicly air private confidences and thrust into the public domain intimacies that are controversial, morally problematic, even squalid. As such, these collections violated Howells's stated belief in the exercise of literary restraint and the production of texts that take seriously their potential influence with readers. In other words, these collections depart from literary professionalism: they do not show the "decorum" he publicly demanded of the literary community in 1891, nor do they "[assume] a higher function, something like that of a physician or a priest . . . bound by laws as sacred of those professions." Moreover, they "betray" and "abuse" confidences in publishing the private correspondence between lovers.[52]

And like literary historians, Howells's outrage at the publication of these letters affords him an opportunity to denounce Fuller for failing to exercise the restraint and decorum characteristic of literary professionalism. Fuller in effect is made to answer for the very sins of which the collections themselves are guilty, a move that communicates not only how Fuller was configured as fundamentally inimical to or out of step with professionalism but also how her literary legacy offered literary men of the turn of the century an opportunity to defend staunchly the culture of professionalism that framed their own work. Howells begins by admitting that his dismay at seeing a publication so at odds with literary professionalism had been born out of his personal impressions of Fuller. His thinking about the impropriety of these collections "began," he wrote, "to say itself with the volubility of a woman whose emotions embody her ideas."[53] At first glance, Howells in this brief statement candidly and offhandedly repeats what were already long-standing clichés about Fuller—her talkativeness, her inability to manage or restrain her emotions, the flimsiness of her intellectual output, her inclination to allow her ideas to be erotically "embodied"—in order to dismiss her altogether.

However, especially important is the inadvertent genealogy of this review that lurks beneath its surface. Howells communicates here that the organizing ideas and argument of this review did not derive from an immediate and visceral response at seeing a trend in American publishing at odds with professionalist doctrine. Instead, he admits that he arrived at this position while reading one of these collections, specifically the collection of Fuller's letters to James Nathan. This review derives, in other words, from his dismay at seeing the unseemly, unorthodox, and even scandalous behavior of an American woman—behavior that is both literary (in the very writing of these letters) and sexual (in her conducting of a flagrant affair with an inappropriate suitor). This direct response to Fuller then gave way to a wider, vocational inquiry, as Howells came to recognize the increasing frequency of such collections. This chronology is important and bears some consideration, for it neatly encapsulates the ways in which literary histories of the turn of the century used Fuller. The engagement with Fuller's personal life—and not her literary work—persistently gave way to assertions of the importance of literary professionalism, which both the collections and Fuller flout, albeit in different ways. The result is the confirmation of limits and boundaries, whether of reading or of literary standards, and the designation of the literary professional—here it is the aptly titled "Higher Journalist"—with the task of protecting those limits.

{ *Rancor's Remains*

Barrett Wendell and the
New England Renaissance

The liberal use of literary history to alter the
status and public perception of literary work found occasional critics
who objected to the historical narratives and claims produced in the
service of this agenda. The 1886 scrap between Edmund Stedman and
William Dean Howells figures as one instance in which different opinions about the literary professional gave way to a disagreement about
the generic features of literary history. The tension that accumulated
around the uncertain class status of literary work, both within and
without the academy, and the evidentiary value of literary history to
that debate was so great that it erupted in one of the ugliest episodes
at the literary turn of the century, as one particularly resistant English
professor attempted to halt the consolidation of these narratives of
literary robustness by contributing his own version of American literary history. In this way, disagreement with prevailing narratives of
American literary history also underwrote the production of knowledge, which, in this case, has proved exceedingly resilient and enduring. Though his literary history was born out of compliance with
the professionalization of the literary academy (of which he was a
staunch critic), it attempts to revise public opinion of the postwar
period by depicting it as an era of decline rather than progress. Consequently, it took issue with the already consolidated periodization
of the nineteenth century and attempted to recuperate the status of
antebellum Brahmin New England as the apex of American literary
achievement. This revisionist literary history, Barrett Wendell's *Literary History of America* (1900), relied heavily upon the execution of
literary evaluation and judgment discussed in the preceding chapter,
which Howells had constituted as a vital hallmark of literary professionalism. But the practice of literary evaluation didn't help Wendell

find a sympathetic reader in Howells, who suspected Wendell's book of overturning much of two decades' worth of literary history. And it didn't help either that Wendell's literary history attempted to liberate literary criticism from its moorings in Howellsian professionalism and restore its associations with aristocratic sensibility and taste.

In 1900, Barrett Wendell published what promised to be one of the more important contributions to the nascent field of American literary history. Whereas most previous literary histories had often been intellectually unambitious, slim volumes issued by textbook publishers and tailored to schoolchildren, Wendell's had been packaged by Scribner's as the first extensive scholarly inquiry into American literature, and its title page, in proudly announcing Wendell as a professor of English at Harvard, stamped the book with the imprimatur of this increasingly high-profile seat of American scholarship. The book was the culmination of Wendell's long-standing interest in American literature: Wendell taught Harvard's first course in American literature and its history, and he frequently delivered the lectures composed for that course in other venues, such as the Lowell Institute of Massachusetts and the Sorbonne. Assembled together, those lectures would serve as the cornerstone of his 1900 literary history. And though the book seemed poised to impart to Wendell the institutional recognition and status that he craved throughout his career, it instead subjected him to one of the more humiliating public routs in academic history, one that would still be talked about at the time of Wendell's death twenty years later.

This thrashing—administered by Howells in a 1901 review published in the pages of the *North American Review*—constitutes a defining moment in the discussion about the nature and methods of narrating American literary history. If the violence with which Howells offered his opinions communicates the intense emotions and deeply held convictions that surrounded the discipline of American literary history in this period, it also communicates how literary history became an important instrument for literary power grabs at the turn of the century, through the production of knowledge that either engendered or took sides in literary rivalries and disputes. This particular episode illustrates how literary history often has personal history overlaid upon it, and this chapter attempts to show how the personal motives at the center of both Wendell's book and Howells's review have been instantiated and reified in American literary history, for the history of this review is in fact a history of one of the more enduring, organizing tenets of the discipline of American literary history: the centrality of antebellum Boston in the history of American literary achievement. In producing knowledge that has had a very long shelf life indeed, Wendell's *Literary History of America* is that rare instance in which the losers write history.

Before Wendell, the geography and time line of American literary historical inquiry had been diverse and far-ranging. The many centenary celebrations of the period had made literary histories of the Revolutionary era particularly popular. Southern literature also received individual attention at the hands of such historians as William Peterfield Trent. Broader surveys of American literature, such as those by Charles Richardson, typically attended to the literary cultures of various cities (Hartford, New York, Philadelphia) and periods (New York in the 1820s, for instance). However, in using merit as a criterion of literary historical attention, Wendell anointed antebellum Boston the undisputed apex of American literary achievement, a claim that had not yet been made in such a persuasive, forceful, and authoritative way.[1] The mission of this chapter is not to dispute the importance of antebellum New England in American literary history, but instead to historicize the disciplinary investment in this belief, which has for generations directed scholarly attention and served as the center of disciplinary gravity in American literary studies. The profession's investment in antebellum New England has made it very easy to forget that there had ever been a moment when this belief had been controversial or had encountered resistance.[2] The continuity of its preeminence has hindered inquiry into the process by which this critical consensus was achieved or, rather, the process by which the impression of critical consensus was achieved. Howells's 1901 review communicates that this now accepted idea did not go unchallenged at the time of its origination, and the terms of his objection offer insight both into the contexts that produced this knowledge and into the now lost timbres in that knowledge heard, and protested, by some early readers. In attending to the contexts of Howells's review, this inquiry pursues a limited reception history of one of the most important tenets in the discipline of American literary history. Moreover, the context that produced both this knowledge and Howells's response to it helps explain the altogether unexpected endurance of such a highly contested, contentious belief.

As a discipline, we forget how truly improbable Wendell's literary history really was, and not solely because of Howells's widely read review. The late nineteenth century had already seen the critical depreciation of several of the central figures of antebellum Boston: upon his death, Longfellow had already declined in literary estimation, and both Oliver Wendell Holmes and James Russell Lowell received visibly tentative respect from their literary successors, less on account of the quality of their work than of their status as literary elder statesmen. Though these Fireside Poets have never recovered from the slide of literary opinion that began at the turn of the century, other writers of antebellum Boston who have since been canonized and placed squarely at the center of a literary scene in which they played lesser and often reluctant roles had not yet achieved such renown. Except for a few passing mentions in late-century literary histories, Henry David Thoreau was hardly regarded as a major figure in American letters, and the writings of Nathaniel Hawthorne, though widely admired, were often regarded by such turn-of-the-century writers as Henry James and William Dean Howells as bloodless, if charming and skillful, romances.[3] Literary Boston at the time of Wendell's literary history was a celebrated ruin, widely recognized even by its most devoted adherents—among them Henry Adams, Henry Cabot Lodge, and Francis Parkman—as a shadow of its former self.[4]

However, the arguments that Wendell presented in 1900 would not have surprised anyone who had been familiar either with him or with his prior work. Before the publication of his literary history, Wendell had already cultivated a reputation as a nay-saying critic who lamented the glories of a receding past set against a lesser present.

Wendell accentuated this critical disposition with a studied affect of exacting gentility that made him seen deliberately anachronistic; with his shrill imitation of a British accent and his mannered wardrobe, he became the physical embodiment of a past he celebrated at every turn. In setting himself apart from the conventional dress and mannerisms of his colleagues at Harvard, Wendell freely advertised in visual terms both his close personal identification with the past and what he felt to be his general incongruity with the culture he saw springing up around him, both at Harvard and in the nation at large. Thus, the arguments at the core of his 1900 literary history were the culmination of a long history of divided allegiances and conflict with his own milieus.

Up until the publication of his literary history, Wendell's career had not been unusual, either for generalist literary men employed at universities or for English professors at Harvard. What set Wendell's career apart, however, was the tenor in which he received the inevitable bumps in any career, academic or otherwise, and this sense of personal disappointment would course through his 1900 literary history. Brander Matthews is a useful site of comparison with Wendell, for the two followed essentially the same turn-of-the-century literary career path. Both men were born into well-to-do families down on their luck and attended Ivy League colleges, where they both sought employment after stalled literary careers. Both men took especial interest in drama and were lifelong Francophiles; both offered the first courses in American literary history at their respective institutions; and both published high-profile American literary histories that met with significant media attention and remained in print for decades. Wendell and Matthews even resembled one another physically: both had dark hair with similar hairlines and styles; both wore the Vandyke beard favored by cosmopolitan men in the late nineteenth century; and both favored idiosyncratic affectations in dress, such as Matthews's monocle and Wendell's spats and cane.

The similarities end there, and the disparity between their careers may be due in large part to the cities in which they worked and with which they became associated. Matthews quickly rose through the ranks at Columbia to become one of the university's most celebrated faculty members and its public representative, whom the university bent over backward to accommodate. As a New Yorker, Matthews paired his academic work with a famously bustling social life and even experienced moderate success in his many extra-academic publications, such as his play *A Gold Mine*. Wendell openly begrudged Matthews's success, describing his work in a lecture given at the Sorbonne during his 1904–5 stay there as "less thoughtful, less scholarly, less punctilious, and decidedly more popular," words that echo many of the comments Wendell would make about New York's literary scene in his 1900 literary history.[5] Comparison immediately reveals Wendell as the less favored and the more sensitive and frustrated of the two. Unlike Matthews, Wendell struggled with professionalism, leaving the ranks of the adjunct composition instructors to gain tenure after eighteen years of full-time teaching at Harvard. Whereas Matthews enjoyed a close friendship with Columbia's president Nicholas Murray Butler (he had been one of the few guests in attendance at Butler's wedding), Wendell balked at the infamous coldness of Harvard's president Charles W. Eliot, whose inattention Wendell took personally, and felt generally unappreciated and undervalued. In the margins of a 1907 letter from Eliot thanking him for filling in at the last minute as commencement marshal, Wendell wrote, "to the best of my recollection—the only expression of general approval received during the 27 years of hard work at Harvard. It is pleasant to be held adequate, even in a procession."[6]

Wendell complained of the "curious persistence" of a "general feeling" that he "did not quite belong" at Harvard, which was indeed a widespread complaint among Harvard faculty members such as William James, but Wendell's particular brand of displacement may simply have been due to the looming obsolescence of untrained, generalist literary men on college campuses such as Harvard, which, as discussed in chapter 4, increasingly required such trappings of professionalism as a doctoral degree, specialization, and scholarly publications.[7] Wendell himself saw numerous English faculty members who had been popular with students denied promotion and contract re-

Class, Authority, & Literary History

newal because of insufficient publications, and he suspected that his two novels—*The Duchess Emilia* (1885) and *Rankell's Remains* (1887)—had obstructed his advancement at Harvard.[8] He disparaged philology, the professionalized specialization destined to replace the belletristic method favored by generalists, as the "pedantry that so embounds [*sic*] linguistic learning [which] . . . makes these dead words seem sometimes ever further from vitality than in truth they are," and sensed that "mere men of letters may be only sporadic survivals of a past epoch, soon to be extinct."[9] In this way, Wendell objected to the dismantling of exclusionary protocols designed to restrict access on the basis of class and pedigree, and their replacement with new institutional restrictions derived from professionalism; he celebrated class-based limitations but deplored the implementation of professionalist ones.

It was in this climate of increasing professional pressure to produce knowledge that Wendell began writing American literary history, and he would channel his grievances about the changing academy into that research. Wendell found his first professional success with an 1891 biography of the late-Puritan cleric and Harvard graduate Cotton Mather. Though it was composed chiefly of extracts from Mather's writings, especially his *Magnalia Christi Americana* (1702), and was by no means a work of scholarship, the book's favorable reception influenced Wendell's decision to make American literary history the primary path by which he attempted to forge a career in the new literary academy. Two years later, Wendell followed *Cotton Mather* with the publication of *Stelligeri*, a collection of essays devoted to Harvard's literary luminaries, among them James Russell Lowell, a former professor of Wendell's and the exemplum of the dying breed of academic literary man. What binds the two texts is not only a concentration on Harvard's literary legacy—which Alan Heimert would dub in 1963 "Harvard filiopietism" and which may have derived from an explicit attempt to curry favor with his own institution—but also the use of literary history to tell narratives of decline and obsolescence.[10] These two strains would be front and center in his 1900 full-length literary history and would provide ammunition to his critics, who detected traces of Wendell's personal history of disappointment and obsolescence lurking beneath the surface of his research.

Wendell's sense of his own incongruity extended beyond the limits of Harvard Yard, though not very far. Though he spent his early life in New York, where his father had worked as a merchant, Wendell came from an old Boston family—he was a distant relation of Oliver Wendell Holmes—and felt a keen identification with Boston and its environs, in whose centrality to American literary and cultural achievement Wendell took especial pride, declaring it "the source of what is best in our America," and freely admitted in his criticism to being motivated by regional loyalties.[11] He felt just as keenly the decline of Boston as the nation's cultural and literary capital after the Civil War. Wendell liked to describe himself as a man born several decades too late: all the trimmings that a generation earlier might have brought him career opportunities and respect—his provenance in Boston, his impressive heritage, the wide span of his literary interests—had depreciated in cultural and financial value by the late nineteenth century, when New York had become the nation's literary capital and, within the university, the generalist literature professor was facing extinction altogether amid increasing professionalization.[12] Both changes heralded to Wendell the collapse of the leisured life of letters and its replacement with blatant careerism in which literary engagement— whether in study or creative writing—derived less from refinement and taste than from transparent ambition. For Wendell, the change in the academy and the decline of Boston were intimately intertwined, and this is nowhere more apparent than in his 1893 essay collection, *Stelligeri*, in which reflection on Harvard's own past offered him a way of talking about the larger changes that had befallen the nation itself. "In brief," he wrote, "it seems to me that the America of the past resembles, in more ways than one, the *Stelligeri* of Harvard. It is a thing we shall not see again; we love to think about it and to cherish its tradition."[13] Even the book's title—*Stelligeri and Other Essays Concerning America*—makes use of this sleight of hand: the Latin word "*stelligeri*," which means "stars," derives from Harvard's annual Latin catalog, which listed newly deceased graduates under the heading "S*telligeri*."

For Wendell, the recession of the academic institutional past indexes a decline both in the literary importance of Boston and in the nation's cultural life.

Similar logic is perceptible throughout Wendell's prolific writings, as in such unlikely places as *English Composition* (1891), Wendell's successful rhetoric textbook. The book steers clear of expository matters such as argument, and is concerned chiefly with matters of style such as "elegance" and "clearness." To this end, the book is overwhelmed by endless lists of common though faulty usages, which Wendell corrects and comments upon. At its core, Wendell's composition textbook is suffused by a pervasive sense of class, for, in meting out countless preferred usages legislated less by grammar than by taste, Wendell's book chiefly evidences his own exacting standards and high level of literary refinement. But in so doing, the very fact of the book's existence bespeaks the disappearance of the conditions that would provide students with that same knowledge before entering college. In other words, the need for such a textbook is already girdled with a sense of an evaporating literary elite that Wendell had associated with Boston, and he gives occasional voice to such concerns in some of the many examples of diction that permeate the book. For example, in a chapter on word usage, Wendell turned to one word whose frequent misuse he discusses at length. "What does a man mean, for example, who asserts that another is or is not a gentleman? To one the question turns on clothes; to another on social position gauged by the subtile [*sic*] standards of fashion; to another on birth; to another on manners; to another on those still more subtile things, the feelings which go to make character; to another still on a combination of some or all of these."[14]

The energy that Wendell commits to what is ultimately a passing example of the subjectivity of diction gives way to a seminar on the increasing inability of Americans to appraise social distinction with any certainty, in large part because of the presumed disappearance of the word's referent. The fading of the elite results in the transformation of the word "gentleman" into a metaphor for sociability rather than a specific denotation of pedigree. To make this point, Wendell tells a story of a largely illiterate fisherman, an "uncouth old figure, not over clean," who is described at his death as a gentleman, a story designed to instruct the composition student to preserve at once the integrity of this word and the social class that it denotes.[15] And in using such a charged word as an example, Wendell conflates verbal precision with class privilege and, in making this case in the context of a rhetoric, Wendell explicitly constitutes the vanishing elite as a literary one.

Wendell's fiction is equally suffused with these concerns. His second and last novel, *Rankell's Remains* (1887), uses several interconnected stories to chart the decline of the Boston elite and the concurrent decline in national culture. The novel begins in a state of social, moral order, with the aristocratic Lottimer family secure on their estate and enjoying a vivid social life, and their acquaintance, the self-made Rankell, depicted as an ethical businessman under whose stony exterior lie a fierce loyalty and strong ethic. It should come as no surprise that these early scenes of moral and social stability take place in the context of antebellum Boston, the site Wendell would appoint as the apex of national cultural achievement. However, as the stories unfold, it becomes clear that the prosperity of both parties conceals shady morals, as the younger Lottimer son squanders the family estate through crooked business schemes and as Rankell's vast wealth is revealed to be the result of regular financial trickery and double crosses, including one particularly devastating intrigue that causes the final collapse of the Lottimer fortune. *Rankell's Remains* chronicles the social decay engendered by waning standards of conduct: the decline of the principles favored by the elder Lottimer brings about both the decline of his family's social status and the increasing influence of men who rise to prominence by flouting the gentlemanly principles espoused by men such as Lottimer. The novel builds toward an episode based directly on the contentious 1884 presidential election that shows in heady detail the wide repercussions of such a shift in national values.[16] In its rendering of the conspiracies of power and wealth that allow Rankell to orchestrate the nomination of an unworthy Republican candidate while simultaneously destroying the genteel Lottimers, the novel suggests that unethical opportunists like Rankell are responsible for the decline of the democratic process itself, which, for Wendell, depends upon the successful implementation of the values he associates with the well-born. What begins with the weakening of New England gentry and its highly refined aesthetics is a downward slide in national values that culminates in the corruption of democracy itself.

In 1940 Van Wyck Brooks situated Wendell's partiality for the elegiac within what he perceived as the larger culture of decay in postwar Boston. "The New England mind was steeped in disappointment and chagrin," he wrote. "The Boston mind, once so cheerful, was full of the sense of last things, as if it hoped for no resuscitation," and he saw Boston "sorting its papers, like a man who is dying, anxious to arrange his affairs."[17] Brooks's affecting figuration of the prominence afforded texts amid imminent demise offers, by implication, a compelling theory of the proliferation of literary histories in the late nineteenth century. The narration of the literary past in the newly trendy genre of the literary history is both a symptom and a result of a culture in decline, attempting to secure its memory and place in history: the narration of the New England past became a way for Wendell to mourn the life that he never had because of the vicissitudes of power and geographical development.

It is telling that Wendell was attracted throughout his life to Cotton Mather and afforded him perhaps unmerited importance in his many literary historical writings, including the *Literary History of America*, in which he committed an entire chapter to Mather. Wendell admitted that Mather had fallen out of favor due to his infamous participation in the Salem witch trials and proceeded, both in this book and throughout his life, to argue for Mather's restoration in national esteem. Wendell even went so far as to suggest that Mather had been justified in his accusations of witchcraft, pointing to the turn-of-the-century phenomena of mesmerism and hypnotism as contemporary analogues of the events Mather had prosecuted. But what seems to have attracted Wendell to this less favored Harvard ancestor was Mather's increasing obsolescence during his own lifetime because of his survival well into the eighteenth century, where his values and beliefs were no longer widespread or honored. Wendell articulated this perception of Mather without delay in his 1891 biography; in the second paragraph of his introduction, Wendell admitted that Mather's "veracity had been seriously questioned; and one can see why. In the first place, he was the champion of a cause that, even in his own time, was hopelessly lost,—the cause of the old hierarchy of New England, that once hoped to govern the Western world in accordance with no laws but those of God and Calvin; and not the least tragic fate of men whose cause is hopelessly lost is that victorious posterity rarely appreciates how they can have been honest."[18] Especially striking here is Wendell's apparent sympathy for a man who, in being out of step with his own time, has much in common with Wendell himself. Both Harvard men, sons of New England, and scions of illustrious families, they found themselves adherents of a culture in decline and undone by the changing spirit of the times. And the epitaph that Wendell wrote for Mather could just as well have described Wendell's own mission as a critic and literary historian: "The life he took in earnest was . . . the life of that New England which we who come of it like to believe the source of what is best in our own America" (3). In affirming that the New England past is responsible for "what is best in our America," Wendell admits his sympathy for Mather's attempts to secure the power and stature of New England's oligarchy, and, in so doing, suggests that Mather's failure in this mission has meant the weakening of Wendell's own cohort of New England elite. That is, Mather's loss is Wendell's loss.

Wendell's regionalist jeremiad found its fullest expression in his 1900 literary history, which is organized so as to put the New England past literally at the center of American literature. In a history composed of over 500 pages and covering both British and American literature over three centuries, Wendell devoted precisely half of the book to antebellum New England, quickly dispensing with its literary successors in New York and elsewhere, which he dismissed as "the Rest of the Story." As if to showcase the depth of his expertise and research, Wendell set exceedingly high goals for his literary history, including numerous chapters on American social history alongside his discussions of American literature as well as chapters on both English literature and history. His lengthy discussion of antebellum New England entailed chapters on particular regional pockets of literary production such as Unitarianism, the *Atlantic Monthly*, and abolition, and devoted individual chapters to the standard roster of New England writers that included Emerson, Whittier, Longfellow, Holmes, and Hawthorne. His abbreviated discussion of American letters before and simultaneous with the New England Renaissance paid particular attention to such regional forebears as Cotton Mather and Jonathan Edwards. Elsewhere, he devoted chapters to Charles Brockden Brown, Cooper, Irving, and Bryant. He also singled out Poe and Whitman for individual attention, though his considerations complied with prevailing late-century assessments and balked at both men's unorthodox personal lives.[19]

Like many literary historians of the period, Wendell complied with the expectation that he pair the production of historical knowledge with aesthetic evaluation, though his all-too-willing and visibly biased fulfillment of this latter responsibility only opened him up to attack from Howells, the period's leading advocate of critical assessment. Central to Wendell's evaluative heuristic was a belief that literature of merit could be recognized only by its larger contribution to the English language as a whole, a method that allowed him to measure American literature by the standard of English literature and authorized the dismissal of all American literatures other than that of antebellum New England. Wendell's comparativist method of literary history and literary evaluation had two results, the more immediate of which was mounting evidence of Wendell's elitist sympathies, which here took the shape of Anglophilia and an overt preference for writers of impressive pedigree, such as James Russell Lowell. The second, and more enduring, consequence was the formal declaration of the primacy of antebellum Boston in American letters. After numerous chapters that in quick succession dispatched all other preceding literary movements and locations as undeserving of considered attention, he announced decisively at the beginning to his lengthy discussion of antebellum Boston, "By the middle of the nineteenth century, in fact, the literary impulse of the Middle States [the Mid-Atlantic] had proved abortive. For the serious literature of America we must revert to New England," and in turning his attention there, Wendell dubbed this literary flowering a "Renaissance," a term he put into wide, enduring circulation.[20]

While we may agree with the importance of antebellum New England, the language in which this knowledge was first produced reveals that it originated in the desire to confirm and consolidate a regional upper-class supremacy whose breakdown Wendell had lamented elsewhere. Wendell's most basic tools of literary evaluation— the terms that he used both in sifting through texts and in exalting antebellum New England—are visibly motivated by class loyalties. One central component of his argument is his persistent claim that New England greatness originated in Elizabethan England, an argument he would reiterate throughout his career and that, in its imprecise command of early modern British immigration history, bends over backward to link New England's literary elite with a political, hereditary elite, to make literal a metaphor of a literary aristocracy. This narrative also conveniently allowed him to evade the pronounced antiaristocratic sympathies of many Puritan sects of the seventeenth century and to position Cotton Mather as a regional forebear, despite his origin in a religious tradition that contested aristocratic prerogatives. Wendell even attempted to overturn the liberal tradition of New England by tracing its activist, reformist energies to England, for "no peculiarity has been more characteristic of the native English than a passion to reform other people than themselves, trusting meantime that God will help those who forcibly help somebody else" (357). For Wendell, what appears to be a regional preoccupation with disassembling hierarchies of power is ultimately only proof of the authentic superiority of those activists; for Wendell, reform evidences the righteousness of extant structures of power.

Similarly, Wendell's heuristic method of determining literary quality markedly relies upon the class-inflected language of inheritance and patrimony. In language that resembles the twentieth-century discourse of the literary classic, Wendell argued that literary quality is distinguished by the endurance of its value over time, its ability to maintain its worth over succeeding generations. In requiring that literary texts maintain their capital, as it were, over time, he envisioned literary texts as metonymic figurations of the prerogatives of wealth and privilege that underwrite them. Similarly, he plainly commends writers for their ability to channel pedigreed social allegiances into their work: for example, he observed, "Emerson and Channing . . . and the historians and the scholars and the public men of New England, belonged either by birth or by early acquired habit to the traditional aristocracy of their native region. . . . As the nineteenth century proceeded, literature in American [sic] tended to fall into the hands of people not less worthy, but perceptibly less distinguished than those who have first illustrated it" (338). Distinction in a literary text is determined by the visibility of the writer's own distinguished lineage. In using pedigree to elevate antebellum New England with one hand, he uses low birth with the other hand as a pretext to dismiss other writers such as Poe and Whitman, whose provenance he detects in their alleged vulgarity and sensuality.

Wendell would make a similar move on a broader scale, for his consecration of antebellum Boston coincides with his frank denunciation of its successor, late-century literary New York, as the height of vulgarity in its apparent preoccupation with money-getting, its privileging of the popular over the tasteful, and the ease with which writers of dubious knowledge and skill could ascend to prominence, as he observed with Richard Grant White and Walt Whitman. New York's editors, Wendell noted, are better known than its writers, a detail that evidences to him the controlling influence of business interests in publishing, and therefore the decline of taste in favor of popularity. For Wendell, the ascendancy of New York was not simply coincident with the decline of literary Boston but was also central to it, for it enabled hierarchies to be overturned and the literary elite to be overrun with arrivistes of questionable integrity and parentage; as he reflected with some uneasiness, "There is now hardly a city in the world where you are so little apt to meet people whose families have lived there for three successive generations."[21] The sheer size of the New York economy contributed significantly to the problem of gatekeeping that Wendell saw compromised by the transience of the city's population. "If you have things to sell, there you can find most buyers," he wrote. "If you would buy things, there you can find most who have things to sell. So if as an artist you have things that you would impart to other men, there you can surely find the greatest number of men to whom they may be imparted" (452–53). That is, the enormity of the New York markets makes literary quality control futile, for a writer there will always find a willing buyer, regardless of unfavorable reviews. In toppling the fortifications of Boston literary society, New York caused the depreciation of the very standards that Wendell used to impart preeminence to Boston. And in this account of literary geography, Wendell dramatically revised the narrative of democratic ascendancy at the core of the periodization of the nineteenth century produced in the 1880s, so that it became a story not of populist triumph and aristocratic overthrow but one of decay and declining standards.

In this light, it is altogether expected that Wendell would have found a formidable opponent in William Dean Howells, who was perhaps the embodiment and chief literary sponsor of all the trappings of late-century literary culture he found distasteful. Though he began his career in Boston, Howells had more in common with the late-century New York literary culture Wendell denounced than with the genteel antebellum Boston he revered. The son of an Ohio printer, Howells was born of undistinguished lineage and received minimal formal education, famously supervising his own ad hoc education in his father's office. Despite these origins, Howells found significant success in literary Boston, where he moved after the Civil War and where he lived for nearly thirty years. In contrast to the language of pedigree and elitism Wendell used to describe literary Boston, Howells's experience there suggests otherwise, for he had benefited significantly from the culture of letters there: James Russell Lowell had been an early and warm sponsor of Howells's career during the 1860s, and Howells spent the 1870s editing the *Atlantic Monthly*, that venerable organ of Boston letters. However, in accordance with changing literary geography, Howells moved to New York in the 1880s to assume an editorial position at *Harper's*, whereupon his criticism and fiction (to use the name of one of Howells's more famous works) became more acutely populist in sympathy, as with his 1890 novel, *A Hazard of New Fortunes*, and with his increasing adherence to Christian socialism. Howells's increasing activism and public involvement in reform movements upon moving to New York smack of rekindled working-class allegiances.

As if Howells's career weren't already sufficient confirmation of Wendell's suspicions about New York, Howells's advocacy of literary realism corresponded with his espousal of the literary populism Wendell associated with New York. Howellsian realism expressly condemned literary elitism, as manifested either in subject matter or in voice, to promote instead the literary representation of what Howells termed "the commonplace," which often entailed treatments of poverty and the lower classes, local dialects and customs, and attention to pedestrian activities typically omitted from literary fare.[22] Howells's espousal of realism pivoted on his distaste for the consolidation of "the pride of caste" with "the pride of taste" at the core of Wendell's literary aesthetics and that Howells perceived in the self-termed "literary elect."[23] Howells construed this literary elitism as "averse to the mass of men. . . . It seeks to withdraw itself, to stand aloof; to be distinguished, and not to be identified."[24] In dubbing realism "democracy in literature," Howells proffered realism as the antithesis of this aristocratic literary spirit out of the belief that representations of the American underclasses would cause readers both to "know one another better" and to recognize that "men are more like than unlike one another."[25]

Howells's own integration of class and aesthetics made him a particularly sensitive reader of Wendell's literary history, and Howells took Wendell to task for his explicit allegiance to the "literary elect," a term that, in its allusion to Calvinist doctrine, implicitly targets New England literary complacency. Howells's 1901 review shocked readers for its rancor and nastiness, and this review is even more jarring for readers familiar with Howells and his usual critical methods. Published in seventeen full, single-column magazine pages, it is unusually lengthy for Howells, who typically glanced fleetingly at individual books within the context of a larger thematic essay, and its length communicates the energy of Howells's indignation as well as his need to discredit fully Wendell's argument. The length of the review may also account for Howells's decision to publish it in the *North American Review* instead of in his usual column in *Harper's*, which was typically shorter. Equally uncharacteristic is the presence of ad hominem attacks that declared Wendell "priggish and patronizing," inimical to democracy itself, and a rabid Anglophile, a strategy that communicates the strong undercurrent of personal hostilities in Howells's response.[26]

Howells pays particular attention to Wendell's regional focus, taking issue less with the intellectual legitimacy of his claim of regional supremacy (though he does object to Wendell's take on Emerson and Longfellow) than with the apparent motives that underlie Wendell's literary cartography. In his detection of intense regional partisanship, Howells sees Wendell's geography of literary achievement within a larger cultural context of postwar Boston. He remarks, "Professor Wendell has certain disadvantages of environment to struggle with, and in this he exemplifies the hardship of such Bostonians as have outlived the literary primacy of Boston" (624). Howells here revises Wendell's position on the changing value of provenance; whereas Wendell lamented the declining value of the circumstances of his birth, Howells suggests that Wendell's provenance is actually an impediment to his literary success rather than an asset in decline. Current Bostonians "can hardly fail to ask themselves whether they were not unduly oppressed by a sense of the vanished grandeur. . . . They occupy the places of those illustrious men, and though they no longer find them so very illustrious as people once fancied, still they cannot resist the belief that they inherit them and have somehow the right to administer upon their estates" (624–25). Strikingly echoing Van Wyck Brooks's metaphor of Boston as a dying man eager to settle his estate, Howells detects self-interest at the heart of this literary history, which he sees as part of a larger regional response to its changing fortunes, as the sons of New England attempt to claim their vanished patrimonies through the narration of regional greatness. As if in anticipation of the readiness of antebellum New England to become a synecdoche of American literature as a whole, Howells takes issue with the imprecision of Wendell's title and suggests that he rename the book "A Study of New England Authorship in Its Rise and Decline, with Some Glances at American Literature"(628).

The acrimony of Howells's review derives from his detection of an undercurrent of class in Wendell's claim of regionalist supremacy, for the commitment to one contingency of birth—geographical provenance—quickly gives way to other kinds of contingencies. Wendell's "general attitude toward his subject," Howells notes, "is the attitude of superiority, but not voluntary superiority: every considered volition of his is towards a greater equality with his theme. It is as if, having been born a gentleman, he wished conscientiously to simplify himself, and to learn the being and doings of his inferiors by a humane examination of their conditions, and a considerate forbearance toward their social defects" (624). Wendell, Howells remarked, is simply slumming. While this haughtiness may simply be "temperamental"—a particularly nasty barb—Howells quickly sniffs out the entangled regionalist and class allegiances at the root of Wendell's affect (624). He observes Wendell's reliance on "distinction" as his polestar, particularly in his willingness to equate the polish of a writer's work with the social polish afforded by privilege, as he did with Bronson Alcott and Thoreau, whose writing Wendell found wanting because they always "remained in temper what they were born,—farmers' sons."[27] Howells counters this belief with the equally class-conscious observation that "most members of most aristocracies, most kings and emperors, are altogether most undistinguished, and no breeding can make them so" (627). Having polished his pins, Howells uses them to attack Wendell's own prose style, pointing out its various mistakes of grammar and taste, to demonstrate the error of using birth as an index of literary quality.

Howells makes the most damning and potentially harmful criticism of all in his suggestion that Wendell's chief "disqualification" is due to the fact that he simply lacks the specialized training to handle such material carefully and well. Wendell, he writes, "is versed in general literature, and he knows a great deal of his chosen ground. But he does not, apparently, know all of his ground" (627). In making this last comment, Howells takes a shot at the academic tradition of the untrained, generalist man of letters—a career track that he himself had rejected in turning down offers from both Johns Hopkins and Harvard—and, in so doing, tacitly upholds the emerging culture of professionalization that jeopardized Wendell's career and caused him to write literary history in the first place. The subtext that seems to make this attack possible is not just Wendell's own equation of class privilege with literary quality but a more general attack on the academy itself, which has for generations invited gentleman to teach on the sole belief that their class-based literary tastes qualified them. And in his observation that "that little which is true in [Wendell's book] is new; and that little which is new is true," Howells attempts to prove that a gentlemanly sensibility neither a gifted stylist nor a scholar makes (626).

Howells apparently detected the motives—both professional and personal—that underlay Wendell's anointing of New England, but it bears stressing that this debate about the centrality of antebellum Boston was the culmination of a long history of hostility between the two men, in which literary criticism served as a pretext for an inflammatory dialogue about the proper relationship between aesthetics and social class, the very matter that would occupy both Wendell's literary history and Howells's review of it. Howells and Wendell had known one another socially, which imparts a particular sordidness to this review, and the archives contain evidence that Howells had reason to take Wendell's literary history personally, and not only for the regionalism and classism that he cites in the review. Howells admits as much in the review's opening, in which he owns up to having had personal biases against the book before even reading it, to having "made up [his] mind against it" (623), though he does not specify why. The archives, though, provide an explanation for this unexplained preliminary bias.

The history of their prior relationship had been studded with conflict and thinly veiled hostility, which seem to have commenced in the late 1880s, when Howells had already left New England and when, at a dinner party, Wendell unbidden and openly criticized Howells's prose to his face. In 1887, Wendell sent Howells a note expressing admiration of his novel *The Minister's Charge*, published six months earlier, but these words of praise served as a pretext for Wendell to apologize for this earlier gaffe: "Perhaps you have forgotten it," he wrote, but "I was impudent enough when I dined with you . . . to say that to my mind some of the detail in much of your work as I know [it] was rather tediously prolix."[28] It was by no means in Wendell's interest to have made an enemy of Howells, for Wendell, though already teaching at Harvard, was still hoping for a successful literary career; with his second novel, *The Duchess Emilia*, issued that same year, his apologetic letter may simply have been an attempt to renew friendly ties with the United States' most powerful literary critic and obviate a negative review written out of retribution. Howells's gracious reply by no means downplays Wendell's slight. While acknowledging the sting of Wendell's criticism, he accepts his praise of *The Minister's Charge*, which is "as sweet to me as if you had never censured my work at all. It is hard, as we all know, not to accuse the morals and motives of those who say they don't like what we've done, but I always try to forbear; and in your case, although I don't agree with you, I found myself consoled by the fact that you must have thought about the matter, that you weren't parroting, anyway. What lessened the pain then seems to double the pleasure now."[29] In describing his difficulty resisting the temptation to attack the character of his critics, Howells admits, however indirectly, to having done that very thing in the wake of Wendell's criticism. Wendell's ill-advised criticism, that is, had afforded Howells an opportunity to reflect on Wendell's literary sensibility, which Howells would in turn see reflected in Wendell's literary history and would condemn in 1901. Howells insinuated as much in his comments about the generally poor reviews that had met *The Minister's Charge*: "Your message was all the welcomer to me because, as you may have noticed, the book was not generally liked. It seemed to me that it was disliked because of a poor fellow whose soul was never ignoble, had had ignoble experiences. This astonished and grieved me; I'll own that at moments it deeply discouraged me. Then, people said that they did not want to know anything about their fellow-beings who served in shops or slept in Refuges, as if God had really made the more prosperous of another blood." To readers of Howells's 1901 review, Howells's reply to his critics seems like an explicit threat to the socially conservative, elitist Wendell. Beneath the surface of what seems to be a defense of literary realism lies an attack on the snobbery and social biases that underlie literary criticism, the very lance that Howells would throw at Wendell over a decade later.

This conflict would remain at the center of their subsequent correspondence and of Howells's review. Three years later, in 1890, Wendell wrote to Howells again, using praise of Howells's most recently published book as an excuse for again expressing contrition. In voicing admiration of Howells's *Shadow of a Dream*, he again admits to having behaved badly. "I had the impertinence to say that . . . to my slightly impatient temper the prolixity of your books had often seemed to me a grave fault."[30] By way of explanation for this unwarranted criticism, Wendell only digs himself an even deeper hole. "The real meaning that is always in what of your writing I have read, too often has hidden itself from me under a mass of—admirably vivacious —detail which I must forget before I can understand which is but worth remembering. I found this truth, I confess, in [Howells's 1890 novel] the Hazard of New Fortunes, which in many respects I heartily admired." The garbled sentence structure—its inexactitude, its backpedaling, and its backhanded praise—communicates the awkwardness not only of explaining oneself to the era's most influential man of letters but also of the ways in which reconciling with Howells entailed renouncing his own literary judgments, which he apparently is loath to do. Wendell goes on to praise *Shadow of a Dream*, in whose "technical quality" he takes "delight . . . from beginning to end." But, again, he can't help but slip in an additional criticism, admitting that he would have preferred the narrator's wife to have occupied a less prominent role. "All this is perhaps rather impudent," he writes. "I really don't know you well enough to write so frankly, or indeed to write at all. But I am sure that when what little I have done has pleased anybody, a word of acknowledgement [would have] been a very keen pleasure. In the hope that you may find a little pleasure in knowing how much you have given to one reader, I send this line. Pray don't bother to answer it." It should come as no surprise that Howells does not seem to have answered this letter, and it was only with the 1901 review that he again addressed Wendell in writing.[31]

Wendell acknowledges the impropriety—the impudence, as he put it—of his unbidden criticisms, and quite a lot can be said about his inability to censor himself in apologies for previously voiced criticisms. Amid the compounding blunders that identify a strong self-destructive streak, his irrepressible desire to criticize Howells reveals that he is motivated by something powerful enough to override the sensitive conscience that caused him to write Howells these apologies in the first place. Again and again, Wendell bristles at having to humble himself before Howells, using his literary judgments at once to exculpate prior comments, to incur further wrath, and to position himself as Howells's equal—superior, even—in literary criticism. In letter after letter of apology, Wendell seems compelled to assert the superiority of his literary taste and judgment, qualities that to him always indicate social station and breeding; in offering an unsolicited running commentary on the weaknesses in Howells's fiction, Wendell indirectly expresses that he has a literary qualification that overrides the difference in standing between the two men and makes him a worthy critic, despite his lesser status: his superior pedigree, which makes possible his presumed cultivation, aesthetic sensitivity, and exacting literary standards. Ultimately, his persistent sabotaging of their reconciliation communicates a reluctance to bow to a social inferior, however powerful, and his uneasiness with the postwar, New York-based literary economy that holds literary pedigree in such low esteem. And it would seem, from the class-based digs of his 1887 reply and 1901 review, that Howells sensed the implicit social snobbery that underlay Wendell's literary judgments.

In three separate instances before the 1901 review, Wendell wrote to Howells to praise various newly published novels—*The Minister's Charge* (1887), *The Shadow of a Dream* (1890), and *The Landlord at Lion's Head* (1897). The broad range of these books in Howells's corpus suggests that Wendell kept up with Howells's voluminous publications and read widely in his work. While these books can give us some insight into Wendell's literary taste, they also offer insight into his relationship with Howells and the prehistory of Howells's review. It should come as no surprise, then, that all three novels depict a steep and ultimately insurmountable incline encountered by social risers, and all three novels propound a conservative belief in the impenetrable limits of birth and social class. All three novels are narrated from the perspective of a well-born, educated, professional man who observes with some concern the pretensions of a lesser-born man who recognizes neither his own vulgarity nor the faults of his own judgments, and all three novels use the domains most familiar to Wendell —literature and Harvard—as the backdrop of these failed attempts at social advancement.

In *The Minister's Charge*, Mr. Sewell—a minister who reappears in several of Howells's novels and who offers Penelope Lapham the final word in pragmatist literary criticism in *The Rise of Silas Lapham* (1885)—finds himself the unwilling sponsor of a literary aspirant devoid of talent, Lemuel Barber, because of a dishonest if polite word of praise. As discussed in the preceding chapter, *The Minister's Charge* proceeds from the foundational assumption that evaluative honesty is of paramount importance in literary criticism, regardless of the pain that it may cause, a belief that Wendell seems to have shared, as evidenced by his impolitic letters to Howells. In his 1887 letter, Wendell uses the language of realism in his praise of the character Lemuel Barber, calling him "one of the living figures that now & then come from fiction into my mental life as vividly as if I had known them in flesh & blood."[32] He claims familiarity with the talentless writer spurred on by careless praise, an admission that suggests that, in his appointment at Harvard, he had encountered many aspiring young writers in need of dissuasion. The affinity between Wendell and Sewell is also made possible by the Puritan evocations of Sewell's name, which summons Samuel Sewall, the Harvard-educated peer of Cotton Mather who also participated in the Salem witch trials; we are, that is, in territory that was comfortable and familiar to Wendell, and so his pleasure in Howells's book is unsurprising.

Howells's allusion to Samuel Sewall throws Wendell's lifelong affection for Mather into a new light, for his novel invites a reading of this later religious leader and amateur literary critic—Mr. Sewell—in the context of his Puritan antecedent and namesake. Reading *The Minister's Charge* in this light draws homologies between two different instances of New England clerics rooting out people whose preferences and practices were perceived to be threatening to an established order, although in Howells's novel that search takes place on the literary front, in the belief that bad literature is of the utmost danger to the public welfare. And in this narrative confirmation of the importance of religious leaders in maintaining standards, *The Minister's Charge* illuminates Wendell's affinity for Mather. The defense of the stronghold of New England undertaken by both Mather and Wendell entails the prosecution of those invaders who would bring foreign influences and therefore destroy it; for Wendell, the fortress to be defended is the Brahmin tradition of literary Boston, and so the maintenance of exacting literary standards is one way by which he may stave off the invasion of those lesser-born New York writers, of whom Howells was chief.

Though Wendell recognizes the necessity of stringent literary criticism in the preservation of his cherished, dying Boston, he also recognizes himself, as a novelist and writer, as equally subject to its violence. In his 1887 letter to Howells, he voices these mixed feelings in typical form, by pairing his expressions of hostility toward Howells with a pacifying concession in which he admits to being more like Barber than Sewell. He writes, "If the temper of a writer who has won his spurs be not very unlike that of one who would like to win them, you will not mind the slight [imposition] on your time in which I venture to" offer praise of the novel.[33] Bent with contortions of logic and syntax, this implied comparison of Wendell to Barber equivocates in its handling of literary stature. He defers to Howells as the writer "who has won his spurs," a curious metaphor that conflates Howells's success with the capacity to inflict pain and violence on others. Seen retrospectively from Howells's 1901 review, this figuration of the brutality awarded with literary achievement communicates an eerie prescience on Wendell's part, as if he had already sized up Howells as the man who held the reins of his career, as it were, and who was capable of abusing the power of that office. As was typical of Wendell, this acknowledgment of Howells's power, and therefore of Wendell's vulnerability, camouflaged Wendell's covert toppling of the differences in stature between the two men, for this statement proceeds from the assumption that men with spurs are "not very unlike . . . [those] who would like to win them." Despite the menace of Howells's spurs, Wendell will not abase himself altogether before Howells, and suggests that the only substantive difference between them is Howells's power to do harm. It remains unclear whether the harm Wendell sensed would be exacted solely in Howells's criticism of other writers, such as Wendell himself, or in Howells's wider literary influence and the decline of taste Wendell associated with realism and postwar New York.

The praise that Wendell lavished on Howells's 1890 novel, *The Shadow of a Dream*, is equally telling of the dynamic between these two late-century literary men. A short novel about an ailing man's recurring dream about the imagined infidelity between his wife and his best friend, it bears many striking similarities to Wendell's own 1885 novel, *The Duchess Emilia*. The novel is imbued with a keen sensitivity to the unexpected workings of the supernatural in everyday life, an interest shared by Wendell's novel, which follows the spiritual kinship between a young American living in Rome and a long-dead, disgraced Roman woman. Both books illustrate the powerful material influence exerted by the imagination, which can bring things into being through sheer suggestion and conviction; both recount the premature deaths of impressionable young men given to imagining the sexual transgressions of others; and both throw into question the enduring literary convention of romantic sacrifice, in which lovers renounce one another out of sympathy with a third party or in response to some obstacle to their courtship (a convention that Howells would examine at length in *The Rise of Silas Lapham*). Also, the main characters of both books are displaced travelers, who leave their native environment—the Midwest, New England—for confusing, unfamiliar places that further expose their naïveté and awkwardness.

While these shared interests may account in part for Wendell's stated admiration for *The Shadow of a Dream*, the book reaffirms one of Wendell's most cherished beliefs in its handling of literary sensibility as a reliable social inventory. Like *The Minister's Charge*, *The Shadow of a Dream* is narrated by a recurring character in Howells's corpus, Basil March, also a literary aspirant who renounced his ambitions for a career in the insurance industry (in *A Hazard of New Fortunes*, published just months before *The Shadow of a Dream*, March gives up the relative safety of both insurance and Boston to edit a literary magazine in New York). Critics have long recognized Basil March as Howells's fictional counterpart, his novelistic substitute: both men are Midwesterners who move east to pursue literary careers, make career sacrifices to support their families, and follow the same geographical trajectory from the Midwest to New York by way of Boston.[34] As Howells's fictional persona and as a man of previously proven character, March, much like Mr. Sewell in *The Minister's Charge*, functions as the voice of reason and reliable literary taste in a novel that overlays this story of the supernatural with a debate about literary taste. The novel begins with March's memories of an old friend from the West, Douglas Faulkner, with whom he'd shared a youthful literary enthusiasm. Each embarking on a separate career path, the men reunite many years later when the Marches visit the Faulkners at their country retreat, where Faulkner is suffering from a worsening nervous ailment. It rapidly becomes clear to the embarrassed Marches that Faulkner is mentally unstable and harbors visible resentments toward his doting, beautiful wife, Hermia. But what is especially important is March's, and Howells's, reliance on literary sensibility as an early indicator of the kind of man Faulkner proves to be. Before we see his conduct toward his wife or his erratic behavior, his literary preferences immediately tip off Basil March and the reader: "He talked about Bulwer and Dickens and Cherbuliez and Octave Feuillet as if they were modern. But nobody came up to Victor Hugo. Of course we had both read *Les Misérables?* Mrs. Faulkner, he said, was crazy about a Russian fellow: Tourguénief. Had we read him, and could we make anything out of him? Faulkner could not, for his part. Were we to have any great poets again? Byron was the last you could call really great."[35] A reader conversant with Howells's literary criticism would have recognized Faulkner as his antithesis in literary taste, in his backward-looking neglect of contemporary literature; in his affection for Dickens, whom Howells dismissed for the superficiality of his characters; and his indifference toward Turgenev, whom Howells had dubbed in 1873 "a man of great genius."[36] And as Howells's literary representatives, the Marches serve as the mouthpiece of Howells's literary views and, in so doing, orient the reader in this stream of literary criticism: in private, they proclaim Faulkner "ignorant and arrogant," "one *sop* of a sentiment," "second-rate and second-hand" (19).

In the flurry of highly dramatic events that follow—Faulkner's death, the engagement of his widow to Faulkner's best friend, the revelation of Faulkner's recurring dream imagining their love affair, their subsequent separation and implied reunion, the sudden and violent death of Hermia's fiancé in a train accident, and her death from a presumed broken heart soon after—this episode of impromptu literary criticism would seem like a relatively minor event. However, the disclosure of Faulkner's literary judgment, or lack thereof, functions as a kind of Rosetta stone in this novel about misinterpretation and faulty judgment. In a consistency of character, Faulkner's literary judgments are of a piece with the other central bit of data about him: his belief in the credibility of a recurring and altogether erroneous dream. Both these details communicate a systemic inability to exercise judgment and make educated distinctions; Faulkner is in both cases easily susceptible, gullible, and inclined to favor emotion over logic. And in equating keenness of literary judgment with social worth, Howells's novel accords with Wendell's own beliefs.

In 1897, Wendell wrote to Howells to praise *The Landlord at Lion's Head* in a letter that, like the 1890 letter about *The Shadow of a Dream*, seems to have gone unanswered. Whereas the other two novels may have found favor with Wendell because of their use of literary sensibility as a social index, *The Landlord at Lion's Head* uses Wendell's own haunting ground—Harvard itself—to the same purpose. In fact, Wendell expressly praised the novel's "presentation of character," a clever expression of praise for a novel that explicitly examines both the ways in which people present their character through their conduct and tastes and the ways in which those presentations go unheeded.[37] The very terms of Wendell's praise indicate, that is, approval of the novel's philosophy of character not as an internal moral calibration but as a social performance or presentation of that interiority. In the logic of the novel, one's sociability is a register of character, a belief in concert with Wendell's own and one that he expressly commended in his 1890 letter to Howells.

Narrated from the perspective of a middle-class professional man, the painter Jere Westover, the novel charts the gradual transformation and financial prosperity of the lower-class family who housed him during a brief painting expedition to the mountains. Of particular interest to Westover is the family's younger son, Jeff Durgin, sent to Harvard by his socially ambitious and newly affluent mother and who conducts himself there recklessly and coarsely. It is to be presumed initially that Jeff's social failures at Harvard derive less from character flaws than from the spotty social education he received growing up in the country. At the request of Mrs. Durgin, Westover functions as Jeff's occasional moral steward there, and the novel follows the circular path of Westover's ever-changing opinion of Jeff's character, as he alternately warms to Jeff's brusque candor and high self-regard and recoils from his total ignorance—rejection, even—of social etiquette. Howells prepares the reader for a novel in the vein of his 1885 *The Rise of Silas Lapham*, in which the social failures of another coarse, rural-born newcomer to Boston, Silas Lapham, actually help him to reveal the true nature of his sterling, honest character; in that novel, social pretensions actually compromise Lapham's innate ethics, and social failure coincides with his moral "rise," as in the words of the novel's title. Jeff, however, never rises, as it were, to these expectations, and his misbehavior toward several women figures as irreducible evidence of an uneducable, dissolute character. Jeff Durgin is not, like Silas Lapham, a moral diamond in the rough, but is an amoral opportunist, and in this way he resembles Howells's other celebrated social failure: Bartley Hubbard of *A Modern Instance* (1881), whose persistent ill-treatment of women serves as final evidence of a disreputable character.

But what is noteworthy for the purposes of this inquiry is the clear field of moral vision provided by Harvard. As Westover and the reader turn over the mounting evidence of Jeff's character and attempt to determine whether Jeff more closely resembles Silas Lapham or Bartley Hubbard, Jeff's Harvard class immediately recognizes him for what he is. His fellow students immediately label him a "jay," a social outcast. In the words of one Harvard student (himself a dissolute alcoholic), Jeff is "not only a jay, but a cad, and [is] personally so offensive to most of the college men that he had never got into a decent club or society."[38] Social stature and moral character are intertwined here, so that social exclusion both derives from and evidences a shady moral disposition. This conviction comes very close to Wendell's own belief in "quality" as a catch-all blending social station with taste and moral virtue, and it is not surprising that Wendell would approve of Howell's use of his own institution—Harvard—as the social setting for the articulation and confirmation of that belief. In somewhat allaying Wendell's own anxieties about the changes he saw at Harvard, the novel offers a more conservative picture of the Harvard that Wendell would have liked to have seen around him.

From his several letters of praise, it is clear that Wendell warmed to Howells's more socially conservative novels, which told stories that seem to defend the class prerogatives of old Boston society—pedigree, literature, higher education, Harvard—as reliable methods of weeding out both social pretenders and the morally disreputable. What's more, these novels entangle these two categories so that social climbing is necessarily an indicator of a dubious character: Howells by no means suggests that the lower classes are immoral, but their acceptance of their rightful social place is used to signal a strong moral fiber. Literary taste in these novels serves as a kind of shibboleth of class membership, a way by which the initiated recognize each other and can espy pretenders and arrivistes. It bears remarking that these conservative novels were authored by a man who began his career as a literary claimant to Boston society; though he was accepted into this society, he was not born into it and was not unlike Lemuel Barber, Douglas Faulkner, or Jeff Durgin in his early life. This biographical detail imparts an added dimension to Wendell's appreciation for these novels. Certainly, Wendell's admiration stems from their narration of the necessity of social exclusion, particularly in the literary arena, but his appreciation rings of social irony in seeing a social riser affirm the importance of keeping people like himself out of literary circles. That is, there is a strong undercurrent of social cruelty in Wendell's letters, which are underwritten by a desire to affirm the superiority of his own social station. In complimenting these already conservative novels, Wendell implicitly concurs with the social sentiments expressed in them: those not to the literary manor born ought to be barred from it. In pairing these compliments with literary criticism, he implicitly reminds Howells of his own lowly origins. From the tenor of Howells's reply in 1887, from his refusal to answer Wendell's later letters, and from his class-conscious 1901 review, it would seem that Howells recognized both Wendell's compliments and criticism as a direct assault on his membership in the literary elite, and his 1901 review can be construed as a rebuttal to these numerous letters of literary criticism.

It is impossible to reconstruct the effect of Howells's review on Wendell, particularly because Wendell seems to have attempted to erase any record of its, and the book's, reception. Wendell did not retain any correspondence received in the wake of the review; though in a 1909 letter to Edmund Stedman's granddaughter Wendell claimed not to save answered correspondence, his papers indicate otherwise, for Wendell typically kept elaborate records of all his other important publications, retaining preliminary notes and manuscripts—both handwritten and edited—as well as clippings and correspondence received in the aftermath of publication.[39] It is notable that no such record exists of Wendell's literary history, especially because in 1904 Wendell issued, in collaboration with his Harvard colleague Chester Noyes Greenough, a revised, condensed textbook version that remained in print well into the 1940s. In the place of the weighty file devoted to the literary history that one expects to find in the Harvard University Archives, where the papers of former university faculty members and administrators are kept, is instead a slim file that contains a single document: Howells's review. The absence of the manuscript file and its replacement with an offprint of the 1901 review suggest that the review had literally obscured or overtaken the book itself in Wendell's consciousness: in a moment of unexpected wit, Wendell's archives suggest that the only thing one need know about this book is Howells's review of it.

The only existing document where Wendell mentions Howells's review is a letter to Charles W. Eliot—hardly the person Wendell would turn to for comfort. He wrote, "In six weeks or so, two thousand copies of the book were disposed of. This unusual success is partly due, no doubt, to the extreme animosity of certain criticism. I venture to hope, however, that it is rather due to the fact that, however [word is unclear] some of my opinions may be, they are carefully thought out, and expressed with a clearness and with a constant effort to set forth with fairness many matters which fail to touch my intuitive sympathy."[40] The syntax of the letter reveals Wendell's inclination to use erasure as a strategy of managing this crushing review, for he refuses even to name Howells or identify the particular article, in so doing symbolically nullifying both. This letter also communicates that, despite the gaps in the archival records, Wendell did write and receive letters about Howells's review. Moreover, this letter appears not in Wendell's own papers but in Eliot's, where Wendell had no jurisdiction and over which he could exert no authority, a detail that suggests that Wendell had indeed destroyed all epistolary evidence of Howells's review.

This letter is also of particular value in its revelation that both Eliot and the professionalization of the academy figured prominently in Wendell's consciousness of the book. Anyone familiar with Eliot's notorious frostiness and Wendell's filial need for Eliot's approval would wonder why Wendell would bring Howells's review to Eliot's attention, when Eliot could most certainly be relied upon to disappoint Wendell in these awkward circumstances. While the letter may function as a kind of confession or institutional unburdening to Eliot, it also shows Wendell's need to broadcast the book's successes to the university president. The syntactical order of the letter shows that the first thing Wendell wants to communicate to Eliot is the book's high sales, and, after acknowledging "the extreme animosity of certain criticism," Wendell then proceeds to state his scholarly mission and technique in writing the book. Although the letter is tempered by a nod to Howells's review, it is visibly motivated by a need to show Eliot the seriousness and success with which Wendell produced literary historical knowledge. If the letter can tell us anything, it shows how this volume of literary history is intertwined with a desire for the institutional acceptance and respect recently rendered conditional by professionalism. Especially noteworthy is the similarity between Wendell's defense of the book and the language Howells had used in reply to Wendell's apologetic letter in 1887: both writings of Wendell's can be excused because of the intellectual motives that underlie them and the spirit in which they were written. In other words, Wendell recycles Howells's own language to defend himself from it.

To be sure, one strategy by which Wendell responded to Howells was in taking frequent potshots at his literary powers and importance, a strategy that seems designed to minimize by implication the importance of Howells's criticism. In revising the literary history for reissue as a textbook in 1904, Wendell seems to have taken direction from many of Howells's comments, eliminating many of the passages Howells had taken issue with, such as his Anglophilic reverence for Queen Victoria, to whom he had referred as "her Majesty."[41] But the fingerprint of Howells's review can be most visibly discerned in the direct, lengthy discussion of Howells's own literary importance, an addition that is particularly striking because Howells had been altogether absent from the 1900 full-length literary history, which alluded to him directly not even once. In that book, Wendell defended his inattention to postwar literature with the claim that "it is hard to resist the conclusion that whoever shall make a new library of American literature, thirty or forty years hence, will by the same token find no place for many of our contemporaries momentarily preserved by our latest anthologists. As you turn their pages, you can hardly avoid feeling that, however valuable these may be to history, they contain little which merits permanence."[42] If Basil March's reaction to Douglas Faulkner's dismissal of contemporary literature in *The Shadow of a Dream* can give us any indication, it is likely that Howells reacted similarly to seeing both his own work and his literary milieu so dismissed and expunged from literary history altogether.

In the 1904 textbook version, however, Wendell and Greenough pay Howells special attention, introducing him with a backhanded compliment that quickly deteriorates into outright hostility. Howells "has written so much, so faithfully, and in a spirit at once honestly American and so kindly, that it is hard to say why he has not achieved more certainly powerful results. His chief limitation seems to be a kind of lifelong diffidence, which has forbidden a feeling of intimate familiarity even with the scenes and the people of his own creation."[43] As was and remains typical of textbooks, this discussion was accompanied by a one-word sidebar summation, "Diffidence," that efficiently distilled, and dismissed, Howells for generations of schoolchildren. This tactic seems designed not only to subject Howells to the same kind of public routing Wendell had endured but also to arrest the reproduction of Howells's readers, as it were, by implanting opinions that might prevent these students from reading Howells later in their adult lives. Wendell exacts particularly trenchant revenge by heading future readers off at the pass, in effect using the medium at his disposal to weaken Howells's position in American literary history itself. At first glance, this appraisal is surprising, for diffidence hardly characterized Wendell's experience of Howells, whose 1901 review was nothing if not aggressive. However, Wendell makes this criticism on the basis of a perceived emotional reserve, a coldness even, in which a "feeling of intimate familiarity" is "forbidden." Howells "never quite sympathizes" and seems to see "the vivid creatures of his imagination . . . externally." In detecting this quality "even" in Howells's attitude toward the characters and settings in his own work, Wendell admits that his judgment of Howells is based in large part on a detection of an aloofness that extends *outside* the limits of his books and into his general demeanor. One cannot help but hear in this criticism Wendell's many rebuffed overtures soliciting greater intimacy with Howells, even if unbidden criticism served as the pretext for those overtures. This criticism also evokes Wendell's frequent complaint about President Eliot of Harvard, whose coldness Wendell found frustrating. At the same time, Wendell's perception of aloofness even toward those figures most immediately subject to the whims and power of Howells's imagination—the characters in his own works—echoes Wendell's 1887 letter to Howells, in which he compares Howells's success to the acquisition of spurs. If the execution of violence is made possible by a lack of sympathetic projection, then Wendell's detection of emotional detachment constitutes an inquiry into the emotional demeanor that made it possible for Howells to use his spurs in the forum of literary criticism. And Wendell suggests that the emotional quality that makes it possible for Howells to pen such a review seems to seep into and compromise his fiction.

By way of explanation for this unsympathetic mien, Wendell suggests that Howells's reserve may "perhaps [be] due to the circumstances of his life," and relates a rough sketch of Howells's early life, including his origins in Ohio, his sojourn in Italy during the Civil War, and his long residence in the Boston area. However, "during his long and welcome residence near Boston [in Cambridge]," Wendell comments, "he never seems to have felt quite at home."[44] In his narration of Howells's personal history as an explanation for his affect and literary style, Wendell subjects Howells to the same biographical interpretive method that he himself had used in 1900 and that Howells had used against him in 1901, when he asserted that Wendell's Boston parochialism had compromised his judgment and hamstrung his tastes. Though Wendell himself had complained of a similar feeling of displacement in Cambridge, he here continues to rely on New England geography and social status as an index of literary quality.

Howells's lack of belonging in Boston at once serves as a reminder of his lesser social status and intimates his larger incongruity within the literary culture in Boston anointed by Wendell. For Wendell, if you feel you don't belong in the elite ranks of literary Boston, then you probably don't, and he intimates that Howells's feelings of displacement indicate his disqualification, both as a lesser writer and as an emigrant, to be included among those ranks.

In 1904, Wendell was invited to lecture on American literature and culture at the Sorbonne in Paris, where, over the course of an academic year, he delivered many of the lectures and arguments that had formed the core of his 1900 literary history. In February 1905, Wendell discussed Howells in more acerbic language than he had used in the textbook the year before. "And there can be no doubt," he asserted, "that when you put his stories beside the poems and essays of his predecessors, they seem petty, trivial—comparatively, though not positively, vulgar."[45] The literary genres that Wendell names here— poetry and the essay—serve as a shorthand reference to antebellum Boston, whose chief literary output was famously composed in those same genres, and his description of Howells's voluminous literary corpus as "stories" also works to diminish the seriousness and importance both of the genre of narrative fiction and of Howells's work. In this moment of comparative literary criticism, Wendell again uses antebellum New England as a gauge by which he evaluates other writers and moments, and, in holding Howells up against this heuristic, he is able once again to use social status as an index of literary merit. When placed alongside the writers of antebellum Boston, Howells is revealed to be "vulgar," a criticism that bears the unmistakable stamp of social snobbery, with an appraisal of social affiliation standing in for literary evaluation.

A less visible but significantly more durable strategy by which Wendell responded to this crisis was his involvement in the design of Harvard's curriculum and its positioning at the forefront of academe. The collapse of standards that Wendell saw in the changing geography of literary power was increasingly apparent to him at Harvard, where curricular changes functioned like the early fissures that herald the coming of an unbridgeable chasm. Though Wendell had been an early supporter of Charles W. Eliot, he became increasingly distressed by the changes taking place under his presidency, such as Eliot's negotiations to unite Harvard with Radcliffe College and the creation of graduate programs modeled after the German university system that had trained the philologists who were rapidly replacing untrained generalists like himself; Wendell was disappointed to witness the university committing to a graduate curriculum that seemed to ensure the decline of institutional standards and the replacement of gentleman professors.[46] Chief among Wendell's concerns was his dislike for Eliot's famed elective system, which decentralized the curriculum by releasing students from long-standing, stringent requirements of ancient languages, theology, and mathematics, and authorized them to elect their own courses. In his refusal to require students to select a defined course of instruction or major, Eliot emphasized broad rather than deep learning, and in an 1895 address, he proffered the elective system as the intellectual heir of numerous cherished American institutions: "The elective system," he averred, "is in the first place, an outcome of the Protestant Reformation. In the next place, it is an outcome of the free spirit of political liberty."[47] Whereas Eliot positioned the considerable freedoms of the elective system as politically correct, as it were, Wendell saw these freedoms as evidence of relaxing institutional standards. Wendell said as much throughout his career; while he disliked the curriculum of ancient languages and mathematics that he had experienced as a Harvard undergraduate and that Eliot dismantled, he equally disliked Eliot's elective system for its lack of rigor and standards. With the erosion of writing skills among students and the laxity of curricular requirements, even Harvard seemed poised to relinquish its role as a gatekeeper of quality.

These concerns about the Eliot presidency put Wendell in an uneasy position, and his pessimism found disfavor with Eliot, who joined Howells in criticizing Wendell's account of American literary history in large part because it associated Eliot's postwar presidency with regional decay. A brief 1899 note from Eliot communicates the overlap between the personal and the institutional that underlay both Wendell's work and its reception. Perhaps as a way to curry favor with Eliot, who had an interest in his own family history (to a degree, Wendell's literary history can be construed as deriving from the same interest), Wendell published a brief tribute to Eliot's recently deceased cousin Samuel Eliot in the *Proceedings of the American Academy of Arts and Sciences* in 1899. In a note expressing appreciation for Wendell's tribute, Eliot took issue with Wendell's use of the word "gentry" to describe the elite Boston circles in which Samuel Eliot had lived and that Wendell would extol in the literary history he would publish the following year, offering instead "the real New England word 'quality' " as the "better" descriptor.[48] While this may seem like a minor semantic disagreement, it communicates that Eliot, like Howells, both recognized and objected to Wendell's desire to map political structures of power onto literary allegiances, to make a literary elite into a political elite. And in quibbling with Wendell's vocabulary, Eliot is doing nothing less than challenging the research conclusions of one of his own faculty members and, just as Howells would do in his 1901 review, indirectly exposing Wendell's lack of specialized expertise and genuine professionalism. In this way, both Howells and Eliot made Wendell an American version of Edmund Gosse, whose 1885 literary history, discussed in the preceding chapter, revealed the dangers of making literary history a vehicle for untrained literary men to professionalize.

Eliot also patently rejected Wendell's account of Boston's decline. "You say several times that the New England virtues . . . are passing away. I doubt it. . . . Objects and pursuits change but qualities endure. . . . All race qualities are wonderfully persistent." To demonstrate this persistence, Eliot identified several New England men whose vigorous, prosperous lives defy the terms of Wendell's narrative of New England's decline. In identifying his own son as a counterweight to Wendell's regional history, Eliot attempts to reorient his own centrality in Wendell's narrative, as his own cousin had provided the impetus for this work. Eliot verges on direct insult here, for he seems to suggest that Wendell speaks only for himself in this narrative of Boston's decline; my family is robust and flourishing, Eliot suggests, so keep me out of your apocalyptic vision. Eliot intimates, that is, that Wendell has conflated regional history with a personal history of disappointment and weakness, that his research generalizes on the basis of very limited, very personal evidence. Moreover, Eliot's response figures as a tacit defense of Harvard, for Eliot was literally at work on preserving the Boston area as the nation's intellectual center, and his rejection of Wendell's narrative of regional decline communicated, however implicitly, the centrality of this particular educational institution in American literary history. The diction of Wendell's 1900 literary history communicates that he took Eliot's comments seriously, for he omits the original word "gentry" and persistently favors Eliot's suggestion, "quality," to describe the elite circles that Wendell credited with the apogee of American literary achievement. But Eliot's note also communicated the centrality of Harvard to Wendell's regional narrative, and his 1900 literary history would markedly revise the position of Harvard in American literary history, and it is important to note that the publication of this volume coincides precisely with Wendell's attempts to reform the Harvard curriculum and restore its role as gatekeeper.

Wendell's suspicions about the elective system were confirmed with the 1899–1900 publication of a faculty report disclosing that the majority of Harvard students were opting only for introductory-level courses; despite Eliot's stated expectations, fewer than a third of the student body had actually pursued their interests systematically by taking courses in a favored department.[49] In response to the revelation that academic standards had indeed wavered, the first years of the twentieth century saw a wave of curricular reform, which included elevating the difficulty of introductory courses, raising the requirements for graduating with distinction, and dissuading students from graduating early.[50] Wendell's contribution to this institutional crisis proved enormously important. He and A. Lawrence Lowell, a government professor who would succeed Eliot as president of Harvard in 1909, formed a committee that drafted a blueprint for a highly rigorous departmental concentration that required intense faculty supervision of student work. Students would be expected to select appropriate specialized courses under consultation with a faculty adviser

(Harvard up to this time had had no system of student advising, which enabled the popularity of introductory courses to pass under the radar), engage in directed readings with a tutor, write a thesis, and take a general exam in the senior year. In its heavy emphasis on faculty direction, this curriculum stripped students of the liberties Eliot had so valued, and reinstalled hierarchy and supervision in Harvard culture. This program exerted considerable influence at Harvard: it was put into place informally as an honors concentration as early as 1906, and when Lowell was instated as president, it was used as the model not only for all honors programs but also for all departmental concentrations in general.

The curriculum Wendell drafted collaboratively still exists at Harvard as an honors concentration: it was and still is known as the History and Literature concentration, a program that put into curricular form Wendell's abiding interest in fusing literature and history. The History and Literature program at Harvard plays a significant role in the history of the American academy, for it signals that interdisciplinarity was by no means a recent invention of the late twentieth century, but emerged simultaneously with disciplinary specialization at the turn of the last century; the establishment of disciplinary limits coincided with the emergence of practices and fields of knowledge that depended upon the traversing of those limits. Nor is it particularly surprising that Wendell had been so instrumental to the development of this program (Elliott Perkins has described Wendell as its "patron saint"), for the change in academic culture that led him originally to fuse literature and history as early as 1890 was also at stake in the development of an interdisciplinary program that implicitly challenges the necessity of specialization.[51] And in establishing this program, Wendell imparted institutional legitimacy to the literary historical work so often performed by untrained literary men attempting to adapt to new institutional demands.

The social and literary context that enveloped Howells's review equally frames the creation of Harvard's History and Literature concentration. Throughout his career at Harvard, Wendell complained of the many institutional responsibilities, such as meetings and grading, that occupy the academic's time, and so, coming from a man already protective of his time, the heavy emphasis upon faculty supervision at every turn in the History and Literature program is especially conspicuous; the disparity between Wendell's avowed complaints about service and his legislation of faculty overload is marked. As Wendell's one opportunity to design a university curriculum from the ground up, the History and Literature program evidences his insistence upon the establishment of clear lines of authority between faculty and students, an aim that is not troubling in and of itself but that assumes an added complexity when Wendell's pronounced conservatism is taken into consideration. The History and Literature program provided Wendell with an opportunity to put into place an educational setting that runs counter to the trends he detected elsewhere, with the erosion of standards and the increasing inclusiveness of literary circles. While operating in accordance with the professionalization of the academy, the insistence on faculty authority in this program also constitutes an attempt to reinstall, at least in this one environment, the elitist structures of gatekeeping whose demise Wendell had lamented. This ambition also helps explain why Wendell would reissue his beleaguered literary history as a textbook amid this climate of curricular revision, for its micromanagement of the student's literary taste and judgment communicates its larger mission of occupying a supervisory role and consolidating critical authority. In this way, Wendell fully complied with the parameters of literary professionalism propounded by Howells and widely absorbed in literary histories of the period at pains to affirm their own social importance.

The creation of the History and Literature program is particularly important in light of Wendell's failed attempts to preserve birth and provenance as important tokens of literary value. Having been publicly exposed and humiliated by Howells, Wendell seems to have turned to the university as the site where he could realize and preserve his beliefs. Just as the History and Literature program—and later the Harvard undergraduate major in general—runs counter to the trends Wendell had observed elsewhere in its insistence on faculty gatekeeping, the program also institutionalizes Wendell's fervent belief in the importance of provenance. After all, the program—like Wendell's literary history—appoints history as an indispensable resource in literary evaluation and interpretation, and, in thinking "facts together," as he described it, students would be able to see the two "in their mutual relations."[52] The insistence on history as a tool of literary evaluation—however forward-thinking it may seem amid the moral emphasis of turn-of-the-century realist criticism, and however much it accords with the New Historicism of the late twentieth century—was by no means a neutral gesture. Wendell had insisted elsewhere on the necessity of history for evaluation, and Howells had suspected that history had served as a discreet cryptogram for pedigree. For Wendell, careful evaluation—whether of a person or a text—requires seeing it within its historical context, but Howells's review brings into sharp relief the context of Wendell's own insistence on context: namely, the equation of social quality with literary quality. And in creating a curriculum that requires students to see literary texts within the contexts of history, Wendell preserved and institutionalized the belief that provenance matters.

In the autumn of 1914, Howells wrote to Wendell for the first time in nearly thirty years. After an initial salutation, Howells got immediately to his purpose in writing after so long a silence. "Once I wrote of a book of yours in a very abominable spirit," he wrote. "Your behavior to me since, as often as we have met, had made me wish to tell you that I was, when too late, immediately sorry for what I had done, and have always been ashamed."[53] A letter written by Howells three days later suggests that a looming social engagement prompted him to write this brief note in an attempt to preempt a socially awkward occasion. However, there may have been other motivations. Howells was at that point seventy-seven years old, and had seen the ranks of his literary peers thin considerably with the recent deaths of Thomas Bailey Aldrich, Edmund Stedman, and Mark Twain, among many others. Two years before, Col. George Harvey, the new head of Harper's, Howells's long-standing publisher, had hosted a dinner in honor of Howells's seventy-fifth birthday, the kind of celebration of aging literary men that Howells had participated in twenty-five years before in honor of writers from the preceding generation such as Longfellow. Though he continued writing, Howells by that point had seen the signals of a literary life near its close, and his writing to Wendell may have constituted his own attempts to arrange his papers before dying, to use the metaphor that Van Wyck Brooks had used to describe the mood in postwar Boston that contributed to the proliferation of so many literary histories in that era.

That Wendell preserved this letter in its original envelope is a sure sign of its value for him, as he claimed to dispose of all answered correspondence. He replied to Howells's letter immediately, and his response is lengthy and garbled, bisected by conflicting impulses that cut through and interrupt his sentences, leaving them virtually unintelligible. Just as in his earlier letters to Howells, Wendell's visible desire for intimacy with Howells is shot through with barely concealed hostility, and, as in a psychomachia, his letter voices both sentiments at once, with each literally interrupting the other. "Your wonderfully kind words came to me only late last evening," he wrote. "It is hard to know whether they bring more pleasure or trouble; they surely bring both, and I know not which is the deeper. For the pleasure I feel in this assurance of friendship means more than I can put into words, without undue confession of the self-distrust which has always made me hesitant, and I fear a little repellant [sic] in the shining humility of disguised self-consciousness."[54] In admitting to feelings of hesitance, he lays claim to the very "diffidence" he had ten years before attributed to Howells, just as he also admitted to the feelings of displacement in Cambridge that he projected onto Howells. In these initial remarks, Wendell admits to having two competing responses to Howells's letter, and he obliquely confesses his suspicions that his prior efforts to conceal his feelings may have indirectly contributed to Howells's former manner to him. In what initially appears to be a gracious attempt to relieve Howells's guilt, Wendell uses conspicuously ambiguous language. "An honest man writes honestly, and he would not be human if his honest words did not now and then stir honest resentment in men equally honest." The problems of clarity and syntax that encumber this letter suggest that Wendell was in less than perfect control of his prose, but the opacity here nevertheless allows Wendell to satisfy both of his apparent impulses: to reconcile with Howells while voicing his resentment.

He continued in this vein. "The more fervid the instant utterance of such genuine criticism, the less it stings. The very rancor of it—if rancor be not too harsh a term—implies something like its transcience, if there be such a word. And can one possibly understand or care for, another human being where temper is always in hand half so well, or half so much, as one where temper now and then, not all wrongly, either, blazes?" The awkwardness of these sentences no doubt communicates the difficulty Wendell encountered in drafting his reply, but it also seems to serve as a furtive cover that allowed him to discuss sensitive matters. After all, Wendell certainly might have revised and edited a reply to one of the most important letters he would ever receive, and his decision not to—to send this letter in such disarray—is something we must take seriously. This statement begins with what seems to be a dismissal of the importance of Howells's review on the basis of an argument about the fleeting nature of wrath; the intensity of Howells's review signaled that it had been nothing more than a temporary flare-up, as such rage is simply unsustainable for long periods, he suggests. This argument is disingenuous at best, for it equates the ephemeral nature of Howells's rage with the inconsequence of the review it produced. But the very language of this dismissal—stings, rancor, temper, blazes—bespeaks both the pain caused by the review and a harsh appraisal of Howells's temperament. The word "rancor" in particular cuts across the grain of Wendell's dismissal, for, in denoting long-standing and deep-seated anger, it intimates that Howells's review had been brewing for some time and had its basis in an earlier injury. But as was typical, Wendell uses a disclaimer to downplay the harshness of this word even as he relies upon it. He signs off in a similar manner: "I write too much, I fear, and too long. Were I more articulate to-day, I could not so clearly show you how deeply your more than kind words have touched me." In acknowledging the excesses and murkiness of his prose, Wendell is able to disarm its latent content while leaving it intact.

Howells's response was archly succinct. "Dear Mr. Wendell," he replied, "From the true magnanimity you have shown I could not have expected less or asked more."[55] That is, Wendell replied just as Howells expected he would. Their abbreviated correspondence during the remaining six years of Howells's life was cordial and brief. In 1917, Hamlin Garland hosted a celebratory gala in honor of Howells's eightieth birthday, and Wendell sent his regrets at being unable to come. He wrote, "Howells is of the few one can't help loving for himself, as well as for the work which has made [him] for long our chief man of letters."[56] Using typical doublespeak, Wendell voices his affection for Howells while admitting to having attempted to suppress that affection. Howells responded in turn with an affectingly sentimental reply. "Of all the letters which my superannuation . . . brought me, I have been thinking none gave me [more] pleasure than your letter."[57] On its own terms, Wendell's note had hardly deserved such distinction among the literally dozens of affectionate, appreciative letters Howells received in honor of his birthday. However, if Howells's letter can tell us anything, it is the enormity of his relief in having received further confirmation that he had been forgiven for his 1901 review. Little did he know that, of the two of them, Wendell's work would endure, at the expense of Howells's own status in literary history. As the literary historian Ellen M. Hutchinson presciently asked of her collaborator, Edmund Stedman, "Where will . . . Howells be 55 years hence?"[58]

Wendell's institutional penumbra may have been in large part responsible for the circulation and endurance of his controversial literary history. Certainly, the longevity of the textbook version helped keep his account in wide circulation, instructing generations of American students well into the 1940s about the centrality of antebellum New England in American literary history. Similarly, Wendell's affiliation with Harvard imparted a particular weight to his opinions that other literary historians—such as the Philadelphia high school teacher Albert H. Smyth or the Wellesley College professor Katherine Bates, for example—did not enjoy, and Scribner's packaging of his 1900 literary history illustrates how this increasingly high-profile seat of American learning came to be used in literary marketing at the turn of the last century. However, these particular channels of circulation do not account for the readiness with which Wendell's core argument was accepted and revised by his academic successors in literary history.

While Wendell's affiliation with Harvard may have attracted general readers, its role in the survival of his work cannot be discounted. In 1924, the literary historian Fred Lewis Pattee detected an institutional bias in Wendell's literary history, noting the concerted attention paid to Harvard graduates and professors, among them Emerson, Holmes, Longfellow, and Lowell. Just as Howells had offered an alternative title that he felt more accurately described the contents of Wendell's literary history, so Pattee joked a generation later that Wendell's book ought to be retitled "A Literary History of Harvard University, with Incidental Glimpses of the Minor Writers of America."[59] With the publication of the revised textbook version in 1904, Wendell admitted to paying Harvard special attention and defended this decision in language that communicates perhaps one explanation for the endurance of his geography of American literary achievement. "It may appear that we have dwelt too long on Harvard," Wendell and Greenough wrote. But "Harvard remains the chief intellectual centre of that part of New England from which the literature of our Renaissance sprang."[60] Harvard, they argue, is inextricably entangled with the literary flowering of antebellum New England, but what is especially telling about this defense is the positioning of Harvard, and not New York, as the rightful intellectual successor to New England's former greatness. From the ashes of New England, Harvard rises to take its place as the nation's "chief intellectual centre."

Institutional affiliation remains one of the most potent and unremarked-upon contexts for the production of knowledge, and the role of Harvard in the endurance of Wendell's literary history cannot be discounted. To trace the various twentieth-century scholars and critics who have revised, confirmed, and reanimated the centrality of antebellum Boston in American literary history is to offer a list of some of Harvard's most distinguished graduates and faculty: Van Wyck Brooks, F. O. Matthiessen, Perry Miller, Vernon L. Parrington, and Robert Spiller, among others. All of these men produced important contributions to the Wendell thesis and nearly all—save Perry Miller—received their first formal instruction in and exposure to the discipline through their work with Wendell, the original source of the narrative that they would retell through their own scholarship.[61] Many of these twentieth-century critics also participated in the History and Literature program designed by Wendell to instruct students in the importance of reading literature within the context of the social; for example, F. O. Matthiessen—best remembered for his 1941 study, *The American Renaissance*, which took its title from Wendell's appellation for the period and reconfirmed the centrality of antebellum New England to American letters—supervised the History and Literature program after Wendell's retirement. The history of this foundational tenet in American literary history is not only a history of Wendell's own frustrated attempts to hold off the barbarians he saw at the gate of American literature but also a history of Harvard affiliation, as generations of Harvard men produced and reiterated knowledge that affirmed, however indirectly, their own institution and their own intellectual pedigree; to use the language Alan Heimert gave to Wendell's own loyalty to Cotton Mather, the survival of the Wendell thesis may be due to the continuation of Harvard filiopietism. In reiterating Wendell's literary geography, these twentieth-century descendants situated themselves, however implicitly, as the protectors and heirs of New England greatness. And as Wendell's students, they imitated the Great Man both through the reiteration of his geography of literary achievement and through paving their own literary histories with professional self-interest.

In revising and adapting Wendell's celebration of Boston, Matthiessen and his cohort tailored it to the changing climate of literary opinion by pointing toward one other Harvard son—Ralph Waldo Emerson—as the central figure in American letters, and it is in the disciplinary agreement upon the centrality of Emerson that Wendell's literary geography endures in revised form. However, what is especially striking about the pull exerted by Emerson on American literary history is the lingering aroma of elitism that still encircles this version of Wendell's argument. In the discipline's continued expectation that Americanist graduate students become conversant with antebellum New England, Emerson has become a disciplinary patrimony or inheritance that retains or appreciates in value as it passes from each generation of scholars to the next.[62] Emerson has become a vehicle by which Americanists showcase their intellectual pedigree and affirm their membership in an academic elite. The profession is full of anecdotal accounts of thinly veiled sparring matches between critics vying for superior Emersonian command, whether in conferences, graduate seminars, or oral examinations. Whereas Wendell had used literary sensibility as a test of social status, the Americanist literary academy still retains antebellum Boston—and Emerson in particular—as a kind of disciplinary litmus test distinguishing serious scholars from the slight and trendy, and in this way the discipline of American literary history not only retells Wendell's literary geography but also continues to use writers of antebellum Boston to determine academic pedigree: antebellum New England and its favored son have become disciplinary status symbols.

Epilogue

Relevance & Its Discontents

Against the grain of widespread perception that the most recent wave of research in literary history, beginning in the 1980s, has corrected the many faults and biases of older research, this book has aimed to show some of the residual ways in which the literary history of the United States is still organized by many questionable beliefs, practices, and aims of late nineteenth-century practitioners. In relating a history of the many causes and disciplinary products of the fad for literary history at the turn of the last century, I have tried to show over several chapters the urgency of literary workers and professors to allay public suspicions of aristocratic elitism by marketing themselves as accessible, valuable contributors to the public welfare, more akin to doctors and civil servants than to aloof, unintelligible priests of high culture. Despite the many, many ways in which literary historians since the 1980s have indeed broken with late-century literary historians, our discipline is still profoundly shaped by the pressure to placate widespread anti-intellectualism by demonstrating our hostility toward elitism and commitment to the public welfare. Numerous critics in recent years—among them Jonathan Arac, Wai Chee Dimock, Linda Hutcheon, David Perkins, and John Carlos Rowe—have attempted to extricate literary history from the thematics of nation, and this book explicates what is at stake in American literary histories' deep-seated and even ineluctable attachment to nation: the authority and stature of literature academics amid widespread American anti-intellectualism.

A telling example: Sacvan Bercovitch's preface to the 1986 *Reconstructing American Literary History*, an edited volume that played an important role in revitalizing the field and drawing attention to new work. Bercovitch's preface begins with the pronouncement that the "need for a new American literary history seems clear and unexceptionable," a statement that implies the inadequacy of past work amid recent paradigm shifts.[1] The volume is more frank than most in acknowledging its indebtedness to the discipline's past, as with its dedication to "the memory of F. O. Matthiessen and Perry Miller" and praise of Spiller's literary history, quoting his famously unfulfilled appeal for continued activity in the field (v). Subsequent to this dutiful acknowledgment of his forebears, Bercovitch cites the intellectual ruptures of "the political-academic upheavals of the late sixties and . . . the recent impact of European critical theories" to declare the need for new work in the long moribund field of literary history (vii). "During the past two decades," Bercovitch writes, "consensus of all sorts has broken down—left and right, political and aesthetic. . . . It was the achievement of the Spiller *History* to consolidate a powerful literary-historical movement. It will be the task of the present generation to reconstruct American literary history by making a virtue of dissensus" (vii–viii). Bercovitch puts his finger on some essential differences between earlier and current work in American literary history, such as the current suspicion of earlier critics' emphasis on unity —whether in national politics or in New Critical aesthetics—and the recent rejection of prior historians' inclination to privilege the exemplary in favor instead of the marginal, fragmentary, and resistant. Yet at the same time, Bercovitch identifies some shared characteristics of American literary historians across time and space: the expectation that they make unifying sense out of national disorder and that their work perform a kind of national service. The fulfillment of the former responsibility was one means, among several, by which late-century literary historians were able to evidence their fulfillment of the latter. Today's American literary historians and scholars, for better or worse, are still beholden to this same expectation of national service, though it would appear that our compliance with this demand seems only to spark further public suspicion of the literary intellectual.

Bill Readings has shown how academic literature departments were created in the nineteenth century with the expectation that they would serve as "producer, protector, and inculcator of an idea of national culture," an expectation made possible by the perception of literature as the artistic expression of national character.[2] The academic study of literature, that is, was founded with the expectation of national service, which quickly made it the centerpiece and heart of the Western university. For late nineteenth-century American literature professors, literary history enabled compliance with this requirement, and even less overtly nationalist researches in philology nevertheless served as proud evidence of American intellectual achievements.[3] Throughout the twentieth century, literature professors of diverse interpretive schools continued to comply with this expectation of national service. Even the New Critics performed vital social services in the aftermath of World War II, despite their repudiations of any social, historical, or political commitments of the literary. Created amid the extraordinary pedagogic burdens caused by the Servicemen's Readjustment Act of 1944 and the consequent millions of veterans who enrolled in college in the 1940s and 1950s, New Criticism participated in a direct way in the rehabilitation and cultural reacclimatization of the American soldier by proffering a reassuring aesthetic of unity and historical erasure.[4]

The twentieth century was studded with similar efforts of literary scholars to make a place for themselves in a culture that equates scholarship with hereditary elitism. During the Cold War, the Myth and Symbol school that produced such works as Henry Nash Smith's *Virgin Land* (1951), R. W. B. Lewis's *American Adam* (1955), and Leo Marx's *The Machine in the Garden* (1964) used American literature in the service of American exceptionalism and to evidence the nation's cultural might and mission in the face of a perceived Soviet threat.[5] It may seem that the Myth and Symbol school and poststructuralism have little in common; the former seems unrepentantly and even sentimentally nationalistic, while the latter investigates the involvement of literary discourse in the construction and circulation of the conservative, oppressive nationalist ideologies that infused some Myth and Symbol works. However, both Cold War methodologies allowed literary academics, once again, to demonstrate their populist allegiances and to illustrate the power of literary study to heal wounds to the body politic. The social thrust of poststructuralism has trained

several generations of American critics to see their work as a politicized activity in which reading, writing, and teaching might better the
nation by exposing oppressive ideologies and training young citizens
to think critically about power and its abuses. While this agenda may
seem a far cry from the conciliatory and power-obsessed literary histories of the late nineteenth century, poststructuralism offered American literary scholars another possible means of pacifying widespread
anti-intellectualism by substantiating their stated identification with
the lowly and commitment to the national good. And one need hardly
bother to place the current revival of literary history in this disciplinary context, for its privileging of the social and political sources of the
literary text clearly identify another strategy of fulfilling the long-
standing nationalist obligations that American literary scholars have
had to fulfill.

The current lamentation of literary study's putative "irrelevance"
in the wake of poststructuralism's demise is yet another manifestation of this continuing disciplinary requirement. This cry of obsolescence derives in part from the participation of universities and literary curricula in various important political movements since the
1960s, and doubtless expresses nostalgia for those moments when
literary study contributed directly to national culture and politics,
whether in the theory-informed antiwar movement of the late 1960s
or the feminist movements of the 1970s and 1980s. But it is worth
asking, irrelevant to whom? Certainly not to us, we scholars of American literature, for we continue to read and take inspiration from each
other's work, attend conferences, subscribe to disciplinary discussion
groups, and collaborate. The oft-heard lamentation from within the
profession evidences the endurance of the belief that the work of
literature academics ought, somehow, to be useful beyond the borders
of the university, a requirement that profoundly shaped the literary
histories published in the late nineteenth century and that we have
clearly naturalized and absorbed. Most troubling, this claim of irrelevance registers a latent streak of anti-intellectualism in the literary
academy itself, as manifested in our own wariness of studying art for
its own sake and the belief that literary study must have wider social

applications to be of value. This century-old disciplinary obsession with "relevance" has been absorbed into the very fibers of the profession, as with the weighing of community service in promotion and tenure decisions as well as annual merit reviews. It is also apparent in the contraction of university presses, whose shrinking rosters now put a premium on works with crossover appeal—that is, books that are somehow "relevant" to general readers and make the academy look less like the aloof, elitist, and cloistered ivory tower that Americans have always accused it of being. In these very direct ways, literature academics are literally rewarded for reducing their participation in seemingly exclusionary disciplinary discourses and crafting their work with an eye to appealing to the wider populace.

The terrible irony, however, is that literature academics seem to have been caught in an irresolvable, Sisyphean struggle, for the more we comply with American anti-intellectualism, the more we are expected to. The many published expressions of outright anti-intellectual hostility upon the death of Jacques Derrida in 2004 bespeak the widespread expectation that the researches of literature scholars somehow be apprehensible to a lay public, and the subsequent outrage upon finding that often it is not. These expectations were partially created by the public intellectual movement of the postwar era, which saw the translation of academic expertise into language and media accessible to more sophisticated lay readers—and which, I would argue, constitutes yet another effort of literary scholars to combat public hostilities by assuming public pedagogic responsibilities. These expectations also derive from a lingering suspicion of abstruse, specialized literary discourse, which, according to Derrida's postmortem detractors, smacks of Old World, aristocratic, and therefore anti-American elitism, as well as an anti-intellectual disbelief in literary expertise altogether. One recently published history of Franco-American relations pronounced poststructuralism the product of an anti-American French conspiracy to hobble the nationalist responsibilities of American literature departments.[6]

The profession's use of poststructuralist and Marxist theory since the 1970s in the service of antielitist, populist sympathies has only caused the escalation of national suspicions of the literary academy and the increase in cries of irrelevance, albeit from the intellectual right wing.[7] The popularity and wide circulation of such works as Allan Bloom's *Closing of the American Mind* (1987), E. D. Hirsch's *Cultural Literacy* (1987), and Lynn Cheney's pamphlet *Defending Civilization* (2001) can be attributed to the enduring currency of the same conflicts that troubled late nineteenth-century literary historians: American anti-intellectualism and the permission of specialized literary study on the sole grounds that it serve as "producer, protector, and inculcator" of American culture.[8] For William Bennett, Allan Bloom, and others, the methodological changes and curricular revisions made under poststructuralism have rendered literary study irrelevant and directly hostile to their own definitions of national culture and citizenry. These recent curricular and disciplinary changes, though derived from the commitment to the public welfare and identification with the subaltern that have always served as de facto work visas for literature academics, have nonetheless armed conservatives in restoring the perception of literary work as innately un-American, claiming that literature departments are now irrelevant to their version of national culture, and causing the removal of the literary academy from its century-old patriotic responsibilities.[9] Sadly, our capitulation to American anti-intellectualism during the last century has steadily caused our further demotion in the nation's estimations.

It should be no surprise that the combination of recent scholarly interest in debating nationhood and its political ideologies, as well as renewed public suspicions about our loyalties altogether, have yielded a disciplinary interest in globalization. Globalization studies have contributed substantially to the recent revival of literary history with the publication of numerous important works—among them Anna Brickhouse's *Transamerican Literary Relations and the Nineteenth-Century Public Sphere* (2004), Brent Hayes Edwards's *The Practice of Diaspora: Literature, Translation, and the Rise of Black Internationalism* (2003), and Kirsten Gruesz's *Ambassadors of Culture: The Transamerican Origins of Latino Writing* (2002)—that have searched out the transnational vectors that failed to interest American literary historians in the field's first century. As if to herald this brand of scholarship as the next wave of the literary critical future, the first issue of the *PMLA* of the twenty-first century was titled "Globalizing Literary Studies" and included contributions by Stephen Greenblatt, Giles Gunn, and Edward Said. The current interest of literature scholars in globalization, however valuable and important a pursuit, rings of disciplinary opportunism. In his assertion that the "globalization of the academy . . . has positioned the literary scholar within a space for which the American empire serves as the horizon of future possibilities," Daniel O'Hara makes a similar claim, though I would temper this claim with a counterargument that the disciplinary preoccupation with globalization is yet another attempt to affirm the relevance of our work in a postnationalist age in which the paramount allegiance of our disciplinary forebears—the nation—has been complicated beyond restoration both intellectually and geopolitically.[10] Relieved of our nationalist responsibilities by the right wing and again perceived as essentially un-American in our leanings, we have turned to globalization studies to try, once more, to differentiate ourselves from a reprehensible and self-interested elite, and to reaffirm our political relevance and commitment to justice. Let's hope that this time our efforts will succeed.

However, history has shown that these attempts to pander to antiintellectualism succeed only in reifying these hostilities and enabling their survival. Our work will always be shaped by the circumstances—personal, disciplinary, professional, institutional—that surround it, and I am not suggesting that we should disavow the political aims of our work as teachers and scholars, for we must take seriously our responsibilities to our students in preparing them to think critically in a world where close reading and ideological scrutiny have never been more necessary or endangered. However, let us stop capitulating to the dual demands that we undergo aristocratic purity tests and make ourselves useful. Teaching our students to read, write, and think critically and with an eye to historical context is sufficient public service, and we must fervently believe that intellectual labor need not defend itself. Whether Marxism, postcolonialism, aesthetics, historicism, or formalism, let us do our work without guilt, apology, or justification.

Notes

1 For a chronicle of literary history in Europe before it found popularity in the United States, see David Perkins, *Is Literary History Possible?* (Baltimore: Johns Hopkins University Press, 1992), 29–51.

2 Robert Spiller, preface to *Literary History of the United States*, edited by Robert Spiller et al., vol. 1 (New York: Macmillan, 1948), vii.

3 See both preface and general introduction, *Columbia Literary History of the United States*, edited by Emory Elliott (New York: Columbia University Press, 1988), xi–xiv.

4 See, for example, Anna Brickhouse, *Transamerican Literary Relations and the Nineteenth-Century Public Sphere* (Cambridge: Cambridge University Press, 2004); Amy Kaplan, *The Anarchy of Empire in the Making of U.S. Culture* (Cambridge, Mass.: Harvard University Press, 2002); Laura Wexler, *Tender Violence: Domestic Visions in an Age of U.S. Imperialism* (Chapel Hill: University of North Carolina Press, 2000).

5 Corynne McSherry, *Who Owns Academic Work?: Battling for Control of Intellectual Property* (Cambridge, Mass.: Harvard University Press, 2001). See, too, Bill Readings, *The University in Ruins* (Cambridge, Mass.: Harvard University Press, 1996), 3.

6 Some works that contest the custom of tethering literary history to nation include Jonathan Arac, "What Is the History of Literature?," in *The Uses of Literary History*, edited by Marshall Brown (Durham, N.C.: Duke University Press, 1995); J. Hiller Miller, "Literary and Cultural Studies in the Transnational University," in *"Culture" and the Problem of the Disciplines*, edited by John Carlos Rowe (New York: Columbia University Press, 1998); Perkins, *Is Literary History Possible?*; Edward W. Said, "Globalizing Literary Study," *PMLA* 116 (January 2001): 64–68; Mario J. Valdés and Linda Hutcheon, *Rethinking Literary History—Comparatively* (New York: American Council of Learned Societies, 1994).

7 For trenchant criticism and more elaborate catalogs of these academic controversies, see Michael Bérubé and Cary Nelson, "Introduction," in *Higher Education Under Fire: Politics, Economics, and the Crisis of the Humanities*, edited by Bérubé and Nelson (New York: Routledge, 1995), 1–23;

Annette Kolodny, *Failing the Future: A Dean Looks at Higher Education in the Twenty-first Century* (Durham, N.C.: Duke University Press, 1998); Cary Nelson, *Manifesto of a Tenured Radical* (New York: New York University Press, 1997), 13–28, 153–70; Cary Nelson, ed., *Will Teach for Food: Academic Labor in Crisis* (Minneapolis: University of Minnesota Press, 1997); Richard Ohmann, *Politics of Knowledge: The Commercialization of the University, the Professions, and Print Culture* (Middletown, Conn.: Wesleyan University Press, 2003).

8   See Adam Begley, "The Tempest Around Stephen Greenblatt," *New York Times Magazine*, March 28, 1993, 201–6.

9   Numerous recent studies of intellectual property laws include Rosemary J. Coombe, *The Cultural Life of Intellectual Properties: Authorship, Appropriation, and the Law* (Durham, N.C.: Duke University Press, 1998); McSherry, *Who Owns Academic Work?*; Meredith L. McGill, *American Literature and the Culture of Reprinting, 1834–1853* (Philadelphia: University of Pennsylvania Press, 2003); Siva Vaidhyanathan, *Copyrights and Copywrongs: The Rise of Intellectual Property and How It Threatens Creativity* (New York: New York University Press, 2001).

10 Nelson, *Manifesto of a Tenured Radical*, 23.

11 June Howard, *Publishing the Family* (Durham N.C.: Duke University Press, 2001), 7.

12 Lora Romero, *Home Fronts: Domesticity and Its Critics in the Antebellum United States* (Durham, N.C.: Duke University Press, 1997), 50.

CHAPTER ONE

1   Julian Hawthorne and Leonard Lemmon, *American Literature: A Text-Book for the Use of Schools and Colleges* (Boston: Heath, 1892), iii. Leonard Lemmon, Hawthorne's coauthor, was a professional educator working at the time of the book's publication as the superintendent of city schools in Sherman, Texas.

2   See David R. Shumway, *Creating American Civilization: A Genealogy of American Literature as an Academic Discipline* (Minneapolis: University of Minnesota Press, 1994); and Kermit Vanderbilt, *American Literature and the Academy: The Roots, Growth, and Maturity of a Profession* (Philadelphia: University of Pennsylvania Press, 1986).

3   See Shumway, *Creating American Civilization*, 19, 25–60. See also Bill Read-

ings, *The University in Ruins* (Cambridge, Mass.: Harvard University Press, 1996), 1–20; David Perkins, *Is Literary History Possible?* (Baltimore: Johns Hopkins University Press, 1992), 6–7.

4   Howard Mumford Jones, *The Theory of American Literature* (Ithaca, N.Y.: Cornell University Press, 1966), 81–82. For a discussion of the effects of the centenary on the discipline of American history and on American culture in general, see Michael Kammen, *Mystic Chords of Memory: The Transformation of Tradition in American Culture* (New York: Knopf, 1991), 134–45. Another useful source attesting to the growth of American history at the turn of the century is Edward Channing, Albert Bushnell Hart, and Frederick Jackson Turner, *Guide to the Study and Reading of American History*, revised and enlarged (Boston: Ginn, 1912).

5   Alan Heimert, "Introduction," in *Cotton Mather the Puritan Priest*, by Barrett Wendell (New York: Harcourt, Brace, and World, 1963), xvi.

6   David Amigoni makes a similar argument in his history of Victorian biography, that "the emergence of the authoritative discipline of history in the nineteenth century was crucial in determining the subordinate space occupied by literature." David Amigoni, *Victorian Biography: Intellectuals and the Ordering of Discourse* (New York: St. Martin's, 1993), 3.

7   In his study of late nineteenth-century English literary criticism, Ian Small concurs that history served a similar function in legitimizing English literary studies. He writes, "Academic literary and art criticism tended to borrow from those other disciplines principles for validating its judgements and procedures: academic literary study also became historical—began to use literary history, that is—and thus began to use archival and empirical research. Literature was perceived as possessing a history which could be systematically described, and its texts could be scrutinized with the same rigour as the texts of theology or history." Ian Small, *Conditions for Criticism: Authority, Knowledge, and Literature in the Late Nineteenth Century* (Oxford: Clarendon, 1991), 57–58.

8   Peter Carafiol, *The American Ideal: Literary History as a Worldly Activity* (Oxford: Oxford University Press, 1991), 16.

9   Theodore Stanton, preface to *A Manual of American Literature*, edited by Stanton (New York: Putnam, 1909), v.

10 For an inquiry into the imperial roots of English literary study, see Gauri Viswanathan, *Masks of Conquest: Literary Study and British Rule in India* (New York: Columbia University Press, 1989).

11 Joan Shelley Rubin, *The Making of Middlebrow Culture* (Chapel Hill: University of North Carolina Press, 1992), 13.

12 For example, subscription salesmen hawking the eleven-volume *Library of American Literature* (1888–90) relied upon circulars mapping out a course of self-education in American literature. For a discussion of this turn-of-the-century vogue for self-education, see Rubin, *The Making of Middlebrow Culture*, 1–33.

13 Kammen, *Mystic Chords*, 145.

14 Ralph Waldo Emerson, "Thoreau," in *Selections from Ralph Waldo Emerson*, edited by Stephen E. Whicher (Boston: Houghton Mifflin, 1957), 393.

15 Scott Casper's discussion of the American Men of Letters series offers the definitive history of this series of author biographies. Scott E. Casper, *Constructing American Lives: Biography and Culture in Nineteenth-Century America* (Chapel Hill: University of North Carolina Press, 1999), 271–83.

16 Amigoni, *Victorian Biography*, 1.

17 Casper, *Constructing American Lives*, 277.

18 In his study of Victorian biography, Amigoni has argued that the genre of literary biography was central to what he has called the "ordering of discourse," the organization of disciplinary fields of knowledge and the consolidation of literary academic authority (Amigoni, *Victorian Biography*, 3). However, the American Men of Letters series, like the English Men of Letters series it was modeled after, was less attuned to pedagogical interests than to middle-class reader interests. That is not to say that literary history and literary biography were uninvolved in the establishment of literary academic authority, for they most certainly were, a matter I discuss at length in chapter 4, in my examination of professionalism.

19 This term is at the core of George Santayana's famous 1911 lecture "The Genteel Tradition in American Philosophy," in which he attacked the insularity of American intellectuals.

20 For a discussion of this internal conflict, see Michael Davitt Bell, *The Problem of American Realism: Studies in the Cultural History of a Literary Idea* (Chicago: University of Chicago Press, 1993); Amy Kaplan, *The Social Construction of American Realism* (Chicago: University of Chicago, 1989); Nancy Glazener, *Reading for Realism: The History of a U.S. Literary Institution, 1850–1910* (Durham, N.C.: Duke University Press, 1997).

21 William Dean Howells, *Selected Literary Criticism*, vol. 2, *1886–1897*, edited

by Christoph K. Lohmann and Donald Pizer (Bloomington: Indiana University, 1993), 45–46. This first appeared in *Harper's Monthly*, April 1887.

22 Ibid., 49–50. This first appeared in *Harper's Monthly*, June 1887.

23 For a discussion of the relationship between realism and anthropology, see Michael A. Elliott, *The Culture Concept: Writing and Difference in the Age of Realism* (Minneapolis: University of Minnesota Press, 2002).

24 Henry James, on the other hand, was markedly less sanguine. In a 1900 letter to Barrett Wendell in response to the publication of his *Literary History of America* that same year, James wrote, "I could have wished you a richer subject—for I think the history, 'American Literature' a poor one. I hate the very name (which I observe, however, you don't directly use). However there are doubtless responsive spots for you to sound with your knuckle—if your knuckle doesn't fear any—or too much—hollowness of answer." Henry James to Barrett Wendell, 10 December 1900, Barrett Wendell Collection, bMs Am 1784 (253), Houghton Library. By permission of the Houghton Library, Harvard University.

25 William Dean Howells to Brander Matthews, 3 May 1895, Brander Matthews Papers, Rare Book and Manuscript Library, Columbia University. Quoted by permission.

26 William Dean Howells, "Life and Letters," *Harper's Weekly*, 28 March 1896, 293.

27 Scott Casper has detected in the American Men of Letters series a decided antirealist bias in works such as Henry A. Beers's biography of Nathaniel Parker Willis, which "called for recognition of, if not return to, the earlier romanticism." Casper, *Constructing American Lives*, 288.

28 Edmund Clarence Stedman, *The Nature and Elements of Poetry* (Boston: Houghton Mifflin, 1892), viii–ix.

CHAPTER TWO

1 I am thinking here of Steven Conn, *History's Shadow: Native Americans and Historical Consciousness in the Nineteenth Century* (Chicago: University of Chicago Press, 2004); Philip J. Deloria, *Playing Indian* (New Haven, Conn.: Yale University Press, 1998); Michael A. Elliott, *The Culture Concept: Writing and Difference in the Age of Realism* (Minneapolis: University of Minnesota Press, 2003); Shari M. Huhndorf, *Going Native: Indians in the American*

Cultural Imagination (Ithaca, N.Y.: Cornell University Press, 2001); Alan Trachtenberg, *Shades of Hiawatha: Staging Indians, Making Americans, 1880–1930* (New York: Hill and Wang, 2004).

2 Some examples of realist texts that engage oral narration include George Washington Cable's *The Grandissimes* (1880); Harriet Beecher Stowe's "The Minister's Housekeeper" (1872); and Mark Twain's "Jim Smiley and His Jumping Frog" (1865) and "The Story of the Old Ram" (1872).

3 See David Shumway, *Creating American Civilization: A Genealogy of American Literature as an Academic Discipline* (Minneapolis: University of Minnesota Press, 1994), 18–21.

4 See Trachtenberg, *Staging Hiawatha*, 98–139.

5 See Jon Reyhner and Jeanne Eder, *American Indian Education: A History* (Norman: University of Oklahoma Press, 2004); Frederick E. Hoxie, *A Final Promise: The Campaign to Assimilate the Indians, 1880–1920* (Lincoln: University of Nebraska Press, 1984).

6 Lucy Maddox makes a similar argument about the literature of the 1820s and 1830s in *Removals: Nineteenth-Century American Literature and the Politics of Indian Affairs* (Oxford: Oxford University Press, 1991).

7 See, for example, Susanna Ashton's account of Matthews's life in *Collaborators in Literary America, 1870–1920* (New York: Palgrave, 2003), 91–126.

8 Matthews's celebrity and high visibility helped Columbia—its literature program in particular—garner public attention and acclaim. Harvard had long employed some of America's leading literary men—Longfellow and Lowell had both held the Smith professorship of modern languages—and used them to stake a public claim as a seat of learning. Columbia's publicity-savvy president Seth Low used Matthews's celebrity to compete with Harvard for prestige and celebrity. For example, in 1895 Matthews served as Columbia's representative in *Four American Universities*, a survey of four prominent universities—Harvard, Yale, Princeton, and Columbia—published by Harper's and appointed with expensive illustrations and fold-out surveys. Composed of extended profiles of each university written by a leading member of that community, the book relates each school's majors and courses of study, faculty credentials, endowments, and campus features and attractions. While it may today resemble nothing so much as promotional literature, the book heralded the commencement of the modern era of higher education, in which universities marketed themselves to compete for a relatively small applicant pool and remade themselves as

research institutions. Matthews's authorship of the chapter about Columbia, meanwhile, signaled at once his emerging role as Columbia's most recognizable and respected representative and the university's exploitation of his fame. Matthews's importance to Columbia was such that the institution took extreme measures to accommodate him. When Matthews's conflicts with the university's other prominent literary man, George Edward Woodberry, prevented their department from functioning altogether, President Low reorganized the Department of English and Rhetoric into two separate departments: Comparative Literature and English. Woodberry was named professor of comparative literature, and Matthews, professor of dramatic literature in the new Department of English. Though this reorganization was by no means the origin of the English department as we know it, the university's desire to accommodate Matthews led to the reorganization of literary study into a local institutional structure that still endures.

9   According to Susan Sheckel, the highly fictionalized story of Pocahontas and her romance with Captain John Smith found wide popularity in melodrama in the first half of the nineteenth century, particularly flourishing in the first quarter of the century. Susan Sheckel, *The Insistence of the Indian: Race and Nationalism in Nineteenth-Century American Culture* (Princeton, N.J.: Princeton University Press, 1998), 45.

10 Allen Staley, "Introduction," in Miriam and Ira D. Wallach Art Gallery, *Unfaded Pageant: Edwin Austin Abbey's Shakespearean Subjects* (New York: Columbia University Press, 1994), an exhibition catalog; Alan Shestack, "Introduction," in *Edwin Austin Abbey* (New Haven, Conn.: Yale University Art Gallery, 1974), an exhibition catalog.

11 This play was composed as a response to the criticisms of Molière's 1662 play *L'École des femmes*.

12 Brander Matthews, *These Many Years* (New York: Scribner's, 1917), 404.

13 In his study of nineteenth-century American biography, Scott Casper shows that portraits of notable American personalities had long served a similar role, though the anxieties caused by late-century immigration ratcheted up the need for such nationalizing pedagogical tools, especially for young readers. See Scott E. Casper, *Constructing American Lives: Biography and Culture in Nineteenth-Century America* (Chapel Hill: University of North Carolina Press, 1999), 4.

14 For a discussion of their long friendship, see Lawrence J. Oliver, *Brander Matthews, Theodore Roosevelt, and the Politics of American Literature, 1880–*

1920 (Knoxville: University of Tennessee Press, 1992); and Lawrence J. Oliver, ed., *The Letters of Theodore Roosevelt and Brander Matthews* (Knoxville: University of Tennessee Press, 1995).

15 For a more involved discussion of Roosevelt's literary interests and sponsorship, see Aviva F. Taubenfeld, "Rough Writing: Ethnic Authorship in the Age of Theodore Roosevelt" (Ph.D. diss., Columbia University, 2003).

16 Theodore Roosevelt, *The Spread of the English-Speaking Peoples*, vol. 1 of *Winning of the West* (New York: Putnam, 1889), 17.

17 Theodore Roosevelt, "An Introduction to American Literature," *Bookman*, February 1896, 519–21.

18 Theodore Roosevelt, "True Americanism," in his *American Ideals* (New York: Putnam, 1900), 66.

19 Hoxie, *A Final Promise*, 103–6.

20 Priscilla Wald, *Constituting Americans: Cultural Anxiety and Narrative Form* (Durham, N.C.: Duke University Press, 1995); John D. Kerkering, *The Poetics of National and Racial Identity in Nineteenth-Century American Literature* (Cambridge: Cambridge University Press, 2003).

21 Brander Matthews, *An Introduction to the Study of American Literature* (New York: American Book Company, 1896), 5. All subsequent page references will appear parenthetically.

22 Christopher Steiner offers a helpful discussion of the Western inclination to conflate Native cultures with antiquity, though his analysis is largely limited to visual representations of indigenous peoples. See Christopher B. Steiner, "Travel Engravings and the Construction of the Primitive," in *Prehistories of the Future: The Primitivist Project and the Culture of Modernism*, edited by Elazar Barkan and Ronald Bush (Stanford, Calif.: Stanford University Press, 1995), 202–25.

23 See Renée Bergland, *The National Uncanny: Indian Ghosts and American Subjects* (Hanover, N.H.: University Press of New England, 2000).

24 Brander Matthews, "The Centenary of Fenimore Cooper," *Century* 38 (September 1889): 796, 797.

25 A copy of Twain's essay is among Matthews's archived papers, as are occasional handwritten references to it among his notes.

26 In a letter clearly designed to recapitulate his 1895 essay, Twain in 1903 wrote to Matthews about Walter Scott, listing a series of questions that directly echoed the language he used to describe Scott's most famous imitator, Cooper. For example, he inquired, "Has [Scott] personages whose

acts and talk correspond with their characters as described by him?" Mark Twain to Brander Matthews, 4 May 1903, Brander Matthews Papers, Rare Book and Manuscript Library, Columbia University. Quoted by permission.

27 Oliver, *Brander Matthews*, 104.

28 Mark Twain, "Fenimore Cooper's Literary Offenses," in *Selected American Prose, 1841–1900: The Realistic Movement*, edited by Wallace Stegner (New York: Holt, Rinehart, 1964), 330. All subsequent citations will be included parenthetically.

29 For examples of similar rhetoric among realist tracts, see William Dean Howells's "Criticism and Fiction," in which he maintains that "literature and art are . . . but the expression of life, and are to be judged by . . . [no] other test than that of their fidelity to it." William Dean Howells, "Criticism and Fiction," in his *Selected Literary Criticism*, vol. 2, *1886–1897*, edited by Christoph K. Lohmann and Donald Pizer (Bloomington: Indiana University Press, 1993), 300.

30 The year before, this poem was reprinted in *Hero Tales from American History*, coauthored by Henry Cabot Lodge and Theodore Roosevelt, a book that, like Matthews's literary history, was designed for younger readers and used stories of important figures in the American past to educate readers in American character. Henry Cabot Lodge and Theodore Roosevelt, *Hero Tales from American History* (New York: Century, 1895).

31 Oliver Wendell Holmes, "Francis Parkman," in *The Complete Poetical Works of Oliver Wendell Holmes* (Boston: Houghton Mifflin, 1923), 298–99.

32 Matthews began teaching at Columbia out of financial necessity when it became clear in the 1880s that his playwriting and criticism would not provide sufficient income.

33 Brander Matthews, *Tom Paulding: The Story of a Search for Buried Treasure in the Streets of New York* (New York: Century, 1892), 2. All subsequent citations will be included parenthetically.

34 Philip Deloria has argued that "Indianness . . . offered proto-Americans a platform for imagining and performing an identity of revolution," a dynamic that may account for the repetitive cycles of history included in *Tom Paulding*. See Deloria, *Playing Indian*, 14.

35 The engineer was imagined as an agent of modernity, bringing technology and improvements to all aspects of daily life. As such, the engineer was popularly regarded as indispensable to and a symbol of American global expansion. Under the rhetoric of modernization and progress, American

globalization was imagined as a beneficent influence abetting the spread of civilization abroad and enveloped by the glamour of exploration; the engineer was construed as a servant of that progress, who, in bringing the American business interests of mining and drilling, brought American-style progress to underdeveloped countries. See Cecelia Tichi, *Shifting Gears: Technology, Literature, Culture in Modernist America* (Chapel Hill: University of North Carolina Press, 1987), 97–132.

36 Philip Deloria offers a useful discussion of the enduring American equation of Native peoples with children. See Deloria, *Playing Indian*, 106–7.

37 Matthews's 1905 correspondence with a literary agent in the hopes of placing the play suggests that this play was composed after Matthews was hired at Columbia in 1891 and had established a national reputation as a public intellectual and university professor. Paul Reynolds to Brander Matthews, 18 May 1905 and 23 May 1905, Brander Matthews Papers, Rare Book and Manuscript Library, Columbia University. Quoted by permission.

38 Matthews's correspondence from Jessop communicates only that Jessop, as the professional playwright of the pair, typically traveled with their productions, while Matthews, an employed professor, remained in New York. However, extant typescripts and manuscripts suggest that Matthews played the more decisive, dominant role in the writing component of their collaboration, as his handwriting alone appears in the notes and margins of drafts. Later versions of these plays incorporate Matthews's comments, and it is clear, at the very least, that his suggestions were treated as law. Matthews's name always appears before Jessop's in manuscripts and printed versions of their plays, an arrangement counter to alphabetical order. While this ordering may simply derive from Matthews's greater celebrity and denote an agreed-upon strategy to attract attention for their work, the sequence of their names may also document an agreement between both parties that Matthews would play the more important role in the authorship of these plays. In her recent study of literary collaboration, Susanna Ashton discusses Matthews's avid and wide-ranging collaborative efforts, though she does not substantively deal with the precise nature of his work with Jessop. See Susanna Ashton, *Collaborators in Literary America*, 91–126. Of all of Matthews's plays and collaborative works with Jessop and others, *A Gold Mine* (1908) is the one play to have a presence, however slight, in theatrical and literary history, primarily because of its unflattering appearance in Dreiser's *Sister Carrie* (1900) as one of the plays that

sparks Carrie's theatrical imagination. Nancy Warner Barrineau, "Brander Matthews," in *American Literary Critics and Scholars, 1880–1900*, vol. 71 of *Dictionary of Literary Biography* (Detroit: Gale Research, 1988), 153–62.

39 Brander Matthews and George H. Jessop, "High Spirits: A Farce in One Act" (n.d.), 6. Brander Matthews Papers, Rare Book and Manuscript Library, Columbia University. Quoted by permission. All subsequent citations will be included parenthetically.

40 In an early draft of the play, Matthews edited out an exchange in which Redding asks Black Hawk, played by Modockawando, whether George Washington is "present" with him in the afterworld, an exchange that again situates the text within the context of early American history. Brander Matthews and George H. Jessop, "Mr. Lo: A Farce in One Act" (n.d.), 45. Brander Matthews Papers, Rare Book and Manuscript Library, Columbia University. Quoted by permission.

41 This plot outline was scribbled on the back of a receipt dated 6 June 1882; however, the actual date of this plot summary remains indeterminate and cannot be definitely traced to the dated receipt; an inveterate note-taker, Matthews habitually recycled scrap paper. Brander Matthews, undated note, Brander Matthews Papers, Rare Book and Manuscript Library, Columbia University. Quoted by permission.

42 Brander Matthews, undated note, Brander Matthews Papers, box 23, file 4, Rare Book and Manuscript Library, Columbia University. Quoted by permission.

43 This nickname derives from a line from Alexander Pope's "Essay on Man": "Lo, the poor Indian! whose untutored mind / Sees God in clouds, or hears him in the wind." "Lo" was a common nickname for Native peoples in the nineteenth century. I am grateful to Michael Elliott for glossing this for me.

44 See Michael A. Elliott, "Coyote Comes to the *Norton*: Indigenous Oral Narrative and American Literary History," *American Literature* 75 (December 2003): 723–49.

CHAPTER THREE

1 Vernon Parrington, *The Beginnings of Critical Realism in America, 1860–1920*, vol. 3 of *Main Currents in American Thought* (New York: Harcourt, Brace, 1930), 4. Of Parrington's pervasive influence, Lionel Trilling wrote in 1953: "His ideas are now the accepted ones wherever the college course in Amer-

ican literature is given by a teacher who conceives himself to be opposed to the genteel and the academic and in alliance with the vigorous and the actual." Lionel Trilling, "Reality in America," in his *The Liberal Imagination: Essays on Literature and Society* (New York: Anchor, 1953), 1.

2 Parrington, *Beginnings of Critical Realism*, 86.

3 Many texts rework or build upon the foundation of Parrington's argument; classic examples include William Charvat, *The Profession of Authorship in America, 1800–1870: The Papers of William Charvat*, edited by Matthew J. Bruccoli (New York: Columbia University Press, 1992); Lewis P. Simpson, *The Man of Letters in New England and the South: Essays on the History of the Literary Vocation in America* (Baton Rouge: Louisiana State University Press, 1973); and Robert E. Spiller et al., *Literary History of the United States* (New York: Macmillan, 1948).

4 William Dean Howells, "Criticism and Fiction," in his *Selected Literary Criticism*, vol. 2, *1886–1897*, edited by Christoph K. Lohmann and Donald Pizer (Bloomington: Indiana University Press, 1993), 300. Howells's essay was originally published in *Harper's Monthly*, May 1886. For critical analyses of realism, see, for example, Michael Davitt Bell, *The Problem of American Realism: Studies in the Cultural History of a Literary Idea* (Chicago: University of Chicago Press, 1993); Nancy Glazener, *Reading for Realism: The History of a U.S. Literary Institution, 1850–1910* (Durham, N.C.: Duke University Press, 1997); and Amy Kaplan, *The Social Construction of American Realism* (Chicago: University of Chicago Press, 1988).

5 In its reliance on associative geography, this qualitative periodization of the American nineteenth century oversimplifies the literary climates in both halves of the century, and the bifurcation itself misrepresents the actual dispersion of literary culture. Casting the aristocrat as the central literary figure before the Civil War fails to consider the degree to which many writers before Twain—Emerson, Hawthorne, Thoreau, Whitman— revolted as early as the 1830s against the dominance of a hereditary literary class that displayed its pedigree with devotion to European letters. Placing pedigreed men at the center of power in the antebellum era similarly obscures the many prominent women authors whose writings challenged the prerogatives of privilege. Also passed over are the many antebellum writers who remained popular and productive far beyond the temporal limits assigned to them, yet this periodized narrative would have us believe that the rise of self-made writers without formal education, such as

Mark Twain, was concomitant with the convenient disappearance of their predecessors.

6   Howells, "Stevenson's and Hawthorne's Romances; Balzac; Realism," in his *Selected Literary Criticism*, 2:300.

7   See "The Author's Rights," *New York Times*, 9 January 1888, 8.

8   See John William Tebbel, *The Expansion of an Industry, 1865–1919*, vol. 2 of *A History of Book Publishing in the United States* (New York: Bowker, 1975), 640.

9   See, for example, the editorial in *Journal of the International Typographical Union of North America*, 15 January 1890, 9.

10   J. W. De Forest, "A Novelist's Opinion of Copyright," *New York Times*, 24 February 1884.

11   Charles Dudley Warner, letter to the editor, *New York Times*, 13 January 1884; reprinted in *Publishers Weekly*, 19 January 1884, 60–61.

12   Washington Gladden, "Open Letters," *Century*, July 1888, 474.

13   Roger Sherman, *International Copyright. An Open Letter* (Philadelphia: Sherman, 1884), 4.

14   Henry Van Dyke, *The National Sin of Literary Piracy* (New York: Scribner's, 1888), 12.

15   See Michael Newbury, *Figuring Authorship in Antebellum America* (Stanford, Calif.: Stanford University Press, 1997).

16   John Jay, *International Copyright: Memorials of John Jay and of William C. Bryant and Others, in Favor of an International Copyright Law* (Washington: Tippin and Streeper, 1848), 2.

17   Thomas R. Lounsbury, *James Fenimore Cooper* (1882; reprint, Detroit: Gale Research, 1968), 166.

18   See letters to the editor, *New-York Tribune*, 18 and 25 February 1884 and 8 March 1884.

19   Brander Matthews, "Open Letters," *Century*, July 1885, 488; quoted in Aubert J. Clark, *The Movement for International Copyright in Nineteenth-Century America* (Washington: Catholic University of America Press, 1960), 148.

20   George Haven Putnam, preface to *The Question of Copyright. A Summary of the Copyright Laws at Present in Force in the Chief Countries in the World*, edited by Putnam (New York: Putnam, 1891), viii.

21   Putnam's inclusion of Irving's plight as literary historical evidence of the wrongs of copyright infringement is complicated by Putnam's involvement as plaintiff in a high-profile lawsuit, *Putnam v. Pollard*, in which he,

as Irving's long-time publisher, challenged a reprinting of Irving's works without the consent of Irving's nieces. In telling this story of Irving's thwarted legacy, Putnam attempts to defuse accusations of self-interest by turning to the literary past, but substantiates those charges by exposing the motives that underlay both his support of copyright and his account of literary history.

22 "Speech of S. Irenaeus Prime," in *International Copyright: Meeting of Authors and Publishers, at the Rooms of the New York Historical Society, April 9, 1868, and the Organization of the International Copyright Association* (New York: International Copyright Association, 1868), 18.

23 Ibid.

24 Quoted in Brander Matthews, *American Authors and British Pirates* (New York: American Copyright League, 1889), 14–15. Matthews here paraphrases comments Lowell made in a speech in England in the 1880s.

25 F. A. P. Barnard, "Open Letters," *Century*, February 1886, 628.

26 Brander Matthews, "Copyright Property," *New York Times*, 28 August 1890.

27 Brander Matthews, "The Evolution of Copyright," in *The Question of Copyright*, 15.

28 Samuel L. Clemens, *A Connecticut Yankee in King Arthur's Court* (New York: Norton, 1982), 44. For a recent study of Twain's involvement in the copyright movement, see Siva Vaidhyanathan, *Copyrights and Copywrongs: The Rise of Intellectual Property and How It Threatens Creativity* (New York: New York University Press, 2001), 35–80.

29 According to Tebbel, Trollope was instructed by the British Foreign Office to work on behalf of copyright. Tebbel, *Expansion of an Industry*, 2:634.

30 See James J. Barnes, *Authors, Publishers, and Politicians: The Quest for an Anglo-American Copyright Agreement, 1815–1854* (Columbus: Ohio State University Press, 1974), 74.

31 Matthew Arnold, "Doing as One Likes," in *Culture and Anarchy*, edited by Samuel Lipman (New Haven, Conn.: Yale University Press, 1994), 56. For realist admirers of Arnold, see John Henry Raleigh, *Matthew Arnold and American Culture* (Berkeley: University of California Press, 1961), 82–83.

32 Arnold, preface to *Culture and Anarchy*, 5.

33 Although Arnold was an avowed copyright supporter, his vision of universal copyright granted upon publication failed to take into consideration the demands of the American book industry. He was thus interpreted as hostile to American labor. Responding to Arnold's 1880 essay "Copyright,"

the *New York Times* invoked his inattention to labor to claim that Arnold "has no sympathy with the American cry, 'free books for free men.'" In a faulty leap of logic, Arnold's indifference to labor was interpreted as evidence of both social and literary elitism (*New York Times*, 20 March 1880; reprinted in *Publishers Weekly*, 27 March 1880, 335).

34 See Raleigh, *Matthew Arnold*, 59. Martin T. Buinicki has recently documented Whitman's complicated position on international copyright, astutely attending to the ways in which Whitman's antiaristocratic sentiments figured prominently in both his reception of Arnold and the literary debate that he represented. Martin T. Buinicki, "Walt Whitman and the Question of Copyright," *American Literary History* 15 (Summer 2003): 248–75.

35 Arnold, "Doing as One Likes," quoted in Raleigh, *Matthew Arnold*, 57.

36 Matthew Arnold, "A Word About America," in *Philistinism in England and America*, vol. 10 of *The Complete Prose Works of Matthew Arnold*, edited by R. H. Super (Ann Arbor: University of Michigan Press, 1974), 5.

37 Arnold gave this lecture many times during his 1883–84 tour of the United States; see Arnold, "Emerson," *Macmillan's Magazine*, May 1884, 1–13.

38 James B. Fry, "Mr. Matthew Arnold on America," *North American Review*, May 1885, 515–19; quoted in Raleigh, *Matthew Arnold*, 78.

39 Ibid.; quoted in Raleigh, *Matthew Arnold*, 77.

40 Twain, speech to the annual reunion of Connecticut's Army and Navy Club, 27 April 1887; see Matthew Arnold, *General Grant*, edited by John Y. Simon (Carbondale: University of Southern Illinois Press, 1966).

41 See H. C. Allen, *The Anglo-American Relationship since 1783* (London: Adam and Charles Black, 1959), 69.

42 W. E. Simonds, "International Copyright," in *The Question of Copyright*, edited by Putnam, 133.

43 Lyman Abbott, "Open Letters," *Century*, February 1886, 627; Henry Holt, quoted in Simonds, "International Copyright," 137.

44 Henry Holt, "Plain Talk to a Professed Pirate," *Critic*, 10 April 1886, 185.

45 Mark Twain, "Open Letters," *Century*, February 1886, 634. This letter was reprinted in *Publishers Weekly* in January 1888 and was issued as a pamphlet by the American Copyright League.

46 Brander Matthews, *Cheap Books and Good Books* (New York: American Copyright League, 1888), 6.

47 Van Dyke, "National Sin," 18.

48 Lowell used both these terms in correspondence with William Dean Howells at the beginning of Howells's career in the 1860s; see Lowell to Howells, 5 July 1868 and 22 September 1869, William Dean Howells Collection,
bMs Am 1784 (301), Houghton Library. By permission of the Houghton
Library, Harvard University.

49 James Russell Lowell to William Dean Howells, 2 November 1865, William
Dean Howells Collection, bMs Am 1784 (301), Houghton Library. By permission of the Houghton Library, Harvard University.

50 Proceedings of an 1888 dinner given by the British Society of Authors in
honor of numerous American guests suggest the success of this mission.
Lowell was roundly toasted and honored by gathered luminaries, including Walter Besant, Wilkie Collins, Edmund Gosse, and Oscar Wilde. *Report
of the Proceedings at the Dinner Given by the Society of Authors to American
Men and Women of Letters at the Criterion Restaurant on Wednesday, July 25,
1888* (London: Society of Authors, 1888).

51 Lowell testified before the Senate Committee on Patents on 29 January
1886. His quatrain was published in *Century*, May 1886, 161–62.

52 See Howells, *Selected Literary Criticism*, 2:96–97. These comments originally appeared in "Editor's Study," *Harper's Monthly*, July 1888.

53 James Russell Lowell, "On a Certain Condescension in Foreigners," in
Lowell's Prose Works, vol. 3 of *The Writings of James Russell Lowell* (Cambridge, Mass.: Riverside Press, 1890), 241–42.

54 Clarence Gohdes, *American Literature in Nineteenth-Century England* (Carbondale: Southern Illinois University Press, 1944), 3.

55 George Haven Putnam, "International Copyright," in *A Library of American
Literature from the Earliest Settlement to the Present Time*, edited by Edmund
C. Stedman and Ellen M. Hutchinson (New York: Charles Webster, 1888),
11:304.

56 In her study of antebellum literary piracy and reprinting, Meredith L.
McGill examines the frequent use of slavery as a metaphor for piracy
among pre–Civil War copyright activists. Meredith L. McGill, *American
Literature and the Culture of Reprinting, 1834–1853* (Philadelphia: University
of Pennsylvania Press, 2003), 4.

57 For a transcript of Lowell's address, see *Critic*, 3 December 1887, 282; see
also William Dean Howells, "Editor's Study," *Harper's Monthly*, October
1887, 804.

58 This metaphor was also deployed by British writers incensed by American

piracy, and slavery offered them a vehicle by which they pointed to the moral imperfections of American culture. For example, in 1889, the British critic and writer George Moore responded to Putnam's claims of innocence with a salient analogy: "America does not yet stand within the morals of civilization; to give up slave trading and to continue to pirate English books is equivalent to saying, 'I will not break into houses, but I must stand at the street corner and pick pockets'" *Athenaeum*, 12 January 1889.

59 Matthews, "American Authors," 206–7.

60 See "International Copyright," *Critic* 18 (1891): 213–14.

61 Ibid.

CHAPTER FOUR

1 This configuration of professionalism is drawn from the following sources: Andrew Abbott, *The System of Professions: An Essay on the Division of Expert Labor* (Chicago: University of Chicago Press, 1988); Svante Beckman, "Professionalization: Borderline Authority and Autonomy in Work," in *Professions in Theory and History: Rethinking the Study of Professions*, edited by Michael Burrage and Rolf Torstendahl (London: Sage, 1990), 115–38; Burton Bledstein, *The Culture of Professionalism: The Middle Class and the Development of Higher Education in America* (New York: Norton, 1976), 80–88; W. Bruce Fye, *The Development of American Physiology: Scientific Medicine in the Nineteenth Century* (Baltimore: Johns Hopkins University Press, 1987), 168–69; Ian Small, *Conditions for Criticism: Authority, Knowledge, and Literature in the Late Nineteenth Century* (Oxford: Clarendon, 1991), 19–28; Thomas Strychacz, *Modernism, Mass Culture, and Professionalism* (Cambridge: Cambridge University Press, 1993); William J. Reader, *Professional Men: The Rise of the Professional Classes in Nineteenth-Century England* (London: Weidenfeld and Nicolson, 1966); Francesca Sawaya, *Modern Women, Modern Work: Domesticity, Professionalism, and American Writing, 1880–1950* (Philadelphia: University of Pennsylvania Press, 2004); John Thomas, *Alternative America: Henry George, Edward Bellamy, Henry Demarest Lloyd and the Adversary Tradition* (Cambridge, Mass.: Belknap Press of Harvard University Press, 1983), 47–48; Michael Warner, "Professionalism and the Rewards of Literature: 1875–1900," *Criticism* 27 (Winter 1985): 13; Anne Witz, *Professions and Patriarchy* (London: Routledge, 1992).

2 See Charles Johanningsmeier, *Fiction and the American Literary Marketplace:*

The Role of the Newspaper Syndicates, 1860–1900 (Cambridge: Cambridge University Press, 1997); Michael Schudson, *Discovering the News: A Social History of American Newspapers* (New York: Basic Books, 1978); and Christopher P. Wilson, *The Labor of Words: Literary Professionalism in the Progressive Era* (Athens: University of Georgia Press, 1985).

3   Numerous critics have examined the history of this belief in Anglo-American letters. Terry Eagleton traces it from its origins in the English eighteenth century to its apotheosis in the nineteenth century. According to Eagleton, the rise of curatorial literary criticism indeed derives from the opening of numerous markets, including literary ones: "As capitalist society develops and market forces come increasingly to determine the destiny of literary products, it is no longer possible to assume that 'taste' and 'cultivation' are the fruits of civilized dialogue and reasonable debate [as he asserts they had been in the English eighteenth century]. Cultural determinations are now clearly being set from elsewhere" (Terry Eagleton, *The Function of Criticism: From* The Spectator *to Post-Structuralism* [London: Verso, 1984], 34). In his study of Victorian biography, David Amigoni offers a different theory in his examination of the British institutional and discursive conditions that led to a similar belief among mid-to-late-century British literary intellectuals. According to Amigoni, the British attachment to this belief may have been due to the religious moorings of many academic positions, such as the requirement that holders of some humanities chairs and fellowships be Church of England clergy. In this case, institutional policy required literary expertise to be bundled together with moral stewardship, a combination that Howells reanimated in the American late century. See David Amigoni, *Victorian Biography: Intellectuals and the Ordering of Discourse* (New York: St. Martin's, 1993), 120–57.

4   William Dean Howells, *Selected Literary Criticism*, vol. 2, edited by Christoph K. Lohmann and Donald Pizer (Bloomington: Indiana University Press, 1993), 180. This essay was originally published in *Harper's Monthly*, August 1891.

5   Nancy Glazener has examined the ways in which the realist formulation of professionalism took particular aim at female readers and their perceived faults. See Nancy Glazener, *Reading for Realism: The History of a U.S. Literary Institution, 1850–1910* (Durham, N.C.: Duke University Press, 1997), 93–146.

6   Howells, *Selected Literary Criticism*, 2:344.

7   Ian Small, citing the research of Bernard Barber, emphasizes the symbiotic relationship between universities and professionalism, as professionalism offers legitimacy to intellectual labor while universities offer formal institutional structures by which professions can train initiates and oversee disciplinary standards. (Small, *Conditions for Criticism*, 21–22.) Thomas Strychacz has also commented helpfully on the centrality of the university to professionalization. See Strychacz, *Modernism, Mass Culture, and Professionalism*, 23.

8   Gerald Graff, *Professing Literature: An Institutional History* (Chicago: University of Chicago Press, 1987); Elizabeth Renker, "Resistance and Change: The Rise of American Literature Studies," *American Literature* 64 (June 1992): 347–65.

9   See Bliss Perry, *And Gladly Teach: Reminiscences* (Boston: Houghton Mifflin, 1935).

10 For example, Barrett Wendell and Bliss Perry both lamented the difficulties of professional advancement without a doctorate, though both were eventually promoted.

11 Barrett Wendell to Edmund Clarence Stedman, 7 January 1892, Edmund Clarence Stedman Papers, Rare Book and Manuscript Library, Columbia University. Quoted by permission.

12 See "Introduction," in *Columbia Literary History of the United States*, edited by Emory Eliott (New York: Columbia University Press, 1988), xx–xxiii. Also, a recent special issue of *American Literature* dedicated to "Aesthetics and the End(s) of American Cultural Studies" sought to redress the current skepticism about literary aesthetics, widely perceived as an agent of the social conservatism associated with New Criticism's aesthetic formalism. See *American Literature* 76 (September 2004).

13 Terry Eagleton's description of the untenable position of late-century English academic men of letters is helpful here. He writes, "Either criticism strives to justify itself at the bar of public opinion by maintaining a general humanistic responsibility for the culture as a whole, the amateurism of which will prove increasingly incapacitating as a bourgeois society develops; or it converts itself into a species of technological expertise, thereby establishing its professional legitimacy at the cost of renouncing a wider social relevance" (Eagleton, *Function of Criticism*, 56–57).

14 Charles F. Richardson, *American Literature 1607–1885*, vol. 2 (New York: Putnam, 1891), 3.

15 Several sources are particularly helpful in recounting the events surrounding this review. See Rachel Cohen, "The Very Bad Review," *The New Yorker*, October 6, 2003, 52–67; Small, *Conditions for Criticism*, 58–61; Ann Thwaite, *Edmund Gosse: A Literary Landscape 1849–1928* (London: Secker and Warburg, 1984), 277–97.

16 John Churton Collins, Review, "English Literature at the Universities," *The Quarterly Review* (July–October 1886), 289. All subsequent citations will be included parenthetically.

17 According to Ian Small, "Gosse's claims to possess a critical and scholarly authority turned out on inspection to be counterfeit." Small, *Conditions for Criticism*, 60.

18 Thwaite, *Edmund Gosse*, 280.

19 Quoted in ibid.

20 William Dean Howells to Edmund Gosse, 7 November 1886, in *Transatlantic Dialogue: Selected American Correspondence of Edmund Gosse*, edited by Paul F. Matthiesen and Michael Millgate (Austin: University of Texas Press, 1965), 193.

21 Higginson occupied the role of fact checker and historical conscience for aspiring literary historians at the turn of the century. Brander Matthews's archives evidence that he sent the manuscript of his 1896 literary history to Higginson, who returned a long letter itemizing errors and disagreements. Higginson's supervisory role was literalized in his appointment to Harvard's Board of Overseers in 1896 to oversee the English department in particular. An 1898 letter from Wendell to Charles Eliot communicates that the formal teaching of American literary history began at Harvard at the urging of Higginson; Wendell wrote that its introduction, "among many other desirable things will greatly gratify Colonel Higginson, who, as visitor, has been disposed to complain that we neglect American matters." Barrett Wendell to Charles W. Eliot, 28 October 1898, Charles W. Eliot Collection, HUG 1876, general folder, courtesy of Harvard University Archives.

22 Thwaite, *Edmund Gosse*, 278.

23 William Dean Howells to Edmund C. Stedman, 23 November 1894, Edmund Clarence Stedman Papers, Rare Book and Manuscript Library, Columbia University. Quoted by permission.

24 Small, *Conditions for Criticism*, 61.

25 In fact, the two reviews were further united by Gosse's sympathetic letter to Stedman in response to Howells's review. Gosse wrote, "I am fully with you in your argument, urged as you would naturally urge it, with every grace and courtesy, against a foe worthy of your steel. Why should criticism ever pass out of this delightful atmosphere?" Edmund Gosse to Edmund C. Stedman, 19 November 1886, reprinted in Laura Stedman and George M. Gould, *Life and Letters of Edmund Clarence Stedman*, vol. 2 (New York: Moffat, Yard, 1910), 167.

26 William Dean Howells, "Editor's Study," *Harper's Monthly*, March 1886, 647.

27 William Dean Howells, "A Hundred Years of American Verse," *North American Review*, January 1901, 148–60.

28 Edmund C. Stedman, *The Nature and Elements of Poetry* (Boston: Houghton Mifflin, 1892), 297.

29 The biography of Stedman authored by his granddaughter, Laura Stedman Gould, mentions the flurry of correspondence he received amid the controversy. Stedman and Gould, *Life and Letters of Edmund Stedman*, 2:167–68.

30 Thomas Wentworth Higginson and Henry Walcott Boynton, *A Reader's History of American Literature* (Boston: Houghton Mifflin, 1903), 5. This volume is based on a series of lectures Higginson gave at the Lowell Institute in 1903.

31 For discussions of the British history of this belief, see Amigoni, *Victorian Biography*, 137–42; Jacqueline Pearson, *Women's Reading in Britain 1750–1835: A Dangerous Recreation* (Cambridge: Cambridge University Press, 1999), 196–218. For discussion of the American attachment to this belief, see Michael Davitt Bell, *The Problem of American Realism: Studies in the Cultural History of a Literary Idea* (Chicago: University of Chicago Press, 1993), 167–75; Glazener, *Reading for Realism*, 93–146.

32 William Dean Howells, "A Modern Instance," in *William Dean Howells: Novels 1875–1886* (New York: Library of America, 1982), 414.

33 Fred Louis Pattee, *A History of American Literature since 1870* (New York: Silver, Burdett, 1896), 231.

34 William Dean Howells, "Diversions of the Higher Journalist," *Harper's Weekly* 42 (1903), 1184.

35 David Amigoni has described this practice as the "cult of exemplarity," in

which biography serves as a synecdoche or minute replica of the subject's own historical moment. Amigoni, *Victorian Biography*, 1.

36 Joan von Mehren, *Minerva and the Muse: A Life of Margaret Fuller* (Amherst: University of Massachusetts Press, 1994), 217.

37 From Scott Casper's study of nineteenth-century American biography, it is clear that the Duyckincks' biographical emphasis comports with the larger culture of biography—and literary biography—of the midcentury. This particular product of that period, however, exerted considerable influence on later treatments of Fuller's life and work. Scott E. Casper, *Constructing American Lives: Biography and Culture in Nineteenth-Century America* (Chapel Hill: University of North Carolina Press, 1999), esp. 202–56.

38 Evert A. Duyckinck and George L. Duyckinck, *Cyclopaedia of American Literature*, vol. 2 (New York: Scribner's, 1855), 524.

39 Though Higginson's 1884 biography of Fuller, published in the American Men of Letters series, differs markedly from contemporaneous literary histories in its affectionate handling of Fuller, it is clear that his biography was designed to set the historical record straight and to rehabilitate her already waning reputation. Higginson's biography was by no means an anomaly in late-century literary history, but instead figures as a point-by-point rebuttal to stories circulating about Fuller. In so doing, however, he recapitulated the distinguishing features of her stock biography: the damage caused by her famously expansive education; her social awkwardness and inattention to her appearance; and the ignominy of her marriage. See Thomas Wentworth Higginson, *Margaret Fuller Ossoli* (Boston: Houghton Mifflin, 1884).

40 Brenda Wineapple's recent biography of Hawthorne discusses at length his conflicted relationship with Fuller. See Brenda Wineapple, *Hawthorne: A Life* (New York: Knopf, 2003), 151–54, 194–95.

41 Henry James, *Hawthorne* (Ithaca, N.Y.: Cornell University Press, 1963), 62.

42 Ibid.

43 Margaret Fuller's "Conversations" between 1839 and 1844 went largely untranscribed, though a record does exist of several conversations held in early 1841, documented by the activist and educational reformer Caroline Healey Dall. It is generally agreed, however, that these recorded sessions in 1841 were by no means typical, not only because they admitted men but also because they included figures such as Ralph Waldo Emerson, whose strong participation famously altered the dynamics of sessions that were

usually single-sex. For a fuller discussion, see Annette Kolodny, "Inventing a Feminist Discourse: Rhetoric and Resistance in Margaret Fuller's *Woman in the Nineteenth Century*," in *Nineteenth-Century American Women Writers*, edited by Karen L. Kilcup (Oxford: Blackwell, 1998), 214–15.

44 For a discussion of female talk, see Caroline Levander, *Voices of the Nation: Women and Public Speech in Nineteenth-Century American Literature and Culture* (Cambridge: Cambridge University Press, 1998).

45 Pattee, *History*, 232.

46 Her memoirs were edited and published posthumously in 1859 and then reissued in 1874, amid the interest in literary history. Margaret Fuller Ossoli, *Memoirs of Margaret Fuller Ossoli*, edited by R. W. Emerson, W. H. Channing, and J. F. Clarke (reprint, Boston: Roberts Brothers, 1874), 15.

47 Parrington, *Main Currents*, 2:428.

48 Fuller herself may have been the originary author of the belief that her education had been responsible for her untimely death. In her memoirs, the reissue of which in 1874 may have contributed directly to the narrative of her life that emerged in literary histories, Fuller observed that her education had "wasted [her] constitution, and will bring . . . a premature death" (Fuller, *Memoirs*, 15). Regardless of the provenance of this belief, literary historians deployed it to substantiate their own labor.

49 Barrett Wendell, *A Literary History of America* (New York: Scribner's, 1900), 300.

50 Howells, "What Should Girls Read?," *Harper's Bazar*, November 1902, 957.

51 William Dean Howells, "Diversions of the Higher Journalist," 1184. The book reviewed is *Love-Letters of Margaret Fuller, 1845–1846* (New York: Appleton, 1903). The collection also included an introduction by Julia Ward Howe and reprinted reminiscences by Emerson and Greeley, among others. The man in question here is James Nathan, who later changed his name to Gotendorf. A German businessman with whom Fuller conducted an affair for several months in 1845–46, Nathan refused to return the letters after Fuller's death and contributed a preface to their publication. For a fuller discussion of this episode, as well as the controversy surrounding the publication of these highly expurgated letters, see von Mehren, *Minerva and the Muse*, 206–14.

52 Howells, *Criticism and Fiction*, 2:344.

53 Howells, "Diversions of the Higher Journalist," 1184.

1 Both David Shumway and Kermit Vanderbilt agree that the celebration of antebellum Boston began with Wendell's literary history. See David R. Shumway, *Creating American Civilization: A Genealogy of American Literature as an Academic Discipline* (Minneapolis: University of Minnesota Press, 1994), 75; Kermit Vanderbilt, *American Literature and the Academy: The Roots, Growth, and Maturity of a Profession* (Philadelphia: University of Pennsylvania Press, 1986), 143–45.

2 Though he encountered considerable resistance in literary circles, Wendell was not alone in his efforts to appoint New England as the apotheosis of national achievement. David Noble has recounted the ascendancy of New England as a national symbol in *Death of a Nation: American Culture and the End of Exceptionalism* (Minneapolis: University of Minnesota Press, 2002), 129–50. Steven Nissenbaum has charted the steady progress of efforts in numerous political venues throughout the nineteenth century to position New England as a synecdoche of the nation as a whole. See Steven Nissenbaum, "New England as Region and Nation," in *All Over the Map: Rethinking American Regions* (Baltimore: Johns Hopkins University Press, 1996), 38–61.

3 Lora Romero has a useful discussion of Hawthorne's literary ascent in the context of twentieth-century modernist opinion. See Lora Romero, "Homosocial Romance: Hawthorne," in her *Home Fronts: Domesticity and Its Critics in the Antebellum United States* (Durham, N.C.: Duke University Press, 1997).

4 Several sources are particularly helpful on this point. See Van Wyck Brooks, *New England: Indian Summer 1865–1915* (New York: Dutton, 1940), 409, 425–33; Henry F. May, *The End of American Innocence: A Study of the First Years of Our Own Time 1912–1917* (London: Jonathan Cape, 1959).

5 Barrett Wendell, lectures (1904–5), Barrett Wendell Collection, HUG. 1876.54, courtesy of Harvard University Archives.

6 Charles W. Eliot to Barrett Wendell, 27 June 1907, Barrett Wendell Collection, bMs Am 1907.1 (406), Houghton Library. By permission of the Houghton Library, Harvard University.

7 Barrett Wendell, "Recollections of Harvard (1872–1917)," Barrett Wendell Collection, HUG 1876.10, courtesy of Harvard University Archives.

8 In his study of Eliot's tenure at Harvard, Hugh Hawkins cites the dismissal

of the popular professor Charles Townsend Copeland because of insufficient publication as evidence of the increasingly stringent publication standards during the later years of Eliot's presidency. See Hugh Hawkins, *Between Harvard and America: The Educational Leadership of Charles W. Eliot* (New York: Oxford University Press, 1972), 108. For Wendell's suspicions, see Robert Self, *Barrett Wendell* (Boston: Twayne, 1975), 34.

9   Barrett Wendell, lecture notes, Barrett Wendell Collection, HUG 1876.54.3, courtesy of Harvard University Archives; Wendell, "Our National Superstition," in his *The Privileged Classes* (New York: Scribner's, 1908), 149.

10 Alan Heimert, "Introduction," in *Cotton Mather the Puritan Priest*, by Barrett Wendell (New York: Harcourt, Brace, and World, 1963), vii.

11 Wendell, *Cotton Mather*, 3.

12 He wrote in 1893, "At this moment, very often, I feel a certain regret that I had not the fortune to be born fifty years earlier. Then I could eagerly have joined in the expression of faith in the future which made New England literature promise something. Now I find my temper doubtful, reactionary. Such moods as mine are not things that literature demands." Quoted in Van Wyck Brooks, *New England: Indian Summer*, 425.

13 Barrett Wendell, *Stelligeri and Other Essays Concerning America* (New York: Scribner's, 1893), 11.

14 Barrett Wendell, *English Composition: Eight Lectures Given at the Lowell Institute* (New York: Scribner's, 1899), 68–69.

15 Ibid., 69.

16 Wendell had been among the ranks of Republicans who defected the party in protest of James G. Blaine's nomination and became Mugwumps. Thus, the novel generated some controversy when it was published, in large part because of Wendell's public position on the election. See Self, *Barrett Wendell*, 25–26.

17 Brooks, *New England: Indian Summer*, 409, 429.

18 Wendell, *Cotton Mather*, 3.

19 It needs to be stated that this was by no means an unusual tactic in the period. Nina Baym has correctly observed the frequency with which Poe and Whitman became targets of turn-of-the-century literary historians visibly uncomfortable with the unsavory details of their biographies and unable to engage literature outside the context of authorial biography. See Nina Baym, "Early Histories of American Literature: A Chapter in the Institution of New England," *American Literary History* 1 (Fall 1989): 459–88.

20 Barrett Wendell, *Literary History of America* (New York: Scribner's, 1900), 230. Other critics acknowledged Wendell as the first purveyor of this term. For example, in his own literary history Thomas Wentworth Higginson both used the term and cited Wendell as its source. See Thomas Wentworth Higginson and Henry Walcott Boynton, *A Reader's History of American Literature* (Boston: Houghton Mifflin, 1903), 109.

21 Wendell, *Literary History*, 462.

22 William Dean Howells, "Criticism and Fiction," in *William Dean Howells: Selected Literary Criticism*, vol. 2, *1886–1897*, edited by Christoph K. Lohmann and Donald Pizer (Bloomington: Indiana University Press, 1993), 301.

23 Ibid., 353, 331.

24 Ibid., 353.

25 Ibid., 353–54.

26 William Dean Howells, "Professor Barrett Wendell's Notions of American Literature," *North American Review*, April 1901, 623. All subsequent page references will be included parenthetically.

27 Wendell, *Literary History*, 337.

28 Barrett Wendell to William Dean Howells, 11 July 1887, William Dean Howells Collection, bMs Am 1784 (531), Houghton Library. By permission of the Houghton Library, Harvard University.

29 William Dean Howells to Barrett Wendell, 17 July 1887, Barrett Wendell Collection, bMs Am 1784 (100), Houghton Library. By permission of the Houghton Library, Harvard University.

30 Barrett Wendell to William Dean Howells, 10 June 1890, William Dean Howells Collection, bMs Am 1784 (531), Houghton Library. By permission of the Houghton Library, Harvard University.

31 The evidence suggests that Howells did not reply. He retained typed copies of the bulk of his correspondence, and no version—typed or handwritten— can be found among either Wendell's or Howells's papers. Moreover, Wendell seems to have kept all of Howells's letters, including their accompanying envelopes, a habit that communicates the importance of this particular correspondence.

32 Barrett Wendell to William Dean Howells, 11 July 1887, William Dean Howells Collection, bMs Am 1784 (531), Houghton Library. By permission of the Houghton Library, Harvard University.

33 Ibid.

34 Howells's biographer Kenneth Lynn attended to the tidy correspondences between Howells and this recurring character. Kenneth Schuyler Lynn, *William Dean Howells: An American Life* (New York: Harcourt Brace Jovanovich, 1971), 8–10.

35 William Dean Howells, *The Shadow of a Dream, and an Imperative Duty*, edited by Martha Banta, Ronald Gottesman, and David J. Nordloh (Bloomington: Indiana University Press, 1970), 18.

36 William Dean Howells, "Turgenev's Novel of Russian Life," in his *Selected Literary Criticism*, vol. 1, *1859–1885*, edited by Ulrich Halfmann et al. (Bloomington: Indiana University Press, 1993), 207. This review was first published in the *Atlantic Monthly* in July 1873.

37 Barrett Wendell to William Dean Howells, 16 April 1897, William Dean Howells Collection, bMs Am 1784 (531), Houghton Library. By permission of the Houghton Library, Harvard University.

38 William Dean Howells, *The Landlord at Lion's Head* (New York: Harper & Bros., 1911), 201.

39 Barrett Wendell to Laura Stedman Gould, 28 January 1909, Edmund Clarence Stedman Papers, Rare Book and Manuscript Library, Columbia University. Quoted by permission. In preparing a volume of her late grandfather's correspondence, Gould solicited copies of Stedman's correspondence with Wendell.

40 Barrett Wendell to Charles W. Eliot, 15 January 1901, Charles W. Eliot Collection, UA.I.5.150, box 110, folder 141, courtesy of Harvard University Archives.

41 Wendell, *Literary History*, 154.

42 Ibid., 462.

43 Barrett Wendell and Chester Noyes Greenough, *A History of Literature in America* (New York: Scribner's, 1911), 396.

44 Ibid., 396–97.

45 Barrett Wendell, lecture XXII, 7 February 1905, Barrett Wendell Collection, HUG 1876.54, courtesy of Harvard University Archives.

46 Heimert, "Introduction," xv.

47 Quoted in Hawkins, *Between Harvard and America*, 94. This quotation comes from Eliot's 1895 address "Experience with a College Elective System."

48 Charles W. Eliot to Barrett Wendell, 24 August 1899, Barrett Wendell Collection, bMs Am 1907.1 (406), Houghton Library. By permission of the Houghton Library, Harvard University.

49 Samuel Eliot Morison, "Introduction," in *The Development of Harvard University since the Inauguration of President Eliot, 1869–1929*, edited by Morison (Cambridge, Mass.: Harvard University Press, 1930), xiv; Elliott Perkins, "The Origins of History and Literature," audiotape of lecture, Cambridge, Mass., 1986.

50 Morison, "Introduction," xlv–xlvi.

51 Perkins, *Origins of History and Literature*.

52 Quoted in Self, *Barrett Wendell*, 72.

53 William Dean Howells to Barrett Wendell, 11 September 1914, Barrett Wendell Collection, bMs Am 1784 (100), Houghton Library. By permission of the Houghton Library, Harvard University.

54 Barrett Wendell to William Dean Howells, 13 September 1914, William Dean Howells Collection, bMs Am 1784 (531), Houghton Library. By permission of the Houghton Library, Harvard University.

55 William Dean Howells to Barrett Wendell, 14 September 1914, William Dean Howells Collection, bMs Am 1784 (100), Houghton Library. By permission of the Houghton Library, Harvard University.

56 Barrett Wendell to Hamlin Garland, 25 March 1917. Garland included this letter in a folio of letters and telegrams in Howells's honor. William Dean Howells Collection, bMs Am 1784.4 (116), Houghton Library. By permission of the Houghton Library, Harvard University.

57 William Dean Howells to Barrett Wendell, Barrett Wendell Collection, bMs Am 1784 (100), Houghton Library. By permission of the Houghton Library, Harvard University.

58 Ellen Mackay Hutchinson to Edmund C. Stedman, n.d. 1887, Edmund Clarence Stedman Papers, Rare Book and Manuscript Library, Columbia University. Quoted by permission.

59 Fred Lewis Pattee, "Call for a Literary Historian," *American Mercury*, June 1924, 134.

60 Wendell and Greenough, *A History of Literature in America*, 390.

61 Robert Self offers a useful list of some of Wendell's more famous students. Self, *Barrett Wendell*, 9.

62 Richard Poirier has made a similar observation about the conservative use that American academics have made of Emerson, remarking that "Anglo-

American criticism has in large part striven to perpetuate the cultural traditions which Emerson chose to write against." Richard Poirier, "The Question of Genius," *Raritan* 5 (Spring 1986): 97.

EPILOGUE

1 Sacvan Bercovitch, "Preface," in *Reconstructing American Literary History*, edited by Bercovitch (Cambridge, Mass.: Harvard University Press, 1986), vii.

2 Bill Readings, *The University in Ruins* (Cambridge, Mass.: Harvard University Press, 1996), 3. See also David Perkins, *Is Literary History Possible?* (Baltimore: Johns Hopkins University Press, 1992), 6–7.

3 See Linda Hutcheon, "Interventionist Literary Histories: Nostalgic, Pragmatic, or Utopian?," *Modern Language Quarterly* 59 (December 1998): 402.

4 For a discussion of the nationalizing valences of postwar literature and criticism, see David W. Noble, *Death of a Nation: American Culture and the End of Exceptionalism* (Minneapolis: University of Minnesota Press, 2002), 129–50.

5 Michael A. Elliott and Claudia Stokes, "Introduction: What Is Method and Why Does It Matter?," in *American Literary Studies: A Methodological Reader*, edited by Elliott and Stokes (New York: New York University Press, 2003), 6; John Carlos Rowe, "Introduction," in *Post-Nationalist American Studies*, edited by Rowe (Berkeley: University of California Press, 2000), 5.

6 John J. Miller and Mark Molesky, *Our Oldest Enemy: A History of America's Disastrous Relationship with France* (New York: Doubleday, 2004).

7 J. Hillis Miller has argued that the recent struggles of literature departments derive from a deliberate strategy to weaken and delegitimize the politically insubordinate work of those departments. In contesting the government, power, corporations, and globalization, we indirectly contribute to our own minoritization. J. Hillis Miller, "Literary and Cultural Studies in the Transnational University," in *"Culture" and the Problem of Disciplines*, edited by John Carlos Rowe (New York: Columbia University Press, 1998), 52–53.

8 Readings, *University in Ruins*, 3.

9 This book offers a different take on the alienation of the university—and its fractal-like synecdoche, literature—than Bill Readings or J. Hillis Miller,

who attribute the decline of the university to the conclusion of the Cold War and the replacement of the university with other vehicles such as Hollywood and the media to affirm American cultural importance. According to Miller, "'Society'... no longer needs higher education in the way it once did—that is, to transmit national cultural values. . . . The work of ideological indoctrination and training . . . can be done more effectively by the media, newspapers and magazines, radio talk shows, and television and cinema" (Miller, "Literary and Cultural Studies," 53). While I agree with these arguments, I also see the decline of the university and the English department within the long-standing bargain the profession has made, promising to do community service in exchange for permission to conduct research. See also Readings, *University in Ruins*, 44–53.

10 Daniel T. O'Hara, *Empire Burlesque: The Fate of Critical Culture in Global American* (Durham, N.C.: Duke University Press, 2003), ix.

Index

Abbey, Edward Austin, 37

Abbot, Lyman, 95

Adams, Henry, 42

Aesthetics, 27–32, 34, 49–50, 55–56, 57–59, 107, 149, 155, 158, 193; and American literary history, 77–78; as benchmark of professionalism, 109–10, 115–19, 151; absorption into American literary history, 109–10, 115–19, 199 (n. 27); 213 (n. 12). *See also* Literary idealism; Literary realism

African American literature, 19, 33, 34

Alcott, Louisa May, 24

Aldrich, Thomas Bailey, 180

Amateurism, 110; perceived dangers of, 113, 114–15, 117, 213 (n. 13), 214 (n. 17); Edmund Stedman's advocacy of, 117–18

American Book Company (publishing house), 42, 44

American character: instruction in, 20, 34, 42–43, 203 (n. 30)

American Civil War, 24, 77, 78, 79, 93, 98–100, 146, 154, 173, 206–7 (n. 5)

American Copyright League, 79, 80, 85, 98, 101

American exceptionalism, 46, 189. *See also* Nationalism

American Indians. *See* Native Americans

American literary history: turn-of-the-century rise of, 1, 3–6, 11–12, 17–18, 20–21, 23, 190, 197 (n. 4); generic formation of, 1, 7, 10, 11–14, 19, 26, 34, 35, 110, 118–19, 126, 139, 140; diversity of, 1, 18–19, 26, 141; in twentieth century, 1–2, 187–90, 193; and immigration, 3, 12, 20, 23, 34–35, 42–43, 45–46, 62, 201 (n. 13); and nationalism, 3, 20, 23, 34–36, 37, 42–46, 56, 59, 73, 187, 188–90, 201 (n. 13), 203 (n. 30); similarity of, in nineteenth and twentieth centuries, 3, 187, 188; revival of interest in, during late twentieth century, 3–6, 11–12, 190; and intellectual labor, 4, 6, 11, 12–13, 77–78, 104, 139; on literary labor, 4, 11; role of history in, 5–6, 57–59, 62, 64–65, 177–80, 197 (nn. 5, 7); emergence as academic discipline, 7, 17, 197 (n. 7); legacy of late-century work in, 7–8, 12, 13–14, 19, 32, 187; omission of Native narratives from, 10, 12, 33–34, 40, 49, 59–61, 74; of antebellum era, 10, 13–14, 96, 139–41, 151–53, 154, 157–58, 163, 183–86; and professionalism, 13, 104–5, 107–10, 113–15, 118, 119–20, 124, 132, 135–37, 138, 158, 170–72; hallmarks of professionalism in, 13, 107, 109–10, 119, 139; influence of Barrett Wendell on, 13–14, 139–42, 152, 174, 177–80, 183–86; teaching of, in American colleges and universities, 17, 19, 34–35, 36, 140, 177–80, 214 (n. 21); and European literary history, 19, 22–23, 26, 195 (n. 1); African American literature in, 19, 33, 34; teaching of, in primary and secondary schools, 19, 35, 41, 55, 140, 171–72; and New York, 20, 146, 150, 153–54, 161, 163; and retrospection, 20, 23–24, 29, 46–47; and centenary celebrations of late century, 20–21, 22, 24, 197 (n. 4); as index of American culture, 21; and self-education, 24, 27, 42, 117–18; elegiac quality of, 24–25, 46, 47, 59; and generational demise, 24–25, 98, 180–81; individualistic thrust of, 26; mediation between expertise and popularity in, 26–27, 144; and aesthetics, 26–32, 33, 49–50, 52, 54–56, 57–59, 77–78, 91, 115–19, 162, 209–10; marketing of, 27, 35, 42, 140, 198 (n. 12); reader preferences in, 27, 198 (n. 18); and literary idealism, 27–28, 31–32; and literary realism, 27–32, 33, 49–50, 52, 53–56, 57–59, 77–78, 91, 162; influence of William Dean Howells on, 30, 105–6, 115–23; controversies in, 32, 110–19, 139–40, 215 (n. 29); oral narration in, 33–34, 200 (n. 2); allure of, 37; engagement with political history in, 40, 43–44, 48, 59–61, 64–65, 66, 73, 77–78, 152; and international copyright, 78–79, 82–85, 86–87, 93–94, 98, 104, 119–20; as form of literary criticism, 109–10, 115–18; quality control of, 112, 114–15, 116–17; centrality of Thomas Wentworth Higginson in, 114, 214

(n. 21); written by nonacademics, 118; treatment of women in, 123, 124, 125–28, 129–30, 131, 132–33; treatment of Margaret Fuller in, 123–37; influence of Harvard on, 183–86

American Literary History, 5

American Medical Association, 103. *See also* Professional organizations

American Men of Letters series, 22–23, 25–27, 30, 198 (n. 15), 216 (n. 39)

American South, 98–100; literary histories of, 18

Amigoni, David, 197 (n. 5), 198 (n. 18), 212 (n. 3), 215–16 (n. 35)

Anglo-American literary relations, 13, 22–23; amid international copyright movement, 85, 88–89, 90–93, 94–96, 97, 100, 151, 152

Anglophilia, 13, 92, 143, 151, 152, 156, 171. *See also* Aristocratic sympathies

Antebellum era, 10, 13, 14, 125; Barrett Wendell on, 13–14, 78, 87, 97, 98, 146, 148, 151–53, 154, 173–74, 184, 219 (n. 12); and periodization of nineteenth century, 77–78, 206–7 (n. 5); and international copyright movement, 82, 87, 97. *See also* New England antebellum literature

Anthologies of American literature, 18, 19, 21, 23, 27, 31, 34, 74, 115–16. See also *Cyclopaedia of American Literature*; *Library of American Literature*

Anti-aristocratic sentiment, 13; and American literary history, 77, 124,

157, 191; and international copyright, 80, 84, 87, 89–90, 91, 92, 94–95, 98–101, 209 (n. 34). *See also* Anglophilia; Aristocratic sympathies

Anti-intellectualism, American, 8, 12–13, 80, 91–92, 94, 187, 190–92, 193

Antiquity, Western, 39, 47–48, 202 (n. 22)

Anthropology, 29, 33

Antony, Mark, 48

Arac, Jonathan, 187

Aristocratic sympathies, 12–13, 85, 87, 89, 95–96, 98–99, 140, 147–48, 151, 152, 155, 157, 168; and antebellum literature, 87–88, 93–94, 206 (n. 5); and presumed beliefs of Matthew Arnold, 91–92, 98–99; at turn of the twenty-first century, 187, 191, 193. *See also* Anglophilia; Elitism; Pedigree; Tastes in literature

Arnold, Matthew, 112, 208–9 (n. 33); tour of U.S., 90–93, 209 (n. 37); missteps of, 91–93; and American Civil War, 98–99

Ashton, Susanna, 204 (n. 38)

Assimilation: and education, 6, 34–35, 37, 40–41; of immigrants, 23, 34–35, 42–43, 45–46; of Native peoples, 34–35, 37, 39–41, 45–46, 64, 67, 69; and American literary history, 35, 37, 42–46; and international copyright, 96, 101

Athens, Greece, 39, 47

Atlantic Monthly, 33, 36, 81, 151, 154

Austen, Jane, 120

Author biographies, 1, 18, 22–23, 25–26, 50, 111, 125, 173, 197 (n. 5), 198 (n. 18); exemplary nature of, 26, 42, 125, 210 (n. 13), 215–16 (n. 35), 216 (n. 37); of Poe and Whitman, 219 (n. 19). *See also* American Men of Letters series; English Men of Letters series

Bacon, Francis, 101

Bancroft, George, 57

Barnard, F. A. P., 89

Bates, Katherine, 183

Baym, Nina, 219 (n. 19)

Bay Psalm Book, 110

Beers, Henry A., 21, 123, 199 (n. 27)

Bell, Michael Davitt, 77

Bennett, William, 192

Bercovitch, Sacvan, 187–88

Bergland, Renée, 49

Besant, Walter, 210 (n. 50)

Black Hawk, 71, 205 (n. 40)

Blaine, James G., 219 (n. 16)

Bloggers, 104

Bloom, Allan, 192

Boas, Franz, 33

Bookman, 43

Boston, Mass. *See* New England; New England antebellum literature

Boston Gazette, 118

Bowker, R. R., 79

Boyhood, 65, 204 (n. 34)

Boys' books, 61, 62

Boy Scouts of America, 62

Bradstreet, Anne, 124

Brickhouse, Anna, 192

British Guiana, 66

British Society of Authors, 210 (n. 50)

Brooks, Van Wyck, 1, 28, 149, 156, 181, 184

Brown, Charles Brockden, 151

Brown, John, 99

Bryant, William Cullen, 25, 42, 151

Buinicki, Martin T., 209 (n. 34)

Bulwer-Lytton, Edward George, 166

Butler, Nicholas Murray, 144

Cable, George Washington, 50, 200 (n. 2)

Calvin, John, 150

Cambridge, Mass., 173, 181

Cambridge History of American Literature, 1, 18, 36

Cambridge University, 111, 112

Carey, Henry, 96

Carpenter, George Rice, 20

Casper, Scott E., 198 (n. 15), 199 (n. 27), 201 (n. 13), 216 (n. 37)

Centenary of American Revolution (1876), 20–21, 22; and American literary history, 20–22, 25, 110, 197 (n. 4)

Century (magazine), 50, 79, 97

Cervantes, Miguel de, 120, 131

Chautauqua movement, 42. *See also* Education; Self-education

Channing, William Ellery, 153

Charvat, William, 77

Cheney, Lynn, 192

Cherbuliez, Victor, 166

Class: and authorship, 11, 12–13, 14, 47–48, 77–78, 86, 97; tensions surrounding, 11, 80, 139; and international copyright movement, 80, 81–82, 84, 88–90, 94, 104; and peri-

odization of nineteenth century, 80–82, 140; and professionalism, 105; and Barrett Wendell, 145, 147–48, 152–53, 155, 157, 158, 162, 168–69. *See also* Intellectual labor; Literary labor

Clark, Aubert, 96

Clemens, Samuel L. *See* Twain, Mark

Cold War, 189, 223–24 (n. 9)

Collection of British Authors series, 23. *See also* Tauchnitz edition

Collins, John Churton, 111–13, 114–15; review by, 111–12; as guardian of professionalism, 112–15; career of, 113

Collins, Wilkie, 210 (n. 50)

Columbia History of American Literature, 2, 109

Columbia University, 12, 13, 22, 29, 30, 31, 32, 35, 37, 39, 53, 62, 89, 108, 144; centrality to late-century production of American literary history, 20, 36; and celebrity of Brander Matthews, 36, 144, 200–201 (n. 8); Brander Matthews Dramatic Museum, 40; in *Tom Paulding* (Matthews), 61, 62–63; building of, 63, 65; School of Mines, 65; competition with Harvard, 200–201 (n. 8)

Columbus, Christopher, 40–41

Constitution (U.S.), ratification of, 21

Cooper, James Fenimore, 25, 29, 51; as proto-realist, 50, 52, 56; faults of, 50, 53–55, 56–57; portraits of Native Americans by, 50–51, 54–55; Brander Matthews on, 50–54, 56–

59, 70; Mark Twain on, 53–54; and international copyright, 83, 85, 86

Copyright reform. *See* International copyright movement

Cornell University, 82

Critic, The, 112, 118

Culture wars, 5, 7, 191–92

Curtis, Natalie Burlin, 33

Cyclopaedia of American Literature (Duyckinck), 21; on Margaret Fuller, 21, 125–28, 130, 131; influence of, 125; historiographical methods of, 126. *See also* Duyckinck, Evert and George

Dall, Caroline Healey, 216 (n. 43)

Dartmouth College, 82

Dawes Severalty Act (1887), 34

De Forest, J. W., 81

Democracy, 77, 80, 90, 92, 95, 101, 148–49

Derrida, Jacques, 191

Dial, 132

Dickens, Charles, 90–91, 166

Dimock, Wai Chee, 187

Doresey, George, 33

Dorsheimer, William, 81

Drama, 36, 39, 40, 67–68, 70, 108, 201 (n. 9), 204 (n. 38). *See also* Theater

Dreiser, Theodore, 204–5 (n. 38)

Duyckinck, Evert and George: on Margaret Fuller, 21, 125–28, 130, 131; influence on American literary history, 125; historiographical methods of, 126. See also *Cyclopaedia of American Literature*

Eagleton, Terry, 212 (n. 3), 213 (n. 13)

Edinburgh Review, 21

Education, 34–35, 36, 37, 40–41, 42, 168; self-education, 24, 27, 42, 117–18, 198 (n. 12), 206–7 (n. 5); and Native Americans, 34–36, 37, 71; and assimilation, 61, 62, 63–65, 67, 70, 72–73, 203 (n. 30); of professionals, 103; of professors, 107–8; of Margaret Fuller, 126–27, 131–34

Edwards, Brent Hayes, 192

Edwards, Jonathan, 7, 151

Eliot, Charles W., 24, 218–19 (n. 8); and Barrett Wendell, 108, 144, 170–71, 173, 175–77, 214 (n. 21); elective system of, 175, 177

Eliot, Samuel, 176

Elitism, 91, 187; and American literary history, 39, 77, 87, 155; and professionalism, 103, 105; and Barrett Wendell, 145, 147–48, 151, 152, 153, 154, 157, 160, 161, 169, 174, 176; and Ralph Waldo Emerson, 185–86; as current problem for intellectuals, 187, 189, 191; and Matthew Arnold, 208–9 (n. 33). *See also* Aristocratic sympathies; Pedigree; Populism: in literature

Elliott, Emory, 109

Elliott, Michael A., 74

Emerson, Ralph Waldo, 24, 25, 26, 31, 78, 91, 93, 151, 153, 156; and Margaret Fuller, 124, 125, 128, 216–17 (n. 43), 217 (n. 51); as status symbol, 185–86, 222–23 (n. 62); and periodization of nineteenth century, 206–7 (n. 5)

Engineering, 65, 66, 67, 69, 72–73, 104

English, study of: nationalist function of, 3–4, 187–93; in crisis, 4–6, 13, 190–93; social roles of, 5–6, 188–93; legitimation by history, 22, 197 (n. 5)

English departments: curricula of, 5, 174–75, 192; of Columbia University, 12, 20, 35, 36, 108, 200–201 (n. 8); creation of, 188–89, 200–201 (n. 8); of Harvard University, 214 (n. 21)

English Men of Letters series, 23

English professors, 26; nationalist responsibilities of, 3–4, 187–93; in twentieth-century crisis, 4–6, 191–93; professionalization of, 104, 107–9, 118, 144–45, 218–19 (n. 8), 223–24 (n. 9); professionalized, 107; graduate training of, 107, 108, 213 (n. 10); pre-professional hiring of, 107, 112–13, 158, 203 (n. 33), 212 (n. 3); belletristic, 107, 145; in England, 112, 213 (n. 13); anti-intellectualism of, 190–91. See also Expertise; Philology; Specialization; Universities

Erskine, John, 36

Eulogies and memorials: in American literary history, 24–25, 46, 47, 59–61, 180–81

Expertise: in scholarship, 26–27, 53, 107, 108, 112, 114–15, 116–17, 144, 176, 178, 212 (n. 3), 213 (n. 13); and professionalism, 105, 191. See also Specialization

Female readers: perceived dangers to, 105, 121, 133–34, 135, 212 (n. 5); William Dean Howells on, 105–6, 116; supervision of, 105–6, 121–22, 134–35; professionalist protections of, 105–6, 121–22, 212 (n. 5). See also Readers

Female writers: in American literary history, 109, 123–24, 128. See also Fuller, Margaret

Feminist scholarship, 12, 123, 190

Feuillet, Octave, 166

Fireside Poets, 97, 142. See also Holmes, Oliver Wendell; Long-fellow, Henry Wadsworth; Lowell, James Russell; Whittier, John Greenleaf

Five Points, N.Y., 52

Franklin, Benjamin, 7, 42

Fry, Gen.a2oJames, 93

Fuller, Margaret, 12, 13; and professionalism, 13, 132, 133, 134, 136; treatment of, in American literary history, 123, 124, 125–28, 129–30, 131, 132–33 216 (n. 39); biography of, 123, 124–25, 126, 129–30, 131, 132–33; and William Dean Howells, 123, 127, 133; rumors about, 124; and Timothy Fuller (father), 124; works as discussed in American literary history, 124; and Ralph Waldo Emerson, 124, 125, 128, 216–17 (n. 43), 217 (n. 51); Fred Louis Pattee on, 124, 131; death of, 125; in *Cyclopaedia of American Literature*, 125–28; education of, 126–27, 131–34; personality of, 127, 128; as liter-

ary critic, 127, 128, 130; Henry
James on, 128–31, 132; cult of, 129,
130–31; salon conversations of, 130,
132, 216–17 (n. 43); as conversa-
tionalist, 130–31, 136; as threat to
professionalism, 132; memoirs of,
133, 217 (nn. 46, 48); sexuality of,
133–34, 135–37; love letters of, 135–
37, 217 (n. 51). See also *Cylopaedia
of American Literature*; Duyckinck,
Evert and George; Female writers:
in American literary history
Fuller, Timothy, 124, 126, 131, 134–35

Garland, Hamlin, 11, 24, 29, 33, 43,
183, 222 (n. 56)
Genius, 116, 117, 130, 166
Genteel tradition, 28, 198 (n. 19)
Gilder, Richard Watson, 79, 97
Gladden, Washington, 81
Gladstone, William, 112
Glazener, Nancy, 77, 212 (n. 5)
Globalization, 192–93, 203–4 (n. 35)
Gohdes, Clarence, 100
Gosse, Edmund, 110, 115, 176, 210
(n. 50); and William Dean
Howells, 111, 112, 113–14, 215
(n. 25); career of, 111, 112–13
—*From Shakespeare to Pope*, 110–12;
dedication to William Dean
Howells, 111; history of, 111; faults
of, 111–12; review of, 111–12, 114;
scandal of, 111–13, 214 (n. 17)
Gould, Laura Stedman, 169, 215
(n. 29), 221 (n. 39)
Grant, Ulysses S., 93, 98–99
Greeley, Horace, 127

Greenblatt, Stephen, 193
Greenough, Chester Noyes, 170, 184
Gruesz, Kristen, 192
Gunn, Giles, 193

Harper's, 18, 36, 42, 87, 135, 180; book
publications of, 18, 28, 200 (n. 8);
William Dean Howells's columns
for, 28–29, 77, 105, 111, 115, 135, 156,
206 (n. 4)
Harris, Joel Chandler, 33
Harte, Bret, 50
Harvard Classics series, 24
Harvard University, 13, 69–70, 72, 97,
107, 108, 143, 145, 218–19 (n. 8); and
Barrett Wendell, 108, 140, 144–45,
146, 149, 162, 167, 168, 170, 183, 214
(n. 21); as center of American
scholarship, 140, 177, 200 (n. 8);
institutional loyalty to, 145; curriculum of, 174–75, 177–80; elective
system of, 175, 177; History and Literature program of, 177–80, 185;
influence on American literary history, 183–86; famous graduates of,
184–85
Harvey, Col. George, 180
Hawthorne, Julian, 14, 17, 18, 118, 123
Hawthorne, Nathaniel, 25, 31, 81, 85,
128, 142, 151, 206–7 (n. 5), 218 (n. 3)
Heart of Oak Books series, 23
Heimert, Alan, 22, 145, 185
Higginson, Thomas Wentworth, 1, 18,
92, 119, 220 (n. 20); as expert in
American literary history, 114, 214
(n. 21); on Margaret Fuller, 128, 216
(n. 39)

Hirsch, E. D., 192
History, study of, 62, 64–65, 177–80; turn-of-the-century enthusiasm for, 20–22; in American literary study, 57–59, 177–80
History and Literature program (Harvard University): history of, 177–80, 185
Holmes, Oliver Wendell, 14, 24, 26, 55, 57, 79, 142, 151; on Parkman, 59–61, 203 (n. 30). *See also* Fireside Poets
Holt, Henry, 95
Houghton Mifflin, 18, 25
Howard, June, 8
Howe, Julia Ward, 25, 128, 217 (n. 51)
Howells, William Dean, 9, 11, 13–14, 24, 97, 129, 142; as American literary history editor, 23–24; and literary realism, 27, 28–29, 30, 32, 77–78, 91, 155, 160, 203 (n. 29); columns for *Harper's*, 28–29, 77, 105, 111, 115, 135, 156, 206 (n. 4); and Brander Matthews, 30, 42; influence of, on literary history, 30, 105–6, 115–23, 171; and international copyright, 80; and Matthew Arnold, 92, 99; and professionalism, 104–7, 109, 110, 135–37, 158; as advocate of literary criticism, 105–6, 115–17, 119, 134; on female readers, 105–6, 116; on readers, 105–6, 116, 121–22, 135; and Edmund Gosse, 111, 112, 113–14; carefulness of, in literary history, 115; and Edmund Stedman, 115–19, 123, 215 (n. 25); use of fiction to

advance beliefs, 123; and Margaret Fuller, 123, 127, 135–37; and Barrett Wendell, 139, 140–41, 151, 154, 158–69 passim, 180–83; review of *Literary History of America*, 140, 155–58, 160, 169–70, 178; career of, 154–55, 158–69 passim, 173; on New England, 156–57; correspondence with Barrett Wendell, 159–62, 163–64, 166–67, 180–83, 220 (n. 31), 222 (n. 56); relation to Basil March, 165, 166, 221 (n. 34); on Dickens, 166; on Turgenev, 166; and revision of *Literary History of America*, 171–74; Barrett Wendell on, 172–74; apology to Barrett Wendell, 180–81; aging of, 180–83. *See also* Literary criticism; Literary realism; Professionalism
—*Criticism and Fiction*, 106, 203 (n. 29)
—*A Hazard of New Fortunes*, 155, 160, 165
—*Landlord at Lion's Head*, 163, 166–68
—*The Minister's Charge*, 122, 159–60, 162–64, 165
—*A Modern Instance*, 120–21, 168
—*The Rise of Silas Lapham*, 121–22, 134, 135, 162, 165
—*Shadow of a Dream*, 160–62, 164–66, 172
Hugo, Victor, 166
Hutcheon, Linda, 187
Hutchinson, Ellen M., 19, 83, 183

Immigration, 67, 73; and American literary history, 3, 12, 20, 33, 34–35, 42–43, 45–46, 152, 201 (n. 13); and

Native Americans, 34–35, 41, 45, 67, 73, 203 (n. 34)

Intellectual labor, 3, 4, 6, 12, 80–82, 104; market value of, 4–7; suspicion of, 77–78, 80–82, 100, 187–93; insularity of, 198 (n. 19); professionalism and, 213 (n. 7). *See also* English professors; Professionalism; Universities

Interdisciplinary studies, 5–6, 57–59, 177 (n. 80), 197 (n. 7); history of, 178

International Copyright Association, 87

International copyright movement, 12, 105; and Revolutionary War, 77, 88; relation to American literary history, 78–79, 82–85, 86–87, 93–94, 98, 119–20; popularity of, 79; American Copyright League of, 79, 80, 85, 98, 101; history of, 79–80; involvement of print media in, 79–80, 86–87; opposition to, 80; and class, 80, 81–82, 88–90, 94; and stresses on American literary market, 80, 95–96, 101; class issues in, 80–82, 84, 88–90, 94, 104, 209 (n. 34); populist orientation of, 80–82, 87, 89–90, 91, 92, 93, 94, 104; antebellum, 82, 87, 210 (n. 56); scarcity of argumentation in, 83–84; and democracy, 90; and Charles Dickens, 90–91; centrality of Britain to, 90–93; and Matthew Arnold, 91–93; as protector of American culture, 95–96; centrality of James Russell Lowell to, 97–98;

formal conclusion of, 98, 100–101; and American Civil War, 98–100; and reliance on professionalism, 104–5. *See also* Piracy

Irving, Washington, 25, 26, 86, 120, 151, 207–8 (n. 21)

James, Henry, 24, 29, 79, 142; on Margaret Fuller, 128–31, 32; on American literary history, 199 (n. 24)

Jameson, Fredric, 2

Jay, John, 82

Jessop, George H., 67, 71, 205 (n. 38)

Jewett, Sarah Orne, 91

Johns Hopkins University, 107, 117, 158

Kammen, Michael, 197 (n. 4)

Kaplan, Amy, 77

Kerkering, John D., 46

Lathrop, George P., 80, 81

Lawton, William C., 24

Lea, Henry C., 83

Leipzig, Germany, 23

Lemmon, Leonard, 196 (n. 1)

Lennox, Charlotte, 120

Lewis, R. W. B., 189

Library of American Literature (Stedman and Hutchinson), 19, 27, 31, 116–17, 118, 198 (n. 12); contents of, 34, 83

Lincoln, Abraham, 99

Literacy, 48, 148

Literary criticism: social importance of, 13, 105–6, 116–17, 119, 122, 179, 187–90, 192; amateurism and its

perceived dangers, 113, 114–15, 213
(n. 13), 214 (n. 17); Edmund Stedman on, 117–18; and Margaret
Fuller, 128, 132, 134–37; authority
of, 128, 198 (n. 18); moral stewardship of, 128, 212 (n. 3); as patriarchal, 134–35; Myth and Symbol
school of, 189

Literary geography, 77, 206 (n. 5);
changes in, during nineteenth century, 141, 142, 146, 149, 150, 153–55,
156, 173, 185–86

Literary idealism, 27–28, 31–32. *See
also* Aesthetics

Literary labor, 57, 94, 116; as interest
of American literary history, 4, 11,
77–78; tensions surrounding, 11,
139; and international copyright
movement, 77–78, 80–82, 90, 93,
95, 96, 100; absorption of professionalism into, 104, 106; improvements of professionalism to, 104,
124, 187; of English professors,
107–9, 187

Literary realism, 27–32, 33, 95–96, 155,
162, 164, 203 (n. 29); on oral narration, 33–34, 200 (n. 2); and American literary history, 49–50, 52, 54–
56, 91, 199 (n. 27); and Francis
Parkman, 57–59; and periodization
of late nineteenth century, 77–78;
populist rhetoric of, 78, 105, 155;
and women readers, 212 (n. 5). *See
also* Aesthetics

Lodge, Henry Cabot, 142, 203 (n. 30)

Longfellow, Henry Wadsworth, 14,
24, 32, 42, 85, 120, 151, 156

Lounsbury, Thomas, 82, 83

Low, Seth, 63, 200 (n. 2)

Lowell, A. Lawrence, 177, 178

Lowell, James Russell, 14, 24, 50, 57,
99–100, 142, 151, 154; and international copyright, 80, 97–98, 210
(nn. 50, 51); and Matthew Arnold,
92; at Harvard, 145, 210 (n. 51)

Lowell Institute, 111, 140, 215 (n. 30)

Lynn, Kenneth S., 221 (n. 34)

Macmillan (publishing house), 18

Maddox, Lucy, 200 (n. 6)

Marvel, Ik, 18, 118. *See also* Mitchell,
Donald

Marx, Leo, 189

Mather, Cotton, 108; Barrett Wendell
on, 108, 109, 144, 149–50, 151, 152,
163, 185

Matthews, J. Brander, 12, 13, 18, 19,
20, 22, 30, 32; career of, 12, 36, 61,
62, 83, 108, 143–44, 203 (n. 33);
dealings with theater, 35, 36, 40,
67–68, 204 (n. 38); attitude toward
Native peoples and narrative, 35,
37, 47, 48–49, 51–52, 58–61, 64, 65–
66; contributions to American literary history, 36; celebrity of, 36,
144, 200–201 (n. 8); interest in
American culture and history, 36–
37; bookplate of, 37–41, 47–48, 63,
73; Brander Matthews Dramatic
Museum, 40; use of assimilationist
rhetoric, 41, 42–43; realist aesthetics of, 49–50, 54–56, 91; on
Francis Parkman, 50–51, 57–61; on
James Fenimore Cooper, 50–54,

56–57, 58–59; and Mark Twain, 53–55, 56, 202 (n. 26); and international copyright, 83, 84–86, 95, 101; and professionalization, 108; and George Edward Woodberry, 201 (n. 8); collaborative work of, 204 (n. 38)
—*A Gold Mine*, 144, 204–5 (n. 35)
—"High Spirits," 67, 69–71, 72–73; history of, 67, 71–72, 204–5 (n. 38), 205 (nn. 41,2043)
—*Introduction to the Study of American Literature*, 12, 22, 35, 61–62; history of, 30, 41–42, 44, 55, 108; contents of, 42–43, 46–49, 55–61; reviews of, 43–46
—*Tom Paulding*, 72; history of, 61–62; contents of, 61–66
—"Two Letters," 66–67, 68
Matthiessen, F. O., 184, 185, 188
McGill, Meredith, 210 (n. 56)
McSherry, Corynne, 3
Miller, J. Hillis, 223 (nn. 7, 9)
Miller, Perry, 184, 185, 188
Milton, John, 101
Mitchell, Donald, 18, 118. *See also* Marvel, Ik
Modernism, 18
Modern Language Association, 36, 107, 108. *See also* Professional organizations
Modern Language Quarterly, 5
Molière, 37–38, 39, 131
Moore, George, 210–11 (n. 58)
Moore, Jedidiah, 88
Morningside Heights, N.Y., 62–63
Morse, James Herbert, 80

Motley, John L., 57
Myth and Symbol school of criticism, 189

Nathan, James, 135–37, 217 (n. 51)
Nation, 42
Nationalism, 3, 20, 21, 23, 34–36, 37, 42–46, 56, 59, 73, 187, 188–90, 192, 201 (n. 13), 203 (n. 30); and omission of Native peoples from American literary history, 34–36, 40, 56; in American literary history, 42–46, 187, 210 (n. 13). *See also* American exceptionalism
Native American narrative, 41; omission from American literary history, 10, 12, 33–35, 49, 60–61, 74; anthropological collections of, 33; ready availability of, in turn of the century, 33, 41; inclusion of, in recent anthologies, 74
Native American peoples: anthropological studies of, 33; turn-of-the-century enthusiasm for, 33; representations of, 33, 37–40, 50–51, 54–55, 57, 58–60, 65, 66–67, 70, 71, 73, 203 (n. 34); American policy toward, 33, 41, 43, 60; assimilation of, 34, 36, 37, 39–40, 41, 45, 46, 69; discourse of Vanishing Indian, 34, 51, 57; education of, 34–35, 36, 37, 39–40, 63–64, 69, 70–72; and immigrants, 34–35, 41, 45, 67, 73, 203 (n. 34); and Western antiquity, 39, 46–47, 202 (n. 22); Trail of Tears, 52; Pawnee, 65; Sioux, 65; and American boyhood, 65, 204

(n. 36); massacre of, at Wounded
Knee, 66; Black Hawk, 71
Nelson, Cary, 6
Newbury, Michael, 82
New Criticism, 2, 188, 189, 213 (n. 12)
New England: perceived decline of,
in late nineteenth century, 142, 146,
149, 154, 181; as cynosure of American culture, 145, 146, 151–52, 157,
163, 176–77, 184–86, 218 (n. 2); Barrett Wendell on, 146, 150–52, 163,
173–74, 219 (n. 12); William Dean
Howells on, 156–57; as nation's
intellectual center, 177. *See also*
New England antebellum literature
New England antebellum literature,
10, 13–14, 57, 77, 87; canonization
of, in American literary history, 10,
13–14, 96, 139–41, 151–53, 154, 157–
58, 163, 183–86; Barrett Wendell on,
13–14, 151–53, 154, 173–74, 184;
depreciation of, 14, 142; and elitism, 140, 153; centrality of, in
American literary history, 141, 149,
150–51, 157, 185–86; objections to,
141–42
New Historicism, 4, 5, 180
New Princeton Review, 85, 117
New York: in American literary history, 20, 62–63, 146, 150; Barrett
Wendell on, 146, 150, 153–54, 161,
163
New York Observer, 87
New York Times, 81, 89–90, 208–9
(n. 33)
New York Times Magazine, 5
New-York Tribune, 19, 83, 127

Nissenbaum, Steven, 218 (n. 2)
Noble, David, 218 (n. 2)
Norris, Frank, 91, 104
North American Review, 36, 93, 140, 156
Norton, Charles Eliot, 23
*Norton Anthology of American Litera-
ture*, 74

O'Hara, Daniel, 193
Oliver, Lawrence, 53
Oral narration, 33–34, 200 (n. 2)
Oxford University, 113

Parkman, Francis, 51, 57–61; biography of, 57–58; as proto-realist, 57–
58; Holmes's elegy on, 59–61
Parrington, Vernon L., 1; periodization of, 77, 78, 79, 80, 87, 93–94;
influence of, 77, 205–6 (n. 5), 206–7
(n. 5); on Margaret Fuller, 133, 134;
and Barrett Wendell, 184
Pattee, Fred Louis: on Margaret
Fuller, 124, 131; on Barrett Wendell,
184
Pedigree, 77, 78, 83, 90, 96; and Barrett Wendell, 147–48, 149, 150, 151,
153, 154, 156, 157, 161, 168–69, 176,
179–80; academic pedigree, 184–
86. *See also* Aristocratic sympathies; Elitism; Tastes in literature
Peer review, 116
Penny Post, 118
Periodization of nineteenth century,
12, 27, 77–78, 93–94; populism of,
12–13, 77–78, 80–82, 89, 206–7
(n. 5); weaknesses of, 27, 77–78,
206–7 (n. 5); as circulated by Ver-

non Parrington, 77–78, 93–94; origins of, 78, 93–94, 96, 101; class issues in, 80–82, 140; and death of James Russell Lowell, 98; revisions of, 139, 153, 154; objections to, 139–40, 144–45, 154

Perkins, David, 187, 195 (n. 1)

Perkins, Elliott, 178

Perry, Bliss, 108, 213 (n. 10)

Perry, Thomas Sargeant, 114

Philology, 13, 107, 108, 132, 145, 175, 189

Piracy: of literary texts, 79–80, 85, 86, 88, 89, 91, 94–95, 100–101, 210 (n. 56), 210–11 (n. 58). *See also* International copyright movement

PMLA (*Publications of the Modern Language Association*), 107, 193. *See also* Modern Language Association

Pocahontas, 37, 40, 67, 210 (n. 9)

Poe, Edgar Allan, 31, 151, 219 (n. 19)

Poetry, 80, 115–17; in American literary history, 31, 59, 60, 111

Poirier, Richard, 222–23 (n. 62)

Pope, Alexander, 205 (n. 43)

Populism: in periodization of nineteenth century, 12–13, 77–78, 80–82, 89, 206–7 (n. 5); in literature, 13, 153, 187, 189, 191; rhetoric of, 77–78, 81–82, 105; and international copyright, 80–82, 87, 89–90, 91, 92, 93, 94, 104; and William Dean Howells, 154–55; and literary realism, 155. *See also* Class: and authorship

Poststructuralism, 2, 189–90, 191, 192

Prescott, William H., 56

Prime, Samuel Irenaeus, 87–88, 93

Princeton University, 108, 200–201 (n. 8)

Privacy, 106, 135–37

Professionalism: and emergence of American literary history, 13, 104–5, 107–10, 113–15, 118, 119–20, 124, 132, 135–37, 138, 139, 158, 170–72; and Margaret Fuller, 13, 132, 134, 136–37; defined, 103; exclusivity of, 103; problems with, 103; social function of, 103; benefits of, 103, 104; traits of, 103, 106; twentieth-century skepticism toward, 103–4; and copyright reform, 104–5; impact of, on American literary history, 104–5, 107, 110, 114–15, 118, 119–20, 124, 132, 135–37, 139, 158; obstacles for writers, 105, 108; service of, 105, 134–35; literary criticism as manifestation of, 105–6, 115–17, 119; as protector of social welfare, 105–6, 116–17, 119–23; and academic specialization, 107, 108, 144, 158, 178; and collection of data, 107, 109, 112, 119; impact of, on universities, 107, 118, 179, 213 (n. 7); impact of, on English professors, 107–10, 144–45, 218–19 (n. 8); centrality of, in American literary history, 110, 170–72; jeopardization of, 116–18; and omission of women from American literary history, 124; and privacy, 135–37

Professional organizations, 103, 107, 108. *See also* American Medical

Association; Modern Language
Association
Professors. *See* English professors
Public intellectuals, 36, 191
Publisher's Weekly, 79
Puritans, 97, 108, 110, 145, 162
Putnam, George Haven, 18, 82, 83, 86,
    100, 207–8 (n. 21), 210–11 (n. 58)
Putnam (publishing house), 18
Putnam v. Pollard, 207–8 (n. 21)

Quarterly Review, 111, 113

Radcliffe College, 175
Readers, 51; professionalist protec-
    tions of, 13, 105–6, 121–22; literary
    historical preferences of, 27, 198
    (n. 18); perceived dangers to, 105,
    120, 133, 135; William Dean
    Howells on, 105–6, 116, 121–22, 135;
    alleged desires for supervision,
    106; Edmund Stedman's advocacy
    of, 117–18. *See also* Female readers
Readings, Bill, 188, 223–24 (n. 9)
Realism. *See* Literary realism
Reconstruction, American, 20
Remington, Frederic, 33, 43
Retrospection: and American literary
    history, 20, 23, 24–25, 29, 46–48
Revolutionary War, 61, 64, 65; and
    international copyright movement,
    77, 88
Richardson, Charles F., 7, 17, 19, 23,
    82, 109–19, 141
Roe, E. P., 79
Romero, Lora, 14, 218 (n. 3)
Roosevelt, Theodore, 43–46, 203

(n. 30); as advocate of assimilation,
    43–44, 45–46; as American literary
    history reviewer, 43–46; on politi-
    cal uses of literature, 43–46
Rowe, John Carlos, 187
Ryland, Frederick, 22

Said, Edward, 193
St. Nicholas magazine, 18, 41, 61
Salem witch trials, 149
Santayana, George, 198 (n. 19)
Scott, Sir Walter, 53
Scribners (publishing house), 18, 80,
    140, 183
Self-education, 24, 27, 42, 117–18. *See
    also* Education
Serviceman's Readjustment Act of
    1944 (G.I. Bill), 190
Sewall, Samuel, 162–63
Shakespeare, William, 44, 101, 131
Sheckel, Susan, 201 (n. 9)
Sherman, Roger, 81, 95
Shumway, David R., 17, 20
Simonds, W. E., 95
Simpson, Lewis, 77
Slavery, 100, 210 (n. 56), 210–11
    (n. 58)
Small, Ian, 115, 197 (n. 7), 213 (n. 7),
    214 (n. 17)
Smith, Henry Nash, 189
Smith, Capt. John, 37, 201 (n. 9)
Smith, Sydney, 21
Smyth, Albert H., 24, 30, 183
Sorbonne, 140, 144, 174
Specialization, 107, 108, 144, 158, 178,
    191, 192. *See also* Expertise
Spiller, Robert, 1–2, 77, 184, 188

Stanford, Charles Villier, 37, 67

Stanley, Henry Morton, 63

Stanton, Theodore, 19

Stedman, Edmund Clarence, 7, 17, 18, 19, 27, 109, 115, 180; and aesthetic idealism, 27, 31–32; and international copyright, 79, 83, 101; contribution to America literary history, 115–16; and William Dean Howells, 115–18; 123, 215 (nn. 25, 29); rejection of professionalism in American literary history, 115–18, 132; dislike of professional literary criticism, 117; advocacy of amateurism, 117–18; career, 118. *See also* Gould, Laura Stedman

—*Library of America*, 19, 27, 31, 116–17, 118, 198 (n. 12); contents of, 34, 83

—*Poets of America*, 110, 115–17, 123

Steiner, Christopher, 202 (n. 22)

Stephen, Leslie, 112

Stowe, Harriet Beecher, 7, 50, 99, 124, 133, 200 (n. 2)

Taine, Hippolyte, 26

Tastes in literature, 23, 31, 32, 105, 124, 140, 153, 162, 164, 169, 212 (n. 3)

Tauchnitz, Baron Bernhard, 23

Tauchnitz edition, 23. *See also* Collection of British Authors series

Taylor, Bayard, 30

Tebbel, John, 80

Tennyson, Alfred Lord, 112

Theater, 36, 39, 40, 67–68, 70, 108, 201 (n. 9), 204 (n. 38). *See also* Drama

Thoreau, Henry David, 25, 57, 142, 206–7 (n. 5)

Thwaite, Ann, 114

Tocqueville, Alexis de, 99

Trachtenberg, Alan, 34, 67

Trail of Tears, 52

Transnationalism: and American literary history, 13, 22–23, 26, 192–93; amid international copyright movement, 85, 88–89, 90–93, 94–96, 97, 100, 151, 152

Trent, William Peterfield, 18, 20, 36, 141

Trilling, Lionel, 205–6 (n. 1)

Trollope, Anthony, 90, 208 (n. 29)

Turgenev, Ivan, 166

Turn of the century: rise of American literary history in, 3–6, 11–12, 17–18, 20–21, 23, 190, 197 (n. 4); intellectual effects of, 23–24; enthusiasm for Native Americans in, 33, 66–67

Twain, Mark, 11, 24, 25, 29, 55, 57, 77, 180, 200 (n. 2), 206–7 (n. 5); on James Fenimore Cooper, 53–54, 202 (n. 25); and Brander Matthews, 53–55, 56, 202–3 (n. 26); and international copyright, 79, 90; and Matthew Arnold, 92, 93; on aristocracy, 94, 99

—"Fenimore Cooper's Literary Offenses," 53–54

Tyler, Moses Coit, 7, 17, 18, 19, 21–22, 82

Unitarianism, 151

Universities: nationalist responsibilities of, 3–4, 188–90; late-century changes in, 4–5, 13, 22, 107,

118, 139, 144–45, 146, 178; in crisis, 4–6; effect of professionalization on, 12, 107, 113, 118, 179, 213 (n. 7), 224 (n. 9); teaching of American literary history in, 17, 19, 34–35, 36, 140, 177–80, 214 (n. 21); marketing tactics of, 200–201 (n. 8). *See also* English professors; Expertise; Philology; Specialization

University of Michigan, 82

Vanderbilt, Kermit, 17
Van Doren, Carl, 36
Van Dyke, Henry, 80, 81, 96
Victoria (queen of England), 171

Wald, Priscilla, 46
Warner, Charles Dudley, 17, 23, 26, 81
Washington, George, 21, 205 (n. 40)
Weissbuch, Robert, 96
Wellesley College, 183
Wendell, Barrett, 7, 13, 18, 19, 27; career of, 13, 108–9, 213 (n. 10); on antebellum literature, 13–14, 151–53, 154, 173–74, 184; elitism of, 14, 145, 147–48, 151–53, 157, 160, 161, 174, 176, 177, 179; class preoccupations of, 14, 145, 147–48, 152–53, 155, 157, 158, 168–69; regionalist biases of, 14, 150, 151, 158; and aesthetic idealism, 27, 32; and Cotton Mather, 108, 109, 144, 149–50, 151, 152, 163, 185; and Charles W. Eliot, 108, 144, 170–71, 179; novels of, 108, 145, 148–49, 159, 164–65; professionalization of, 108–9, 170–71; on

Margaret Fuller, 123, 134; and professionalism, 139, 158, 170–71; and periodization of nineteenth century, 139–40, 154; career of, 140, 142–45; and Harvard University, 140, 144–45, 149, 168, 170, 183–86; and William Dean Howells, 140, 151, 158–69 passim; evaluative criteria of, 141, 151–53; reputation of, 142–43; mannerisms of, 143; and Brander Matthews, 143–44; pessimism of, 145–49, 164–65, 169, 175; on New York, 146, 150, 153–54, 219 (n. 12); on New England, 146, 150–52, 163, 174, 219 (n. 12); Anglophilia of, 151, 152, 156; dealings with William Dean Howells, 158–69 passim; letters to William Dean Howells, 159–62, 163–64, 166–67, 180–83, 220 (n. 31), 222 (n. 56); self-destructiveness of, 161; responses to William Dean Howells's review, 169–70, 171–74; on William Dean Howells, 172–74; and Harvard curriculum, 174–75, 177–80; akin to Edmund Gosse, 176; apology of William Dean Howells, 180–81; survival of work of, 183–86, 220 (n. 20); students of, 184–86; politics of, 219 (n. 16)
—*Cotton Mather*, 108, 109, 144, 149–50, 151, 152
—*Duchess Emilia*, 159, 164–65
—*English Composition*, 147–48
—*Literary History of America*, 13–14, 139, 141, 145; review of, 13, 140, 155–58, 169–70; history of, 140; con-

tents of, 149, 150–54; textbook version of, 170–74, 179, 183, 184
—*Rankell's Remains*, 148–49
—*Stelligeri*, 145, 146–47
Wheatley, Phillis, 9
Whitcomb, Selden L., 22
White, Richard Grant, 27, 153
Whitman, Walt, 78, 92, 151, 206–7 (n. 5), 209 (n. 34), 219 (n. 19)
Whittier, John Greenleaf, 24, 55, 151
Wilde, Oscar, 210 (n. 50)
Willis, Nathaniel Parker, 26, 199 (n. 27)
Wister, Owen, 26, 43

Women readers. *See* Female readers
Women's health movement, 103–4
Women writers. *See* Female writers
Woodberry, George Edward, 27, 31, 32, 201 (n. 8)
World War I, 18
World War II, 189
Wounded Knee massacre, 66

Yale University, 82, 118, 200–201 (n. 8)

Zangwill, Israel, 43
Zitkala-Sa, 33